The Advisory Guide

IN THE **PARTNERS IN LEARNING** *SERIES*

DESIGNING AND IMPLEMENTING EFFECTIVE
ADVISORY PROGRAMS IN SECONDARY SCHOOLS

RACHEL A. POLINER AND CAROL MILLER LIEBER

EDUCATORS *for* SOCIAL RESPONSIBILITY

Acknowledgements

We greatly thank the many educators we have worked with and interviewed for this guide: Boston Arts Academy, Boston MA: Linda Nathan, Ann Clark, Ali Abdi; Buckingham, Browne and Nichols School, Cambridge MA: Tom Ware; Cambridge Rindge & Latin School, Cambridge MA: all the faculty of School Five; Cincinnati Country Day School: Dr. Charles Clark, Robert Tuckman, Richard Schwab; Deerfield High School, Deerfield IL: Amy Bricker; East Palo Alto High School, Menlo Park CA: Nicky Ramos-Beban; Fenway High School, Boston MA: Larry Myatt, Luz Padua, Keith Hammitte, students; Health Careers Academy, Boston MA: Peggy Pickering, Seneca King, Carmen O'Hara, students; Health Careers Academy, Boston MA: former faculty Kim Herrera, Christopher Mee, Bethany Wood, Jennifer Tanner; Highland Park High School, Highland Park IL: Kris McKavanagh; Lyons Township High School, LaGrange IL: Michele Harbin; Needham High School, Needham MA: Jennifer Roberts, Deanna Riseman, Maureen White, Elaine Christopulos, Marie Allen, Paul Madden, Susan Bonaiuto, George Johnson; Park Junior High School, LaGrange IL: Lynn Heth; Pike School, Andover MA: Michele Tissiere; Sacajewa Middle School, Bozeman MT: Diana McDonough; Souhegan High School, Milford NH: Alan Gordon; Westerville North, South and Central High Schools, Westerville, OH: everyone on the advisory design teams and the 9th grade academy teams. We also appreciate Larry Dieringer's interest in the this project, his illuminating preface, and his encouragement to combine the design manual with activities. Lastly, we thank Jeffrey Perkins for his insightful conceptual suggestions and for seeing the Guide through to completion.

ESR wishes to thank the following funders for graciously supporting the development and production of this work: Shinnyo-En Foundation, Lippincott Foundation of the Peace Development Fund, and Working Assets.

EDUCATORS *for* SOCIAL RESPONSIBILITY

23 Garden Street, Cambridge, MA 02138
617-492-1764
www.esrnational.org

The Advisory Guide by Rachel A. Poliner and Carol Miller Lieber

Printed in the United States of America.
ISBN 978-0-942349-01-6

Original Design: Elan Design
Book Production: Schwadesign, Inc.; John Kramer Design
Proofreader: Dorothy Miller, EdEx
Cover image: © Chuck Savage/CORBIS

Inquiries regarding permission to reprint from The Advisory Guide should be addressed to Permissions Editor, Educators for Social Responsibility, 23 Garden Street, Cambridge, MA 02138

The Advisory Guide

Designing and Implementing Effective Advisory Programs in Secondary Schools

Table of Contents

PREFACE

Over twenty years ago, I facilitated a group of ten students in my high school's advisory program. We met on a weekly basis. The students were in different grades and had different interests. Some were in classes that I taught; others were not. My main goals were to build a sense of community and to get to know each one of them well enough to support them with academic and life decisions.

Initially, my students didn't care much about one another and couldn't see why we were together. Slowly but surely, however, we became a group. We talked about meaningful issues, contributed input to the student-faculty council, did "workshop-like" activities, and shared food that we brought to our meetings. They began to look forward to seeing one another. Meanwhile, I developed personal relationships with these students, some more than others. I succeeded in connecting with young people who had been unwilling or unable to make connections with other adults in the school. I knew the relationship with me mattered to them, and I saw the ways it helped them do better at school.

Throughout the process, colleagues and I improvised as we went along—fortunately we had wise and talented staff. At the time, there were not very many advisory programs around to learn from. And there were few, if any, resources that could help us plan and implement a program from A to Z.

Since then, advisories have grown in popularity. The Coalition of Essential Schools played a significant role in the expansion of advisories. One of its ten Common Principles states that, "Teaching and learning should be personalized to the maximum feasible extent." Starting in 1984, many Coalition schools chose advisories as one vehicle for achieving personalization.

In 1989, the Carnegie Council on Adolescent Development published *Turning Points: Preparing American Youth for the 21st Century. Turning Points*, a call for transforming the education of early adolescents, accelerated the middle-school movement. The first of its eight essential principles stated that "large middle grade schools are divided into smaller communities for learning." Assigning an adult advisor to each student was seen as a key strategy for achieving smaller communities. *Turning Points* also suggested that "Every student should be well known by at least one adult. Students should be able to rely on that adult to help learn from their experiences, comprehend physical changes and changing relations with family and peers, act on their behalf to marshal every school and community resource needed for the student to succeed, and help to fashion a promising vision for the future."[1]

Turning Points 2000 goes further and states that, "Among youth at risk from health or behavioral problems, family dysfunction, poverty, or other stresses, the most important school factor fostering resilience—defined as 'successful adaptation despite risk and adversity'…—may be the availability of at least one caring responsible adult who can function as a mentor or role model…".[2]

High schools have generally lagged behind middle schools in seeing the importance of personalization and utilizing advisory programs. In 1995, the National Association of Secondary School Principals published *Breaking Ranks: Changing an American Institution*. *Breaking Ranks* challenges high schools of the 21st century to be "much more student-centered and above all much more personalized in programs, support services, and intellectual rigor."[3] In its section called "School Environment: Creating a Climate Conducive to Teaching and Learning," it recommends that, "Every high school student will have a personal Adult Advocate to help him or her personalize the educational experience." Moreover, according to the *report*, "The relationship between the student and the advocate should ensure that no youngster experiences the sense of isolation that frequently engulfs teenagers during this critical period of their lives."[4]

More recently, the Gates and Carnegie Foundations and the federal government have supported the development of small learning communities in high schools. Advisory programs are seen as one of the key building blocks for creating a small learning community, whether it's in a brand new small school or a traditional high school that is being restructured into smaller units.

Yet another development supports the creation of advisory programs. There's a growing body of research—much of it from the study of resiliency and the field of prevention—that shows an integral connection between school success and healthy development among students. This connection is especially true for students who find it more challenging to navigate the dominant culture of secondary school successfully. In a nutshell, the research says that if we create safe, supportive, respectful learning environments, personalize young people's learning experience, help them develop social and emotional competencies, and provide opportunities to practice using these competencies, they will grow more attached to school, avoid risky behavior, and achieve more academic success. Effective advisory programs meet all of these goals.

The research reveals an interesting and complex set of cause and effect relationships. To begin with, initiatives that make the learning environment safer, more caring, better managed, and more participatory have been shown to increase student attachment to school. In turn, students who are more connected and attached to school are more successful, as measured by indicators like better attendance and higher graduation rates, as well as higher grades and better standardized test scores.

The National Longitudinal Study of Adolescent Health, a survey of 75,000 students from 127 schools,[5] found that school connectedness is maximized when the school environment meets core adolescent developmental needs. These needs include opportunities for autonomy, opportunities to demonstrate competence, caring and support from adults, developmentally appropriate supervision, and acceptance by peers. In other words, meeting basic developmental needs is the foundation for academic and school success. This makes good common sense. Students need to feel safe first (both physically and psychologically), feel like they belong, feel respected, and feel cared about in order to be successful in school.

Positive personal relationships with teachers and sufficient bonding with peers are keys to students' success. Academic personalization emphasizes differentiated instruction, collaborative learning, multiple intelligences, and the social construction of knowledge. In addition, student work that has personal meaning and value, and strengthens metacognition and problem solving skills, makes learning both relevant and rigorous. One study showed that when students perceive their teachers as caring and respectful, they participate more in class, complete more of their homework, and cheat less often.

Research also indicates that interventions that improve the climate for learning, enhance student attachment to school, and increase student achievement decrease the rates of high-risk behaviors. The Adolescent Health survey cited above found that adolescents' sense of connectedness to school is the single most important factor associated with significantly lower rates of emotional distress, suicidal thoughts and behaviors, violence, substance abuse, and sexual activity. In other words, when students connect positively with peers and adults, they are more likely to avoid high-risk behaviors. A meta-analysis of 165 prevention programs found that initiatives that focused on creating a more positive environment decreased the prevalence of delinquency, alcohol and drug use, drop-out and non-attendance rates, and behavior problems.

Despite these many findings, school reform efforts and prevention programs evolve separately in most schools. The assumption that students' thinking, feelings, and behavior function independently of each other continues to drive the organizational culture of most secondary schools, especially high schools, where the myth of the divided self goes unchallenged. Relentless departmentalization sanctions specialized roles of adults in secondary schools—the content expert in the classroom, the child expert in the guidance center, and the discipline expert in the dean's office. One group is entrusted to take care of young people's physical, social, and emotional needs, while the other group serves as students' intellectual guardians. If we fail to appreciate how students' academic success is linked inextricably to efforts that support healthy development, then we are unlikely to change the outcomes of the students we want to help the most. Improving the quality of relationships among and between adults and young people can stand at the center of an integrated approach to successful prevention and instructional reform.

Advisory programs promote healthy student development, support academic success, and provide multiple opportunities to bridge the divide between healthy development and academic success. For example, they help ensure that all young people have at least one adult who knows them well. Advisory groups help create stronger bonds among young people, usually cutting across the typical exclusionary social groups that form in schools. They are the "safe container" for discussing adolescent concerns that kids care about. Advisory programs provide an ideal setting to teach and practice important life skills. In addition, advisories encourage student voice on school-wide issues. Finally, they establish a forum for academic, college and career coaching, and advising that cuts across subject areas.

More and more secondary schools are deciding that they want to set up advisory programs. However, good intentions don't translate into successful programs. There are many obstacles that can sink an advisory program, from lack of buy-in from teachers and conflicts over contract issues to confusion over goals and inadequate preparation of those who will serve as advisors.

Rachel Poliner and Carol Lieber have created the guide that I wanted twenty years ago—and that still didn't exist until they wrote this book. Other resources about advisory programs may describe a particular model or suggest activities for the advisor to use. What distinguishes this guide is its comprehensive nature. The guide does not recommend one right advisory program design—rather, it helps schools recognize the choices they face and the plusses and minuses of various choices. Rachel and Carol use the metaphor of a puzzle to help planners think through nine major issues that have to be addressed in order to assemble an effective advisory program. They then offer a guide to facilitating an advisory group, effective activity formats, and a wealth of activity suggestions. Their fifty years' combined experience working with secondary schools across the country is readily apparent in their depth of understanding about both big-picture issues and the important details associated with advisory programs.

Five years ago, ESR made a strategic decision to establish a new focus—helping secondary schools succeed with reform, redesign, and continuous school improvement. We consolidated learning from fifteen years of training and consulting with secondary schools under the banner "Partners in Learning." We found that we could make an important contribution to the field with a new emphasis on integrating instructional reform, prevention, and student support in order to simultaneously promote academic success and healthy development.

This guide is the first in an ESR series on secondary school climate and culture. It complements and builds on the foundational work in ESR's guide to classroom practice, *Partners in Learning: From Conflict to Collaboration in Secondary Classrooms*. I am confident that advisors and those who design advisory programs will find this new guide to be an invaluable resource.

— Larry Dieringer

Larry Dieringer is the executive director of Educators for Social Responsibility and has over twenty years of teaching experience at the secondary and university level.

Endnotes

[1] Carnegie Council on Adolescent Development. *Turning Points: Preparing American Youth for the 21st Century* (Washington, DC: Carnegie Corporation of New York, 1989), 40.

[2] Anthony W. Jackson and Gayle A. Davis. *Turning Points 2000* (New York: Teachers College, Columbia University, 2000), 143.

[3] National Association of Secondary School Principals. *Breaking Ranks: Changing an American Institution* (Reston, VA: National Association of Secondary School Principals, 1996), vi.

[4] Ibid., 31.

[5] Ibid., 31.

INTRODUCTION

Over the years we have led many workshops with secondary teachers to help students develop self-management and conflict resolution skills. A story from one of those workshops serves to introduce this advisory guide. While working with a series of activities about emotional intelligence and managing anger, we found that an activity about identifying anger triggers revealed an important aspect of school climate.

We identified words to describe an anger continuum ranging in intensity from irritated to enraged and read aloud brief scenarios. For each scenario the teachers were to stand at a place on the continuum that would represent how they might feel in that situation. The exercise helps participants note that people feel differently about situations and encourages reflection about one's triggers and reactions. While using typical scenarios that affect teachers, it was also an opportunity to imagine what students might learn in a parallel activity with situations that might trigger young people. For each scenario teachers in this workshop ranged widely on the continuum. "A parent enters your classroom and argues with you about a grade that his/her child was given" resulted in heated comments throughout the continuum. Another example, "The photocopier breaks down for the third day in a row," also drew many different reactions and explanations. We went through several scenarios.

Then we read the scenario, "A teacher yells at one of your students in front of you in the hallway." Nobody moved. A teacher asked for the statement to be reread. Still nobody moved. Some of the teachers looked confused; others looked unaffected. They asked, "What do you mean by *your* students?" It was the word "your" that hadn't registered and hadn't carried meaning.

Further comments and questions gave more information. "Isn't that scenario only for elementary teachers? I don't have students I think of as mine." Another commented, "When students are in my class, they are my students. After class, they're not."

This reaction from secondary school teachers, while understandable, was also enormously meaningful. It exemplified the relationship that students have to their secondary schools—feelings of anonymity and alienation. It is easy for a teacher to know how a student is doing in algebra or in history, but not know how the student is doing in school or in life.

Adolescents, like all students, learn best when they have a sense of community and connection, when they feel heard and known, when they feel safe enough to take risks. Conversely, we consistently hear that the students who are most at risk of dropping out or committing a dangerous act against themselves or their schools are those who are most isolated. Regarding one student who committed a violent act, a high school principal said, "I did not know that student. I've had conversations with our five assistant principals; none of them knew this student either." Occasionally we hear about a student who reports to authorities that friends will be committing an impending danger. Inevitably, the reporting student reveals that there is a teacher (sometimes only one teacher) who had been showing personal concern for the student. The reporting student has chosen loyalty to that one caring adult over the peer pressure to commit a violent act. Kids are searching for authentic acknowledgment and mentoring.

Unfortunately, secondary schools are often organized so that vast numbers of students feel alienated or uncomfortable. As one teacher said, "When I went to school, the only kids who had consistent adult contact were the jocks and the trouble-makers." He now teaches at a school committed to an environment that values community and personal connection. Many schools, however, have not changed in basic structure since he was a teenager.

There are many structures and practices that schools can implement to create a greater sense of community among students. For example, schools can create longer learning blocks; assign teachers, guidance counselors, and/or grade-level administrators to loop with a specific grade of students; or organize teachers and counselors in houses or teams. There are also practices for personalizing the classroom learning environment. See Educators for Social Responsibility's guide, *Partners in Learning*, by Carol Miller Lieber, for extensive discussion of rationales and descriptions of these and other options.

ESR is supporting the creation of a series of guides to accompany *Partners in Learning* to explore specific options outside the academic classroom that can further personalize secondary schools. These initiatives can help create a sense of community and offer students skills related to their social, emotional, and academic development.

How to use this guide

This guide will help educators design and implement an advisory program, including the crucial (and all too often overlooked) tasks of building buy-in and selling the idea.

Chapter 1 introduces basic descriptions of advisory programs, encourages the establishment of a research and design team, checks on your school's readiness, and suggests initiating a process for building buy-in. **Chapter 2** offers ten short profiles of advisory programs in middle schools and high schools throughout the United States to portray a range of designs. We hope they offer inspiration, encourage creativity, and identify a few pitfalls. Further, we hope the snapshots establish a sense of the whole design, since an advisory program is more than a grouping and schedule arrangement. **Chapter 3** introduces the Advisory Design Puzzle, a metaphor for creating a program that takes nine components into account. Each of nine puzzle pieces is taken in turn with questions and support to guide the design team. **Chapter 4** suggests a process for the design team to proactively sell their plan to their colleagues, parents, and students. **Chapter 5** focuses on facilitation tips for advisors, and activity formats particularly appropriate for advisories. **Chapter 6** offers a range of activities on each of ten themes that model different format, grouping, and frequency variations. While Chapter 6 offers activities, please note that there are content ideas throughout the Guide, especially in the snapshots, in the design puzzle sections, and in the formats.

CHAPTER 1

Getting Started

What are advisory groups?

A range of advisory group programs now exists in middle schools and high schools. The National Middle School Association describes advisories as structures in which an adult and a small group of students meet regularly for academic guidance, to coordinate between home and school, and to find ways for students to be successful, and to connect to a peer group.[1]

Some schools have advisories for ten minutes every day so each student is well known by an adult. Others have advisories that include longer, less frequent meetings where students improve interpersonal skills or engage in career exploration. Still other advisory programs include frequent and significant blocks of time, providing the cornerstone of students' personalized, academic development.

Most advisory programs share a few common purposes, even if their program designs, school missions, demographics, and structures vary. These programs are a consistent home base dedicated to

- helping students adjust to school, particularly the entering grade;

- building community among students—that is, encouraging a sense of belonging and respect while decreasing anonymity and alienation;

- academic advising and coaching, helping students succeed by giving them behind-the-scenes support in a proactive, organized way.

Despite the variety of advisory programs that exists, no one has created exactly the right program or the perfect prepackaged activity book for your school. If your school is considering establishing an advisory program, it would serve you well to visit other schools' programs and read articles chronicling other schools' processes. However, the advisory program that will serve your school will be of your own making. Every school has its own schedule and sacred cows in that schedule. Every school has its own building, its particular array and number of spaces. Every school has its own mission, whether it is to prepare students for careers in a certain field, to continue their education, to be global citizens, or to serve another mission. All of these goals and other factors help shape the advisory program that will fit your school.

Think of creating an advisory program as putting together a puzzle. All pieces have to be in place and those pieces have to fit, if advisory is to function well. This guide is organized to help develop those pieces and fit them together. As one component is developed, it will influence other components.

This guide offers questions to foster the decision-making process for each of the major puzzle pieces:

- goals and outcomes for advisees, advisory groups, and school climate and culture

- grouping—that is, the size, mix, and continuity of the group and the advisor over multiple years

- schedule—that is, the length and frequency of meetings

- content, themes, formats, and routines

- advisors' role and expectations

- advisors' skills, planning for professional development

- accountability for students, advisors, and the program as a whole, coordination, and supervision

- materials and resources

- linking advisory to other school programs, policies, structures, and the curriculum as a whole

The Advisory Puzzle

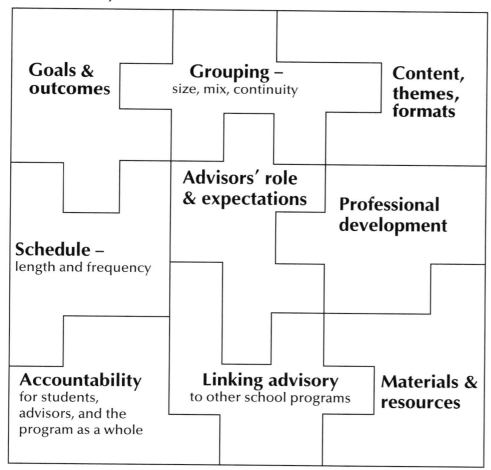

The context for advisory

Advisory programs are implemented best when they are not in a vacuum; advisory alone will not change a school environment that feels alienating and fractured to students. Schools use many different structures to personalize the learning environment and create a sense of community. They can have low teacher-student ratios, or they can limit the number of students assigned to teachers in a given semester. Advisory should be designed in a way that is organizationally consistent and reinforced in the school. For example, if the school has teams, advisory is best assigned within those teams.

Further, advisory should be consistent with the vision and values of the school. An integrated discipline and student support system that provides opportunities for instruction, self-correction, and problem solving demonstrates ways of valuing personalization. Incorporating differentiated learning strategies into every course is another example.

Some middle schools are organized into teams, with two to five teachers responsible for core subjects. As a result, those teachers interact with their shared students repeatedly each day and get to know them well. Schools utilizing grade-level teams often emphasize community via class meetings, team-teaching, looping, long learning blocks, or other structures.

Advisory might be implemented in those schools, or other structures might serve the functions of advisory, such as class meetings, team rituals, and activities.

Currently, hundreds of large high schools are involved in efforts to reconfigure school size by creating small autonomous schools or small learning communities by size, by grade, or by academic emphasis. Advisory programs are a core component of high school redesign. These opportunities enable a specific group of teachers to know and take responsibility for a specific group of students for one or more years.

Yet some middle schools, junior high schools, and the majority of large high schools have not yet implemented many structures that personalize the learning environment and welcome all students and families into school with the same enthusiasm and support. In these schools, the perception of invisibility is especially true for students who are neither "stars" nor "trouble makers." Advisory programs can become powerful vehicles for breaking down anonymity and fostering a sense of belonging.

Are You Ready?

The literature on advisory programs is littered with stories of schools that implemented programs before they had a plan, consensus, or resources. Our experience reveals similar rocky stories. One school put two half-hour advisory group times into the schedule for all teachers and all students, without building buy-in or identifying themes or content, and set aside only a few hours for faculty training and planning. As with so many programs, if advisory is poorly implemented, the program can die an ugly death, taking trust and confidence with it. If that happens, it might be years before the structure can be tried again. Is your school ready for advisory groups?

- Can your advisors finish the following sentences with ease and confidence? The goals of our school's advisory program are... ❏ Yes ❏No
My goals for my advisory group are...

- Can advisors easily and confidently list the major projects or the types of activities they will use to reach their identified ❏ Yes ❏No
goals? Can they name what outcomes are expected for students?

- Are parents and students in support of an advisory program? ❏ Yes ❏ No

- Does the school schedule have time assigned for advisory groups to ❏ Yes ❏No
be held and for advisors to do preparation?

- Is there a professional development program for all new advisors? ❏ Yes ❏ No

- Is there a person or committee that will monitor progress, make decisions, and trouble-shoot problems? ❏ Yes ❏ No

- Are materials easily available to advisors? ❏ Yes ❏ No

- Will anybody know if advisors are fulfilling their roles effectively? If so, who and how? ❏ Yes ❏ No

- Has the relationship between advisory and other school structures been articulated? For example, in what ways are advisors to be involved in disciplinary matters? In what ways are advisors to beinvolved with grade reports? ❏ Yes ❏ No

If you answer the questions above, "No," you may have more planning to do. The Advisory Design Puzzle chapter will walk you through the planning steps. Even if you are able to answer all of the above questions affirmatively and are ready to implement a program, expect your advisory program to go through lots of changes in the first few years. Advisors may find that they need more skills or materials, or the schedule might have to be altered. The design committee should establish lots of ways to assess how things are going. Voicing concerns is part of the process people have to go through to feel ownership. The design committee needs to show that it is listening and willing to problem-solve along the way. With ongoing assessment and adjustments, advisors, students, and parents should be able to see that their concerns will be taken seriously. This will help to avoid a scenario in which concerns become entrenched complaints undermining the program.

Establish a research, design, and PR team

Creating an advisory group program and shaping the environment to implement it successfully are not simple or small tasks. Establishing a research, design, and public relations team (or teams) will be crucial. The research function will include learning about students' academic needs and developmental hurdles, visiting other schools, reading and sharing articles, and exploring the challenges of structural change. The design function will involve envisioning a fabulous program and shaping both the program and the current context to make it work.

The PR function is often overlooked. How many times has your school proposed a new program, even implemented it, only to have it wither or become marginalized? Building buy-in takes time and careful attention, and changes shape at different stages.

Two warnings:

- Do not spend two years with a small design team learning, reading, visiting, planning and getting inspired, and waiting until you have a firm proposal to inform others. Building buy-in has to start early, and last as long as it takes.

- On the other hand, it won't help to publicize the program prematurely or haphazardly.

Therefore, think of building buy-in through two phases. One phase needs to start early in the process, focus mostly on small informal forums, sharing articles and stories from other schools, soliciting questions and concerns. Phase one will help people notice some drawbacks in the current structure—after all, if everyone thinks things are fine, they are not likely to desire change. They need a chance to speak and feel heard by the design team. People who don't feel heard are not likely to listen. Phase one is described in this chapter.

The second phase can begin as the advisory design becomes clearer. Think of it as a PR campaign. A group has to develop a great plan, encourage people to know such a plan is needed, and sell it to people if it is really to be implemented. The PR campaign phase is outlined in Chapter Four. In either phase, the PR team might be the same group as the research and design team, or might be a subset of the group.

The varied research, design, and outreach tasks described above require different knowledge bases, skill sets, and collegial relationships. By including people in various roles, the team will be more efficient in knowing what resources can be brought to bear and what decisions are possible. You will need information about and influence over budgets, schedules, and professional development plans. You will need to include people who have credibility with faculty, counselors, administrators, parents, and students. You will need people interested in and able to do research, planning, and communicating. Thus, the team should include people with different skills and from various positions in the school. Building buy-in among faculty is likely to be easier if the chairperson or cochairperson is a teacher.

In the process of designing your advisory program, there are broad questions about purpose and themes. There are more narrow questions about how to assign students and facilitate discussions, and there is a myriad of preparatory decisions to make. The design committee would do well to include people who naturally think about visions and large structures as well as those who naturally think about steps and details. The committee members will need to embrace the full range of topics involved and to appreciate each others' strengths.

In the first year or two of implementation, the research, design, and PR functions will still be important, though the group will likely be called a coordinating or steering committee. The research, design, and certainly the PR tasks do not end with the announcement of a design and implementation schedule. The team should monitor the program, solicit feedback, and propose any necessary changes to the design or the professional development workshops supporting the program. They might need to do more research about materials or activities. The PR function, especially, will still be needed. Some people can commit themselves to a program when they hear a well-crafted plan and vision. Many, however, do not. Throughout the early years of the program, PR efforts can highlight the benefits to students, teachers, and the school as a whole, and thus preempt negativity.

Over time, the team will be able to fulfill a coordinating role that makes assignments for new students to advisory groups, arranges speakers to address multiple groups, provides materials and coaching to new advisors, and generally supports the smooth running of the program.

When might an outside consultant or curriculum be helpful?

No outside consultant can take the place of the design team, but such a person can be helpful to the process. A core team of people inside the school needs to identify the goals, content, schedules, and other aspects that might be appropriate to that school. The team needs to converse with all constituencies to create buy-in. A consultant can be a resource person if he/she knows about advisory groups at other schools, can lead the team through the design options, or can skillfully facilitate conversations that are difficult to manage. Further, a consultant may be helpful in providing professional development, supporting materials development, and identifying steps to facilitate implementation and buy-in.

We have not yet found a school that could find the set of activities and exercises that they needed conveniently packaged in one resource on the market. Most schools use materials from several resources and create materials of their own, resulting in binders for grade levels or topics (or other organizing schema). If a school uses a consultant or a packaged handbook early in the process, they can be tempted to look to that person or book for the content, goals, and structures.

Remember, no perfect model can be dropped into place from the outside. The design team needs to feel a sense of ownership of the design process and be empowered sufficiently to accomplish its task.

Background for building buy-in

Secondary schools and teachers have long focused primarily on students' academic achievement. Building buy-in before implementing a program and throughout its early years will be crucial. Think of this as an outreach and internal PR campaign. Be sure to plan for lead-time, often a year or more, to hold discussions, read articles, get input, host speakers, visit other schools, and to publicize carefully. Informal and formal meetings with union leaders and school board members will be critical. Discussions and presentations with parents and students should also be part of the process.

Advisory proponents need to be prepared and proactive in representing the benefits and addressing the fears and discomforts associated with taking on the advisor role. It should not be underestimated how different the roles of advisor and teacher are, or how a little bit of sabotage and negative attitude can destroy a new effort. Use small forums whenever possible (rather than large forums, which can too easily fill with complaints and attacks) for teachers and parents to raise concerns and become familiar with the idea. Also, use the written word to promote and establish certain phrases. By the time advisory groups are implemented, everyone should be able to recite basic rationales: "We're making sure every student is monitored and coached" or "We are consciously promoting positive thinking and steps toward success in school and beyond." Whatever your mantras are, have them, repeat them, and proudly make them known.

The benefits that can be highlighted are many

For students
The benefits of advisories start with being and feeling less anonymous. This will be especially true if the advisor group stays together multiple years and/or meets frequently. In high school, students will likely take classes from two to three dozen teachers, but may have one or two advisors throughout those years. Students will feel a greater sense of belonging and will have an opportunity to know and be known within a small circle of students and an adult. A given advisor will have eight to eighteen advisees as compared to a guidance counselor who serves several hundred students.

Some adolescents have received considerable support and modeling from home about how to "do school." These kids know how to keep a schedule, and someone monitors whether homework gets done, or talks to them about patience. Some kids don't have those advantages. Educators are increasingly aware of achievement gaps between kids of different socio-economic backgrounds, racial and ethnic groups, and English fluency. These educators often see advisory as a way of supporting all students to do their best. Advisors can help students keep a schedule and a homework log, map out steps in a long-term project, notice specific learning and/or emotional challenges for referral, identify pairings for peer tutoring, or just create an atmosphere that encourages and celebrates perseverance.

Staff at one Indiana high school identified that 9th graders lacked preparedness for high school academics, had weak attitudes about homework, and lacked effective study skills. They created a pilot advisory program that involved one-third of the ninth grade class, randomly chosen. The program focused on organizational skills and academic progress. Students in that program made more progress in adjusting to high school than the other two-thirds of their class.[2]

Depending on the goals and amount of time allotted for advisory, there are many potential benefits for students. See the content section in Chapter 3 for more ideas.

For staff

Advisor groups are forums to support students in developing the skills and focus that make both teaching and learning more successful. Many teachers wish the students in their academic classes had better communication skills, kept better track of their assignments, knew how to focus their attention, and possessed many other skills that might be referred to as "soft" or "nonacademic." Advisory groups can be a great place to learn and practice these skills.

Further, staff will know and better understand their students, something many teachers wish they had time for.

Becoming an advisor can have indirect benefits for teachers' instructional styles. It is not uncommon for teachers to develop new skills for facilitating discussions, increase their commitment to and skills for personalizing learning, and even change their understanding of their own authority. Advisory can be a means for that growth, specifically because it is distinct from academic pressures and teaching habits. After a year as an advisor, one very dedicated teacher who was mostly traditional in his teaching style summarized his greatest learning when he said, "I've done a 180-degree turn on authority. Did you know that authority is about group buy-in?!"

For parents

The advisor may be parents' first and most consistent contact person with the school. Parents will be able to have a conversation with the advisor about their child's overall progress, not just in one class. Many parents are alienated from their child's school and/or feel intimidated when they interact with the school. Having a consistent person to talk to, especially if their child stays with that advisor for multiple years, makes parents' contact with the school easier. The process allows them to be more informed about and supportive of their child.

For the school

Advisories can be used to solicit student input for decisions, to problem-solve, and to set or reset school norms. Many schools involve not just teachers as advisors, but also the principal, secretaries, media specialists, coaches, and others. When all adults in a school have an advisory group, they share an experience and a commitment to paying personal attention to students. One administrator noted that advisory affects school culture by giving focus to adult conversation. When necessary, advisory groups can be a crucial component of a school's crisis plan.

Schools feel great pressure from standardized tests to help all students achieve higher standards of learning. Students who have not scored well in the past can be supported in proactive ways within advisories. Testing alone won't raise scores, nor will political pressure, but providing support to all students can help them achieve.

Confer with the union and the school board – soon

As part of the process of building buy-in, it will be crucial to confer with the teachers' union and the school board. In some districts, advisory programs were implemented partially and on a volunteer basis until it was time for a new teachers' contract with advisor responsibilities formally added. The design team should include a key union representative and establish a liaison relationship with several board members who are kept informed throughout the planning process. The design team members and one key board member will need to be prepared to respond to many questions that are reasonable and predictable, such as those below.

- Will faculty be compensated or will they exchange some type of responsibility?

- How can the educational program retain the required number of instructional minutes per week and include time for advisory? Some schools introduce advisory at the same time as other scheduling changes. For example, block scheduling reduces the number of passing minutes from one class to another during the week. When students are assigned to a "house" or learning community in one location, passing minutes between classes can also be reduced. Some districts negotiate an agreement to add an extra hour to the school week.

- How will advisory be counted in a teacher's set of responsibilities? Some schools have taken a few minutes out of class time to create the advisory block, so that teachers are teaching the same number of instructional minutes per day. Other schools require that teachers have five responsibilities, such as five classes, or some other arrangement that adds up to five responsibilities. In a school where advisory meets one to two hours per week, it might count as a half-responsibility, matched by another half-responsibility somewhere else in the program. Another option is substituting advisory responsibilities for other assigned duties within the school day. In this scenario, teachers who choose to be advisors are not assigned other monitoring, clerical, supervisory, or departmental responsibilities.

- Will leading an advisory group be voluntary or mandatory?

- What arrangements are being made for preparation time? Advisory is a responsibility; the longer the sessions are, the more they represent another preparation for faculty. Advisory will endure only if advisors feel that the arrangements are fair.

- What professional development process will support faculty assuming the advisor role? Will all new advisors receive a comprehensive orientation? What guarantees will teachers have that training, coaching, and continuing support will be provided after the first year?

- Will the district make a commitment to set aside financial and human resources to build leadership capacity for sustaining the advisory program over time?

- Will there be supervision for advisors?

- To what extent and how will facilitating an advisory group be part of a teacher's evaluation?

- Will the school or district assess the advisory program on a regular basis?

Your advisory design team will get considerable practice thinking about these and other questions as you conduct your research, visit other schools, and read and discuss the information presented in this guide. The snapshots, the puzzle, and the PR campaign chapters offer many suggestions for designing your advisory program, setting the stage for implementation through outreach, and working through resistance.

Endnotes

[1] NMSA website.

[2] Rost, Jacquie and Marceil Royer. "Evaluating the Effectiveness of Charger Connection Class." ERIC No. ED430189, 1999.

CHAPTER 2

Advisory Program Snapshots

Advisory programs vary from school to school. Below are a few descriptions that will demonstrate how some schools have designed their advisories. None of these descriptions can possibly include the richness of each school's experience, how they got to the model they now have, what they tried along the way, or what their next improvements will be. Each one of these schools has identified aspects that need to be formalized, reshaped, or better supported. Designing advisory, just like any other aspect of school programming, is an ongoing process.

These snapshots are meant to portray a variety of ways some schools have shaped their advisory puzzle. The snapshots are from small, medium, and large schools; urban, suburban, and rural; middle and high schools. Some snapshots highlight highly structured and content-driven advisories, while others show less formal group-building and coaching goals. Some of the advisory programs have been in place for decades. They are well supported and a normal part of the school culture, while others are quite new.

High Schools

Souhegan High School, Amherst, New Hampshire

Souhegan High School, built in 1992, has grown to over 1,000 students. Since its inception, it has been in the Coalition of Essential Schools. This high school has had advisory groups since the school opened. Advisory meets 25 minutes per day, nearly every day. Groups meet nine days out of ten. On the tenth day, students get a double lunch, while advisors meet in teams with the Advisory Coordinator. The school's Counseling Coordinator serves also as Advisory Coordinator, which consumes about 25 percent of his time.

According to the advisory coordinator, "Advisory is the most significant way in which we evidence our commitment to personalization. It is the only class that all students take. It is the only class that nearly all our adults teach. Nothing we do here is more student-centered. Nothing we do here is more important."[1]

Almost all teachers have an advisory group (a few choose to teach a fifth class instead of advisory). Administrators have groups, and staff may choose to have an advisory. Some highly effective advisory groups have been led by secretaries, paraprofessionals, custodians, and cafeteria workers. Souhegan has an advisor rubric that delineates aspects of the role and what constitutes effectiveness. Counselors do not have groups; instead they are available to groups as needed.

Groups have about a dozen students. Assignments are random, within grade levels, with most students changing groups and advisors each year, though some groups decide to stay together. Advisory is held opposite the lunch blocks, thus not all groups meet at the same time, allowing extra use of rooms. Over the years, a few groups have included students from multiple grades and have focused on particular themes, but in general this has not been popular with students, who want to eat lunch with their grade-level peers. Holding advisory other than first thing in the morning at Souhegan protects it as much as possible from filling with bureaucracy and announcements. Attendance is taken in every class.

The focus of each grade level is very broad: 9th grade advisory helps with the transition to high school; 10th grade groups support students' preparation of a mid-high school exhibition; 11th graders focus on their postsecondary plans (a graduation requirement). That focus, along with supporting students' senior projects, continues in 12th grade. Many groups engage in community service; one group in the past created a section for the AIDS quilt. Within those general parameters, groups vary widely. No matter the grade level, the underlying focus is on providing support, fostering communication skills, building community and trust, and providing one adult who knows each student well. Advisory is graded Pass/No Credit (based on attendance) with an effort grade assessment rubric that emphasizes positive group participation. While failing advisory is possible, it is usually accompanied by failing multiple courses, in which case individual plans are constructed.

At the inception of Souhegan's advisory program, the school did not supply curricula to advisors, expecting advisory content to be self-generating. Advisors needed more support, which led to the creation of a resource notebook with a wide range of activities, poetry, discussion-starters, and background on group dynamics and educational theory. New advisors participate in a half-day of training, followed by the biweekly meetings. Advisors are organized in a buddy system, so they can get support informally, as needed, from their buddy and/or the Advisory Coordinator. Training for advisors encourages many of the skills Souhegan expects will be modeled in academic classes such as asking open-ended questions, carefully facilitating discussions, and debriefing insightfully.

Comments from advisors include the following:[2]

"I understood more clearly the forces in the lives of students. I accepted my advisees for who they were, was honest with them, and confronted them when needed."

"It [advisory] is a place to round out the rough places of my relationships with kids, serving to remind me that they are people, not just students."

"Kids can't fall through the cracks when one adult is in charge of fishing them out of whatever puddle they have just fallen into. I wonder if the tragedy of Columbine would have happened if each of those boys had had an adviser, someone who knew him well."

Describing the intervention and guidance role of advisory, the coordinator says that advisory serves as an early warning system, explaining that most counselor referrals come from advisors. He says, "conversations take place in the bathrooms, hallways, and parking lots all the time.

Kids talk about parties, about dieting, about cheating, about finding a job. If we are successful and fortunate, kids will trust us enough to bring those conversations into Advisory. That gives us an opportunity to inject into the conversation timely thoughts and suggestions and to create teachable moments."[3]

At times, advisors were put in evaluative roles, such as with senior projects. That practice ended, as it clashed with the need to serve as a supportive coach. Advisors hand out report cards and progress reports. Advisory is central to the high school's crisis plan, though it is only needed one to two times per year.

Deerfield High School, Deerfield, Illinois
Highland Park High School, Highland Park, Illinois

These two high schools have approximately 1,400 and 1,800 students, respectively, and are located in a suburban district north of Chicago. While serving fairly different student populations, they have the same model of advisory program. Only the 9th grade is enrolled in advisory groups, which are led by trios, including one teacher and two 12th grade students. Becoming a student co-leader is a highly sought after and selective role.

The advisory program is scheduled every day for 42 minutes, includes about 25 students, and can be scheduled for any period of the day like any other class. Two of the five weekly sessions are guided study halls. The other sessions focus on getting acclimated to school, building community, academic planning, and monthly themes, including diversity, service projects, substance abuse, sexually transmitted diseases, career exploration, how to study for final exams, and other topics. There are fun activities woven throughout the year. The Advisory Coordinator distributes activities each month to the leaders. The Advisory Coordinator role is held by a school social worker at Deerfield and by a Family and Consumer Science teacher at Highland Park. The role comprises 20-40 percent of their responsibilities.

During the summer, advisory leaders (both student leaders and teachers) participate in a half-day of training together, and the student leaders receive an additional half-day. During the school year, the student leaders participate in one to two lunch meetings per month with the Advisory Coordinator, and one meeting per month with the teacher co-leaders. At Deerfield, the January group meetings are replaced with individual meetings so each senior co-leader receives more specific support.

In addition to the Advisory Coordinators, the counselors actively support the advisory program. At Highland Park, they are involved in the trainings during the summer and the academic year. Advisory groups are the counselors' vehicles for working with students on four-year plans and specific challenges.

At Deerfield High School, four of the sixteen advisory groups are designated music advisories. These students do fewer of the activities than other advisory groups, but still build a sense of community. The school has found this arrangement allows more students to fit music into their schedules.

Teachers who have an advisory group teach four academic classes plus their advisory. Each administrator teaches one class; several choose to make that an advisory group each year. Advisory is not graded, and though progress reports are sent to parents, ensuring that it is taken seriously is an ongoing challenge. Teacher-advisors are supported and supervised, but not evaluated.

The advisory program started about twenty years ago at Highland Park High School, when school board members, who had experienced advisory groups during their own high school experiences in neighboring communities, promoted the program. With success at Highland Park, Deerfield implemented the same model. Highland Park had separate advisory groups for non-English-speaking students; now each recent immigrant student is matched with an advisor and a student leader of similar background to provide the extra support needed to acclimate to school.

Both schools adjust their advisory programs as needed, changing the themes and piloting new arrangements. For example, Highland Park is experimenting with linking advisory to the humanities curriculum. The goal, however, is constant: creating a stronger connection for students, which seems only to become more important in recent years as enrollments increase.

Needham High School, Needham, Massachusetts

Needham High School has over 1300 students in a building whose additions and renovations reflect the growth of this Boston suburb. In the mid-1990s NHS created Mentor Homerooms, a 10-minute block every day. Students are assigned a faculty mentor when they enter 9th grade and stay with that mentor throughout their high school years. Each homeroom group includes students from each grade level, with a few new students added to the group each year as a few graduate.

Mentor homerooms are scheduled between the first and second class periods of each day, when both tardy students or those who don't have a first-period class can be involved. When mentor homeroom was first implemented, all teachers and administrators had groups. At present, not all faculty serve as mentors as there are fewer rooms than potential mentors. Groups have 18 to 20 students, more than they would like, but that is a result of the number of rooms. Students are assigned randomly within a counselor's load, except for six special homerooms filled with students who work on the yearbook, student newspaper, literary magazine, student council, or students with social/emotional issues and attendance challenges.

Needham High School found, however, that creating the time slot and assigning groups was not sufficient for implementing a real mentoring effort. Though homeroom had been designed purposely to mix 9th through 12th graders, in too many homerooms most students sat in fixed, separate groups. Despite being together multiple years, they knew very few of the other students. Without intentional effort, the mix of students was simply physical proximity. Further, alumni, who are surveyed one year and five years after graduating, too often reported that they did not feel a close connection with a teacher during their high school years, and that they would have liked feeling more known. So, in 2002, NHS embarked on a renewal of mentor homerooms. This effort complemented work the district had undertaken to reduce the achievement gap, and has been a component of district-wide work on improving social and emotional learning in grades K-12.

At first, the Mentor Homeroom Initiative (MHI) team, as they are called, was small—a counselor and a science teacher, with an assistant principal serving as liaison to administration, and a consultant supporting the effort. Several changes were implemented, starting with protecting the homeroom time from intercom announcements, which are now mostly limited to two days. It was also agreed that mentor homerooms would have one 30-minute block per month for longer tasks and topics, such as report card discussions, and reflecting on the anniversary of the September 11 attacks.

The MHI team was conscious that teachers could resent a new responsibility and that only a little professional development time would be available. With several days of planning and writing over the summer, they created a safety net of activities and tips that are very easy for teachers to use. The 2002-03 school year included specific activities for the first week of school, every Wednesday thereafter, and more when needed. The MHI team has grown to five, so more teachers are sharing the work. With planning meetings every other month, and each team member taking responsibility for a month, the process has been quite smooth.

Activities appear in mentors' homeroom folders each week and cover a wide range: peer interviews, fun brain-teasers, group "quizzes" about African-American history, problem-solving about cafeteria issues, report card discussions, and adolescent issues. Student groups, such as Students Against Drunk Driving, have organized some of the homeroom topics. The range of activities is designed to build familiarity, school involvement, and a respectful atmosphere, despite the short time slot.

The half-hour blocks of mentor homerooms have been critical for processing tragedies and serious topics. For such times, mentors are given background materials, suggestions for discussions, and a co-leader, if needed. For instance, the school held assemblies last year on sexual assault among teens, and mentor homerooms provided background information and a week of discussion prompts to offer preparation and follow-up to the assemblies.

The activities supplied by the MHI team are meant to be a safety net; mentors are welcome to choose alternatives. Most choose to use the activities, and their success has been noted. Student representatives to the school board reported that discussions with mentors about report cards and goals for the next term proved meaningful, and showed that their mentor was monitoring and caring about how they did in school.

The first year provided a clear and supportive way for teachers to ease into the role. During its second year, the team worked to recruit a member from each academic department and organized monthly themes. Now that more teachers are comfortable as mentors, the MHI team looks forward to offering more professional development to improve students' experiences further.

Cincinnati Country Day School – Upper School, Cincinnati, Ohio

Cincinnati Country Day School is an independent school whose 310 Upper School students are divided into advisories of seven to ten students each, mixing grades 9-12. The groups stay together with the same advisor all four years of upper school. The mixed grade groupings create peer mentor relationships, with older students helping younger students to sort out participation in clubs and activities, a well as to manage stress. The small group size prevents cliques within advisory groups, which are put together using random and intentional placement processes. This structure and their chosen advisory content led the dean of student life to describe advisory as carrying forward the culture of the school.

Advisory at CCD Upper School meets briefly every morning and each Friday for 35 minutes. The focus of advisory changed dramatically a few years ago. It had been quite informal. Food and the accompanying discussion of food were central, giving advisory its nickname, "doughnut time." CCD Upper School now uses a format that is quite unusual, however. Each Friday session (except for seven spread through the year that focus on grades and courses) is organized around a weekly questionnaire. The advisory leaders are three school administrators—the dean of student life, the dean of diversity, and the dean of students—leaders who have a good sense of what the pressing issues on campus are, and thus can craft meaningful questions.

The questionnaires are small—three to four questions each—providing access points for discussion. Because these are questionnaires, not just questions, the responses are collected. This structure helped advisors make the transition to more intentionally designed time. In the first two years, the questionnaires focused on school life and programming, giving students a voice and sense of school citizenship—what it means to be a thoughtful member of a community. For example, one set of questions asked for students' thoughts on how CCD promotes athletics; another allowed students to vent about specific discipline actions that were bound to stimulate controversy. Responses were collected and some were published in a weekly column of the school's newspaper. More recent topics have dealt with larger issues, such as affirmative action, how it plays out on campus and in the world. The advisory discussions led to further exploration in an assembly.

Other advisory activities include a Community Service Day. CCD also promotes student mentor relationships by having 12th grade students lead an orientation program and co-lead health classes.

Now that CCD has used the questionnaire structure for three years, they've been through many topics, with weekly practice discussing issues of import and impact. Faculty have become more skilled at facilitating discussions and have learned more about students' perspectives. Advisors are well-supported, though not formally trained. The dean of student life coaches advisors as needed on the tougher or more sensitive topics.

All faculty serve as advisors. The advisor, the primary contact for parents, supports students through discipline proceedings and is a liaison with faculty. Advisors coach advisees on how to communicate with faculty, inform faculty of special circumstances in students' lives, and respond to faculty requests to work through particular student issues. A student who is called to the discipline panel would be accompanied by her/his advisor. Serving as an advisor is part of faculty members' overall evaluation, with focus on such responsibilities as communicating effectively with parents.

Fenway High School, Boston, Massachusetts

What began as Social Issues Class when the school opened in 1983 became advisory in the mid-1990s. Fenway High School is a small urban pilot high school within the Boston Public Schools serving 270 students. Advisory groups, which meet three times per week for one hour, are one way that Fenway ensures that students feel a sense of community. Other ways include an extended orientation program and a 9th grade adventure off campus, both of which involve community building, teamwork, and getting acclimated to school. The entire school has a Community Building Day each September, as well as other advisory-driven events that encourage a positive school climate. The school is divided into three houses of 90 students each, with one counselor per house. Advisory groups include students from within a house. The advisors and the counselors within each house meet to monitor students' progress.

Advisory groups include students from one grade level. They are larger than at many schools, ranging from 18-25 students per group. The 9th and 10th grade groups each have two advisors, one male and one female. Some advisors loop with their groups for two years (grades 9-10 or 11-12). Almost all faculty members have a group; it is part of the teacher job description. Advisory is graded. For grades 9-10, most advisors opt to give Pass/Fail rather than letter grades; for grades 11-12, many advisors opt to give letter grades. The assistant principal oversees advisory.

Like most schools, content varies from group to group within certain parameters. Advisory in 9th grade focuses on building the Fenway Tool Kit—that is, time management, presentation skills, and interpersonal and organizational skills. The 10th grade group focuses on community service. There is no separate health education class at Fenway, so 9th and 10th grade advisories include a number of adolescent health and wellness topics. Advisory in grades 11 and 12 is quite structured and centers around planning for the future. Students take interest inventories, identify potential careers, interview people in those careers, and undergo an extensive process preparing for "Junior Review," a major exhibition of each student's work. In 12th grade advisory, students get support for writing college essays, planning for their futures, and developing their portfolios.

All advisory groups support students to take responsibility for their own learning plans, to identify challenges, and to problem-solve creatively and effectively. Several students distinguished the atmosphere of advisory from academic classes as involving more teamwork and communication, adding that advisory feels more like a family.

Advisors are the primary contact for parents. Students were unanimous and adamant in voicing the big difference it made to them that their advisor and parents communicate. Advisors are coaches, not advocates in discipline matters. Progress reports and report cards are given out by the counselors, not by the advisors.

Lyons Township High School, LaGrange, Illinois

Lyons Township High School has 3200 students on two campuses in a town west of Chicago. Advisory was instituted fully during the 2001- 02 academic year after much discussion over three years, the creation of a pilot curriculum, and inclusion in the new teachers' contract. It meets once a week for 25 minutes with about 20 students per group. On the day that advisory is held, periods are five minutes shorter to make time. Advisory is added to a teacher's class load.

Groups include students from a single grade level, computer-generated and heterogeneously grouped within a counselor's caseload. Students in an advisor group stay together all four years of high school. The group has one advisor while at the grade 9 -10 campus, and a new advisor when those students move to the grade 11-12 campus. The organizing committee would have suggested staying with the same advisor all four years if students stayed on one campus.

Teachers, administrators, librarians, and other professionals have advisor groups, though not first-year teachers or paraprofessionals. Counselors do not serve as advisors; they are available to support advisor groups. The 12-person committee that oversees advisory includes administrators, counselors, and teachers. Advisors are not involved in discipline, and though some do contact parents, the advisor was not designed to be the primary parent contact, and most advisors are not in touch with parents.

Since advisory has only been in place a few years at Lyons Township High School, advisors are still getting accustomed to the role, and the design committee is still figuring out how much structure to offer. During the first year, advisors had explicit activities for every session; this, however, provided too much structure. In the second year, advisors were given more general support. Now, in the third year, topics and lessons are identified on LT's intranet web site. While some are assigned to specific dates, others offer more flexibility. Advisors can print out lesson plans if they choose.

Overall, advisory focuses on establishing a sense of community and improving students' communication skills. It is organized on monthly themes and five "First Class Principles" addressing respect for each other and for the school setting, creative problem-solving, self-management, responsibility, and accountability. New topics and materials are added as needs arise, for example, offering students a place to talk about world crises.

Some advisory topics involve setting goals and considering study habits, but these lessons are used to support students' academic work indirectly. Advisors do not focus on progress or problems in particular classes. Emphasis is on connection and not directly on academic coaching.

Preparation for advisory included some time in school to review materials the year prior to implementation, a four-hour summer workshop, and quarterly follow-up meetings in the first year. After the introductory year, advisory training is one of the options on professional development days, though a design committee member wished they had been able to offer more intensive training and support.

In the latest phase of LT's advisory program, advisors have nominated students from their groups to be trained as co-leaders. Thus, students in grades 10, 11, and 12 are co-leaders of their own advisory groups. The academic year 2002-03 is the first year of this arrangement, so the co-leader's role is still developing.

Boston Arts Academy, Boston, Massachusetts

As Boston Arts Academy (BAA) prepared to open in 1997, staff interviewed numerous people in the arts community, asking them what the most crucial skill is for young artists. Whether they interviewed visual artists, musicians, arts administrators, or people in other arts fields, they consistently heard that young artists have to be able to write. The art professionals stressed that learning to write is part of the process of learning to express oneself as an artist, a crucial skill for applying for grants, and many other important tasks. School leaders at BAA, a pilot school within the Boston Public Schools with 400 urban students, decided an intensive and personalized instructional approach around writing would be the most effective. So BAA's advisory program is Writing Advisory. Imagine a high school where all teachers, no matter what else they teach, share responsibility for one skill area and everyone is learning and teaching writing skills!

Writing Advisory meets every day for 45 minutes. It used to be scheduled first thing in the morning, unfortunately just when many students are tired and hungry, so it was moved to follow lunch. The change in schedule also better conveyed that advisory is a serious commitment, not to be skipped.

Advisory serves many of the same purposes as at other schools—adjusting to high school and supporting students' progress—but adds an emphasis on writing. Advisory is organized by grade, with a writing focus that develops over the high school years. The 9th grade writing goal is to write a lot, with a focus on personal stories and community. The 10th grade goal is to write with purpose; while 11th graders focus on writing with purpose on complex issues. Seniors write college essays and a grant proposal for an original arts project. (The school's foundation is able to fund some of the proposals!) It is a graded class; if students fail Writing Advisory, they go to summer school.

Advisor/advisee assignments are designed to offer maximal support for students' transitions into and out of high school. The 9th grade advisors provide considerable structure so students acclimate to the high expectations and rigors of the Arts Academy. The 11th and 12th grade advisor groups are assigned according to arts focus. For example, an advisor who is a dancer leads an advisory group of dancers. Since those students need postsecondary advice from those instructors, grouping them together in advisory is efficient and effective.

A lead teacher oversees advisory and the professional development needed for it. Because BAA's advisory program has such a strong content focus, advisors get significant professional training on the skills within one grade level, and stay with their group for one year. Advisors meet monthly in grade-level teams. BAA's first parent conference each fall is with advisors, which reinforces the seriousness of Writing Advisory to parents, students, and to the advisors themselves.

Middle Schools

Cincinnati Country Day School – Middle School, Cincinnati, Ohio

The Middle School at Cincinnati Country Day School has an advisory program that is very different from its Upper School, and also unusual. Their groups are separated by gender, include students from only one grade level, and stay together from grade 6 through grade 8.

CCD Middle School is organized in grade-level teams, with all the important benefits that come with teams, including holistic connection with students, coherent instruction, and sense of community. Some 15 years ago, their advisories included students from multiple grades who were with an advisor multiple years, but that schema ran counter to the purpose of teams. They restructured advisory to be consistent with teams, forming grade-level groups led by an advisor from within the team. The Middle School division head describes this structure as "reinforcing the same comprehensive unit of identity and relatedness."

While a group of advisees stays together for three years, the group gets a new advisor as they advance to each new grade, always having an advisor from within the grade-level team. Having experienced two very different advisor arrangements—advisors who continue for three years, and advisors who are consistent with the one-year team structure—they find the latter to be more effective.

The switch to single-gender groups was more recent. CCD Middle School administrators and teachers learned from research on early adolescent development that 11-14-year-olds benefit from time with same-gender peers. While students might find the contact they need at informal times, CCD chose to ensure that it would happen (and not just through physical education classes). So, five years ago they reorganized advisory to be single-gender groups within grade-level teams.

After the initial uproar from students, benefits started to become evident. The advisors of girls' groups noted that the girls were more relaxed, less self-conscious, that they were not spending time preening, and were instead having more meaningful discussions. These observations confirmed the research. The boys' groups did not measurably improve, but were at least as good as the earlier ones, so this structure has remained.

Each advisory group has ten to twelve students. The school used to assign groups intentionally, striving for "compatible groupings," and unwittingly found that they had reinforced some cliques. Now the school assigns groups alphabetically. Though this arrangement met with some initial resistance, it has proved far better. There are fewer parents advocating for special placements, and the groups reinforce the code of conduct that everyone should treat others with respect. Students (and parents) are reminded that treating others with respect is consistent with a willingness to work with any and all of one's peers.

Because the team structure at CCD Middle School is so strong and advisories are consistent with the teams, the term "by advisory" connotes a group that is relationally strong, thoughtfully planned, developmentally appropriate, and institutionally aligned. In the first two weeks of school, lunch is by advisory, eliminating student anxiety about where to sit. Community service day projects are by advisory. Seating at assemblies and locker assignments are by advisory. Student council election is by advisory, with important consequences: each advisory is represented, making communication easy, there are an equal number of boys and girls, and campaigning for election requires speaking to one's advisory group—a task far less intimidating than campaigning across the school.

Advisor groups meet first thing every morning for five minutes and for thirty minutes after lunch and recess. One session per week involves affective topics or school business, such as trip arrangements or discipline issues. Two sessions per week are "choice days," when the group can decide what to do. The remaining two are guided study halls. The affective focus changes yearly to suit students' needs. CCD Middle School does not use a set curriculum, nor do they expect to find one that would be individualized enough to meet their needs or last more than a year.

Advisors monitor advisees' social, emotional, and academic growth. They are fully involved with all aspects of their advisees' experience at CCD; they hold the comprehensive overview of each advisee's progress. Because of the team structure, they are aware of their advisees' classes and requirements. Advisors are the primary contact with parents; they distribute report cards; they support advisees through disciplinary actions. CCD advisors are trained through the school's mentor program for new teachers and through the team structure.

Sacajawea Middle School, Bozeman, Montana

"An advisory program is a critical element in a school where you want to have every kid connected to an adult. I don't know how you'd ensure that sense of connection and community without it," Sacajawea's principal states. Clearly, advisory is a core element of life at this school.

Sacajawea Middle School is in Bozeman, Montana, a university town, with approximately 650 students in grades 6, 7, and 8. Sacajawea had advisory for at least a decade in its former building and for the six years it has been in its new building. The school is organized in grade-level houses with two teams per house, providing another vehicle for decreasing anonymity and increasing support for kids. Each team includes 110–125 students and 4–5 teachers.

Advisory in this middle school is grade-level specific and is held every day for 25 minutes. The 6th and 8th grade teams hold advisory first thing every morning, while the 7th grade teams hold it just before lunch. This allows them to extend advisory and use it for celebrations. Advisor groups have 20–22 students each.

Themes have changed over the year, but the current array focuses on interpersonal skill-building over the three years. The 6th grade advisory theme is respect and responsibility; the 7th grade theme is conflict resolution and diversity; the 8th grade theme is mediation and communication. Advisory has five main objectives: developing social skills; establishing shared vocabulary and language for school norms; emphasizing cooperation, caring, communication, appreciation of diversity, responsible problem-solving and conflict resolution; getting personally involved in making a peaceable school culture; and (particularly through the 2001–2002 school year) understanding what is happening in the world. The themes and skills addressed are revisited periodically as the advisors and principal identify important student needs.

Lessons are drawn from materials by Kreidler, Crawford, and Bodine. (See Recommended Resources) While advisory does include helping students with some organizing and self-monitoring skills, it is deliberately not focused on academics. Comments are written about student participation; advisory is not graded.

After Sacajawea moved to its new building, they dedicated a few days to professional development for advisory. Since then, the structure and focus has been collaboratively driven as the principal and teachers spend time annually considering how to adjust advisory to better support students.

All core teachers and elective teachers who are on teams serve as advisors and are the primary contact for parents. For teacher evaluations, the principal observes subject area classes and advisory sessions. Advisors are not involved directly in office disciplinary matters, though they are behind-the-scenes coaches to their advisees.

Park Junior High School, LaGrange, Illinois

Located in a suburb west of Chicago, this grade 7-8 school of 650 students has an advisory program linked to its team structure. Park had a personal development class that became advisory groups when the school went through various reforms to embrace the middle school concept. The school day was lengthened slightly as these reforms were implemented. Given the team structure, advisors work with students on their team, thus groups include students from only one grade level. Students change groups and advisors for 8th grade.

Advisors are the main contacts for parents and are key in supporting students' academic development. Via advisory, students plan and then host their own parent-teacher conferences, where they show their work. Advisors distribute grade reports and teach students to use assignment notebooks in 7th grade. Advisors are involved in disciplinary issues by working with students on behavioral contracts.

The broad themes for advisory are goal-setting, decision-making, team-building, and personal and interpersonal responsibility, which are outlined in a two-year cycle of curricula. Materials are given out weekly to advisors, who have flexibility to address new issues as they arise. There are several options offered so teams can select activities to suit their group. Students engage in small local service projects, building up to more significant projects later at Lyons Township High School. At Park, advisory serves as the main vehicle for helping students develop social and emotional skills. Advisory is not graded, though the school is implementing a feedback process for parents based on benchmarks about social and emotional learning.

Groups meet for twenty-two minutes, first thing in the morning, four days per . Advisory at Park includes basic homeroom tasks. Advisory groups have grown in the seven years since they were started, from fifteen students on average to 17-20 per group. All full-time teachers serve as advisors. In order to reduce the size of the groups, some administrators or part-time teachers might be involved in the future. The program is coordinated by a steering committee, including one teacher from each grade who has primary responsibility for producing the content materials.

Endnotes

[1] Peggy Silva and Robert A. Mackin. *Standards of Mind and Heart: Creating the Good High School* (New York: Teachers College Press, 2002),. 63.

[2] Ibid., 58, 63.

[3] Ibid., 60.

CHAPTER 3

The Advisory Design Puzzle

This chapter takes each puzzle piece and offers questions and information to guide a design team through its planning. We recommend creating a rough draft as you work your way through the puzzle, then come back to refine—like roughing out a construction project on a house or outlining a research project. Think of past students who became frustrated when they had to do revisions and third drafts of a paper. Groups that have spent hours fine-tuning one particular aspect may feel stubborn or discouraged if that piece doesn't fit when they focus on the rest of the plan. Thus, avoid fine-tuning any one puzzle piece until all are beginning to take shape.

When we interviewed school leaders where advisory had existed for several years, and asked them to describe their advisory program, the almost universal response was, "Which iteration should I describe? This year's, last year's, our ideas for next year, … the model we started with?" They uttered these questions matter-of-factly, only occasionally with frustration, because the expectation existed that advisory would shift to meet different needs at different times. The design questions in the puzzle sections are for use at the inception of your advisory program, and through its revisions and restructurings.

Fitting the Pieces Together

As you design your advisory program, keep in mind that some pieces fit together well and others simply do not. Below we offer a few examples of combinations that are likely to succeed and some that are likely to be problematic. For example, if the goals and associated professional development are not aligned, faculty will feel (and be) set up to fail. Or when the content does not meet students' needs, students can revolt via nonattendance or parent complaints. We have seen some poorly designed advisory programs result in distrust of leaders, union complaints, schisms among faculty, and many other challenges. Thus, we have identified scenarios below that are optimal, sufficient, and doomed. Badly designed programs can more than problematic; they can be doomed.

Goal: community-building among students, promoting a positive peer culture

Optimal: at least a half-hour block, held at least weekly, in addition to more frequent, if shorter, contact
Students can engage in peer interviews, group exercises, service projects, and build a strong practice of discussing important topics.

Sufficient: at least a half-hour block, held at least monthly, with shorter time slots held more frequently

If advisors use the short time slots carefully, making sure that isolated students are brought into the fold, and students are mixing, rather than sitting in static cliques, then there will be enough of a platform for the occasional longer blocks to include discussions and group projects.

Doomed: infrequent or only short time blocks, such as one monthly gathering, or only daily ten-minute slots

While daily ten-minute slots may work for some purposes (see academic advising, below), they will not be sufficient for group activities or real community-building. Exercises done without time to process can backfire. Community-building is about relationships, and relationships take time.

Goal: academic advising and coaching

Optimal: individual contact each month through daily ten to fifteen minute sessions, plus occasional longer blocks and private meetings; or private contact each month plus group sessions two to three times per week for 20 minutes

Advisors will have private time with each student to discuss course selection and grades. With frequent contact, they can monitor how students are doing, have two-minute check-ins with individual students at least weekly, and have time for longer conversations and reflections after grades are announced, before exam season, or around major projects. The occasional longer blocks will allow students to celebrate successes, brainstorm study tips, and maybe even peer tutor. In this way, advisors will help students create a positive peer culture around academics.

Sufficient: frequent (daily or almost daily) contact for short amounts of time

All students will be helped by daily contact with an advisor who is watching out for students when they need encouragement, special services, even occasional nagging about big projects. There will be time for short individual check-ins, quick group exercises about handling stress, and group energizers before exams.

Doomed version #1: infrequent contact

Long monthly blocks may be useful for encouraging school spirit, for example, but they will not be frequent enough to monitor student progress, watch for students who need a referral, or to offer study tips.

Doomed version #2: unscheduled contact

If advisors do not have scheduled time for meeting with advisees, they are likely to have rushed, haphazard, or inequitable contact. Gifted students will seek out the advisor, and the advisor will make a point of monitoring struggling students, but the kids in the middle will be overlooked. This design also makes no intentional impact on peer culture.

Doomed version #3: no private time with advisees and/or no expectation of contact with parents

Academic advising becomes real when it is specific and personal, and makes an effort to partner with parents.

Goal: prepare students for college and career

(In this case, we focus on grouping rather than scheduling choices.)

Optimal: use this focus for grades 11 or 12, separately or combined

Students in grades 11 and 12 are thinking about life after high school. Interest inventories, sharing information from career exploration interviews or college visits will be immediately meaningful.

Sufficient: use this focus for grade 11 and/or grade 12 groups as support to college and career guidance and counseling services

Advisors can play a supporting role in the college and career exploration process, even if they are not the small, highly personalized, and long-term shepherds of the process.

Doomed: use this focus with mixed groups of grades 9 through 12

What a 14-year-old and a 17-year-old think about are different. While career exploration might be structured to be interesting to a 9th grader, it will be a very different design from me for students who are feeling all the pressures and immediacy of senior year.

Design Considerations

Ask reality-testing questions throughout the design process

As your design team considers what the goals will be for your advisory program, there are likely to be specific schedules, professional development needs, and other puzzle pieces that are optimal, sufficient, and doomed to be problematic. It will be important to do frequent reality tests throughout the design process. Building a habit of asking reality-test questions will help connect the abstract ideas to the concrete tasks.

For example, ask yourselves:

- If our goal is career exploration, what kinds of activities and reflections will we need to do and how much time do those exercises take? If our goal is improving students' interpersonal skills, what kinds of exercises will be effective, in how much time, and with what training?

- If we are planning to combine students across grades, let's say, grades 9 through 12, what specific exercises and tasks during advisory will take advantage of that mix and serve each student's needs?

- If we plan to make advisors the primary contact for parents, have we made time for that task? What procedures should we establish so advisors get the information they need to be helpful to students and parents? What training, protocols, or coaching might our teachers need to communicate effectively with our parent population?

- How will advisory coordinators, advisors, and students know that the program is working? Which goals will have observable outcomes expected?

Three suggestions for the design team to keep in mind:

- Keep asking the questions that connect the vision to the daily reality.

- Remember, no puzzle piece should be considered finished until all puzzle pieces fit.

- Return to the design questions throughout the first year of implementation (and maybe longer or every few years) for refining.

Consider implementing advisory all at once or in stages.
Building buy-in, developing competence, and creating a good program take time and strategic thinking. What arrangement will be successful at your school?

Staging advisory can involve decisions about:

- the frequency of sessions

- the length of sessions

- involving the whole faculty and student body, or only some grades or clusters

There are potential advantages and drawbacks with each decision to phase in implementation.

Your program can start with infrequent sessions that become more frequent, or start with short sessions, building up to longer advisory meetings over the year. Advantages of phasing in frequency or length include not scaring faculty and alleviating some of the planning. Disadvantages can be not developing a sense of community or having enough time for academic advising.

Phasing in students and faculty—that is, starting with one grade level or cluster, and adding other grades or clusters the second year—also carries advantages and drawbacks. If your school has self-contained clusters, starting with those groups might be possible and easier to manage. There will be fewer lessons to plan and fewer advisors to train. This design might mean that advisors have volunteered for the role (rather than being forced into it), and might be able to model and mentor new advisors in the future. However, if students can take classes outside their cluster, or if teachers occasionally teach outside their cluster, the scheduling dilemmas can be nightmares.

The decisions made by the advisory design team at Westerville South High School (Ohio) serve to illustrate these staging decisions. Advisory is one of the first components of their overall high school redesign process. Westerville South High School's design team decided to start with a fairly modest plan—30 minutes every other week, with all activities supplied, and with all students and all faculty involved. They hope to deepen the activities over time and increase the frequency to a half-hour each week starting in second semester. They expect this staging to maximize use of space, minimize advisor-advisee ratios, and enhance the sense of community ("we're all in this together"), while they jointly develop the program.

Design Checklist

This checklist previews the components and choices identified throughout the design puzzle. It may be useful as your design team develops the plan and the timeline for implementing an advisory program in your school.

Implementation components

____ Team(s) are formed of people who will do research, design, and PR.

____ There are at least six months (more is far better!) for the planning phase.

____ A timeline is set with sufficient days and hours identified for

> ✔ research

> ✔ visits and/or calls to other schools

> ✔ design meetings

> ✔ PR tasks for fielding questions, communicating design components, spreading inspiration, and building buy-in with faculty, staff, students, parents, and other community members in the year prior to launching advisory and throughout the first year.

____ Financial resources and time are available for sufficient professional development of advisors.

____ We have outlined how to phase in our advisory program—that is, launching it with all faculty involved from the beginning, starting with one grade level, starting with short or infrequent time slots, or other arrangement.

Design components

Our design articulates the following:

____ Goals and rationales of the advisory program as a whole.

____ Goals and rationales for specific grade levels.

____ Expected outcomes for advisees, advisory groups, and school climate and culture.

____ People (or at least positions) who will coordinate the advisory program and offer supervision and/or support to advisors as needed. Who will be in that role? Will that role be full-time or combined with other duties? What authority and responsibilities will the advisory coordinator have?

____ Schedule—i.e., length and frequency of sessions, how sessions will fit in the schedule, whether or not all groups will meet simultaneously.

___ Grouping arrangements

- ✔ size of groups
- ✔ mix of students (grade level, gender)
- ✔ how assignments will be determined (random or intentional by certain factors)
- ✔ continuity of the group of students
- ✔ continuity of the students with the advisor

___ Content and themes for advisory groups (by grade level, by month, by whatever organizational strategy makes sense for your school), and to what extent groups are expected to do the same activities.

___ Routines, formats, and style of advisory groups.

___ Advisors' responsibilities are clarified regarding

- ✔ academic advising, report cards, progress reports
- ✔ exhibitions and portfolios
- ✔ parent contact
- ✔ discipline
- ✔ career and college preparation
- ✔ school business and school involvement
- ✔ referrals for tutoring, counseling, or other needs

___ Professional development sessions are scheduled prior to launching advisory groups, and throughout the first year of implementation.

___ Materials and resources are available for advisors.

___ Accountability processes are identified that will

- ✔ influence students to take advisory seriously and participate effectively
- ✔ document outcomes achieved
- ✔ influence advisors to take advisory seriously and facilitate effectively
- ✔ assess the advisory program's impact on the goals identified

___ Links to other school programs, procedures, events, and structures are well understood and happen smoothly.

Goals & outcomes

Start with your school's mission. What goals could advisory serve to better achieve that mission?

Perhaps your school's mission emphasizes certain character traits, habits of mind, preparation for a specific career field, or building skills for democracy. Any of these missions can influence your advisory goals.

Consider your student population. What goals could advisory serve to help them be more successful?

Be sure to think about *all* of your students. There may be some for whom advisory could make a significant difference in their experience of school.

Listed below are a few examples of goals that schools have set for their advisor groups, with similar goals grouped together.

Goals related to sense of connection:

- Advisees will be known and feel known consistently by one adult.

- Advisors will get to know advisees well as learners and as people.

- Advisees will feel a sense of belonging to a peer group.

Goals related to academic advising and coaching:

- Advisees will have easy and regular access to academic advising from an advisor who actively monitors their progress.

- Advisees will engage regularly in goal-setting and self-assessment.

- Advisees will develop study and organizational skills that will support academic success.

- Advisors will provide oversight of and coaching around major projects and portfolios.

- Advisees will learn to advocate for themselves and deal effectively with adults.

- Advisors will help advisees see the connection between success in school and options for the future.

Goals related to adjustment to new grade levels and academic work:
- Advisees will adjust more effectively to high school or middle school, and to new grade levels. They will adjust to the schedule, to special benchmark projects, and to the rules and expectations.

- Advisory groups will provide advisees with opportunities to learn about, and encouragement to participate in, extra-curricular activities.

Goals related to development of interpersonal and intrapersonal skills:
- Advisees will learn to be more self-aware, self-managed, and self-directed.

- Advisees will develop cooperation and teamwork skills.

- Advisees will offer and find peer support.

- Advisees will contribute in a positive way to a school's climate.

- Advisees will develop constructive peer relationships.

- Advisor groups will be a means for participating in school decisions (student government, use of common spaces, organizing school events, and celebrations).

Goals related to parent/guardian contact:
- Advisors will be the primary and consistent contact for parents and guardians, so that parents can access holistic information about, and be more supportive of, their child.

- The advisory program will strengthen parents' and guardians' awareness of, involvement in, and support of the school.

- Advisors will develop partnership with parents and guardians to encourage their child's progress.

Goals offer purpose and inspiration. They also will help the design team select content and decide on logistics and many other aspects of the process, so don't leave your goals in a file—bring them into the practical planning conversations.

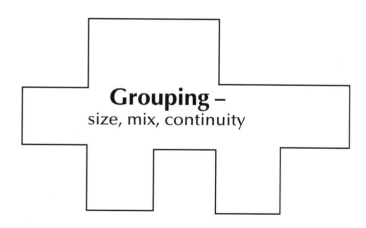

Grouping –
size, mix, continuity

Research and interviews for this guide showed as many variations in how advisory groups are organized as there are advisory programs. Arrangements varied as to the size of the groups, whether students were from one or more grades, whether or not the advisor stayed with the group for multiple years, and many other aspects, each addressed in the questions below.

What size group would best serve your goals?

If your goals are to provide intensive coaching around portfolios and career preparation, or an intimate environment for interpersonal skill development, having small groups will be crucial. Many schools find groups of 12-15 students to be effective, though several schools have found that even smaller groups of eight to twelve students provide greater personalized support and avoid cliques. Depending on your goals, frequency of meeting, and availability of advisors, other sizes might be appropriate, or at least workable.

Are you stepping slowly into advisory or diving right in?

Some schools start with one grade level, often the youngest grade level in the school – grade 6 in a middle school or grade 9 in a high school. Others start with everybody. If you start with one or two grade levels, what will the other grades do during that block? Can the schedule accommodate this variation? Schools might choose to hold advisor groups for 9th graders, a silent reading time for 10th graders, career and college preparation sessions for 11th and 12th graders.

Which adults can be advisors? How many adults are there?

Advisors can be faculty, administrators, counselors, librarians, coaches, aides, coordinators, secretaries, and custodians. There are different rationales for including or not including some of these roles in the pool of advisors. (See below for more on the pros and cons of counselors serving as advisors.) Including secretaries and custodians as advisors may fit with the goals and content expectations of your advisory program, or may not, depending on that piece of the puzzle. If they do fit, schools have found several advantages to including them, such as breaking down hierarchy, spreading credibility more widely, and giving all adults in a school the chance to build relationships, which helps in their other roles.

If all faculty are expected to serve as advisors, does that really mean all of them?

Several schools reported that an ongoing challenge is that not everyone is necessarily suited to, or sufficiently willing to fill, the role of advisor, and that the whole purpose of advisory is defeated if the advisor is alienating to students. See the professional development section (p.65) for some suggestions on this dilemma, since many who are at first resistant and unskilled may become effective advisors over time. There can be, however, occasional faculty members who are inappropriate or deeply uncomfortable in the role. Most schools make arrangements for them to teach an extra class, supervise a lab, or take some other responsibility.

Should administrators be advisors?

In many schools, principals and/or assistant principals have advisor groups or share a group with a co-advisor. When administrators serve as advisors, they demonstrate the importance of advisory and have close connections with kids. In some cases it can be politically crucial for administrators to have advisor groups, especially if the program will involve all faculty, some of whom are resistant. In these cases, the administrators are showing their commitment to the program and experiencing the early rough edges along with the teachers.

Should counselors serve as advisors?

In some schools, counselors have appreciated the chance to have an ongoing relationship with a small group of students that is different from the relationship they normally have. Advisory in those schools becomes a forum shared by faculty and counselors. Sometimes counselors have the 12th grade groups and focus on the postsecondary transition. However, in many schools, counselors are the only adults who specifically do not have advisor groups. In those schools, counselors are available to advisor groups for career and college discussions, or, if needed, to help deal with the illness of a classmate, a horrible event in the world, or even a group dynamics problem within the group. Sometimes this backup support allows faculty to be less anxious about becoming advisors.

Will advisors facilitate a group alone or in pairs, or maybe you'll have some of both?

Some schools pair a new advisor with an experienced one for a term or a year. Others have larger groups with two advisors, paired for particular reasons, such as gender or race.

How many advisor group spaces are in your school?

Be sure to consider large offices, the library, conference rooms, and other spaces not generally used for classes. In many schools, all advisor groups are held simultaneously, so the number of spaces is a critical limiting factor. In a few schools, however, advisory is held at different times (see the schedule puzzle piece), allowing for more flexibility.

How many groups can you create?

Based on how many adults can serve as advisors and how many spaces there are, you can calculate how many students could be in each advisory group. What is that number? Groups vary from eight to twenty-five, but many advisors interviewed spoke strongly about preferring groups of 16 students or fewer. Does your calculated number fit with your goals? If not, what part of the formula can you alter?

How will you organize the groups of students?

Separate grade levels or mixed? Mixed with two grades, three, or four? Interviews and research for this guide found each of the following arrangements:

- Grade-specific advisory groups, no mixing of grades, whether at high schools or middle schools (especially within clusters or teams)

- 9th grade groups dedicated to the transition to high school, while 10th, 11th, and 12th were mixed

- 9th and 10th grades mixed, and 11th and 12th grades mixed

- 9th, 10th, and 11th grades mixed, and separate groups for 12th grade students

- Separate groups for 9th graders and for 12th graders to meet their needs to transition in and out of high school, while mixing 10th and 11th graders

- Groups that included all grades

In general, schools with a specific and strong content focus for advisory draw groups from single grades. Schools with a stronger interest in school-wide community building see greater value in crossing grade-level barriers. Some schools include students from all four grades who stay with the same group and advisor for four years, thus a few students graduate and a few new students are added each year. Schools that mix grades, even if they are drawing from only two grade levels, reported the benefit of older students being able to give advice that might never have been accepted from an adult, passing on the culture of the school, modeling what to expect in future years, and peer tutoring. Some advisors reported some of the same benefits even with students drawn from a single grade.

Will you have mixed-gender advisory groups or separate groups for boys and girls?

Several middle schools have found that advisory groups separated by gender have allowed for deeper discussions than had been the prior experience. High schools where advisory includes topics such as sex education, sexual harassment, and dating violence sometimes split groups by gender temporarily.

What process will you use for assigning groups?

The choices range widely, including having advisory group be the same as first-period class, assigning every nth name on an alphabetical list, or intentionally mixing groups. Schools that have used alphabetical or random assignments as well as intentional assignments have found that the latter caused more parent complaints.

How will faculty be assigned?

Will it be by grade/group they teach? Some advisors prefer to work with students they specifically do not have in class. Most, however, prefer advising students they are getting to know through class, since that allows them to know fewer students in greater depth. If you are creating an advisory program within clusters, houses, or teams, then this decision is clear. A set of teachers/advisors will work with a set of students in a holistic and coherent way.

Will advisors loop with a group for none, some, or all years?

Since the goal of advisory groups is to have advisors know their advisees well, keeping the same advisees for multiple years has obvious advantages. If groups meet frequently for significant amounts of time, that goal might be met within a year, even if advisors do not loop.

There are also strong reasons against looping. Where advisory groups are organized within grade-level clusters, as described above, advisors generally do not loop. Some of the advisors interviewed described feeling torn about not following their students for multiple years, yet they felt even more strongly about advisories being created within clusters.

Where advisory group content involves specialized knowledge, most schools do not loop, or loop only for two years. For example, in schools where 12th grade advisory involves supporting students in their processes of applying to college or other postsecondary opportunities, for financial aid or building a resume, advisors generally stay with 12th grade or work with 11th and 12th. In many schools, the process of postsecondary planning and preparation remains the province of guidance counselors, or there is a separate senior seminar, keeping this specialized area out of advisory.

Will the students in an advisory group stay together for multiple years, with or without the same advisor?

Groups that meet for small amounts of time per day or only one to two times per month can benefit from staying together multiple years. The group builds trust and interdependence. Groups that meet every day for 20 minutes or more might find that the group becomes cohesive during the fall, and that students benefit from going through the group-building process each year.

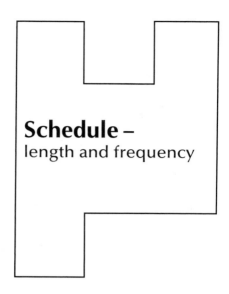

Schedule –
length and frequency

Some schools have chosen to hold daily advisory groups for ten minutes, 25 minutes, 45 minutes, or even an hour. Others hold sessions two or three times per week for 20 minutes to an hour per session. Still others hold sessions once a week, with limited goals. The questions below will help your design team think through important considerations about scheduling your program.

Keep in mind that facilitating an advisory group is a significant role. It is not hall duty. The longer the sessions are, the more preparation time advisors will need. Also, the more responsibility advisors have for monitoring student progress, the more the school will benefit from scheduling time for advisors to meet with counselors, teachers, and parents. As the design team ponders the scheduling options, remember to think about the schedule for the groups, for preparation, and for meetings.

What time arrangements can be considered at your school?
Design teams may need to consider any number of influences on the schedule: the teachers' contracts, special schedules with which people are already familiar (like assembly day schedules), cooperative scheduling arrangements with other schools involving students or potential advisors (if multiple schools share some teachers), or open campus norms for students who don't have first or last period classes. Perhaps your goals could be met by integrating advisory into already existent health education or career development courses, or senior seminar. Maybe advisory can be on a rotating schedule, so it replaces a class, but not the same class twice in any month.

To deal with contract constraints, some districts have shaved a few minutes from each period to stay within instructional minutes limits, or implemented advisory with thoroughly planned sessions to moderate additional preparations. When advisory has been implemented with a subset of a school's students and faculty, some schools have arranged for faculty to trade a duty for advisory, or have made stipends or professional development credit available for the tasks involved in creating and documenting the new effort. In some districts, advisory was implemented only on a pilot basis until a new teachers' contract was negotiated.

Also, think about what schedule will be accepted by faculty and parents. We do not mean to suggest that you plan pessimistically or over-conservatively. Teachers and parents might feel served and inspired by a terrific design. It is important, though, to keep reality in mind, knowing that you can at least strive a bit beyond it.

Whatever your considerations are, be creative about logistics, incentives, trade-offs, and supports.

What time arrangements will serve your goals?

Think about your goals and how much and what kind of time advisors and advisees will need to achieve the goals. You may need daily or less frequent contact, time for the advisory group and/or for private advisee meetings, or even larger blocks of time for off-campus projects. The more frequent and/or long the sessions are, the more preparation will have to be done as well —by the coordinator or committee, and by the advisors. If you cannot identify enough time to realistically work toward your goals, you may need to shape more modest goals. Here is one example from a school with significant goals and significant time for advisory.

New Mission High School in Boston, Massachusetts—which describes advisory as "the hub of students' experience" at the school—has extensive goals and thus, considerable time for its advisory groups. Advisory meets for 15 minutes every morning when students participate in connections and goal-setting rituals. They meet for a similar time slot at the end of each day for reflection rituals, checking whether they met the goals set that morning. During three additional blocks per week, of more than an hour each, advisees conduct extensive independent learning projects, prepare portfolios, and practice for portfolio presentations. Successful portfolio reviews are required for advancing to the next grade level and for graduating, so advisory is a serious commitment. Keep New Mission in mind as you read the puzzle sections about content and accountability.

Will your school hold advisory group first thing in the morning? Will it serve the purpose of homeroom as well, or will it serve your students better to keep those functions separate?

If advisory is held first thing in the morning, will all students be able to participate? Some schools hold ten-minute advisories after the first block of each day to ensure greater attendance. Many schools have moved advisory away from first block, specifically because it gave too many students a reason to arrive late to school, and because the school wanted advisory at a time of day when students were not tired and hungry.

Would it help your students to hold advisory at the end of the day?

Some middle schools, in particular, have scheduled end-of-the-day advisories, which give a structure for making sure students are conscious of homework assignments and of how to prepare for the next day.

Will all advisory groups be held simultaneously?

As you read in the snapshots, Souhegan High School holds advisory opposite the four different lunch blocks, which allows more advisory groups than rooms in the building. Deerfield and Highland Park High Schools schedule advisory like any other course, so different groups are meeting throughout the day.

Will advisory be held Mondays and Fridays to open and close the week, or will it be used to provide more frequent contact?

This arrangement can help students set and reflect on weekly goals. If advisors are trying to manage feisty or possibly volatile relationships between groups of students, advisory at the beginning of the week can offer a chance to monitor tensions, hear what happened over the weekend, and reframe the mood for the school week.

If your school can't have regularly scheduled time with all students, are there other ways to meet the needs of some students?

For example, some schools recruit mentors for students who don't seem to be self-directed, arrange dialogue groups that meet once per month with a teacher, or pilot advisory for students who sign up for study hall.

What about occasional long blocks?

Some small schools have chosen to hold half-day advisory groups once per term for service projects or off-campus community building. Would that arrangement fit your schedule and serve your goals?

Would a mixed schedule fit your school?

Some schools, like Needham High School, hold ten-minute daily advisory groups, plus one half-hour session per month to provide time for discussions after important assemblies, advising, or other group activities.

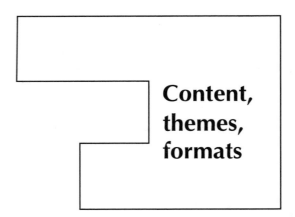

Content, themes, formats

There is some debate in the field about whether advisory programs should have a highly structured curriculum, a loosely organized curriculum, or no curriculum at all. While writing this guide, we found many schools that used to have very open-ended advisories, and none of them were satisfied with that structure. All of them have since changed or are in the process of changing to more clearly defined themes, formats, and activities with expected outcomes. Leaders from one school without sufficient content said it best when they commented, "TA is supposed to stand for Teacher Advisory, but half the time it looks like nothing but Take Attendance." Many schools are quite specific about activities and topics. The most successful advisory programs, however, commit to themes that reflect chosen goals and outcomes, and allow for variation from group to group based on the group's needs and the advisor's skills.

This puzzle piece introduces an array of content and focus areas, some that are common to most advisory programs, others that are more specialized. It also asks the design team to consider formats and routines. Think of the difference between a lecture, a lab experiment, a role play, and a provocative discussion. Each of these formats is effective for learning some concepts and skills, and ineffective for others. We have identified 15 formats to consider for your advisory program.

We offer three overarching questions to discuss, with more specific questions and suggestions following.

Given your school's advisory goals and time structures, what activities and projects might be effective?

Design teams can easily accumulate volumes of activities to make sure the time is filled, but they can overlook evaluating how each activity connects to the goals and themes. Make sure your array of activities builds incrementally to important stated goals.

Given your school's advisory goals and time structures, what routines and formats should be established?

If, for example, your goals are focused on leadership development or career preparation, and you're planning on a significant time allotment, you'll be able to use more time-consuming formats, such as projects, class meetings, and interactive exercises. If your advisory time is limited, formats like pair/shares and personal conferencing will be more suitable.

What are the expected learning outcomes for students? In advisory, students will do _____, and they will learn _____.

Discussing learning outcomes is crucial and often overlooked. Design teams need to consider not just what activities will be used, but what students are expected to learn. Identifying outcomes will influence what formats are used, how long a given topic will last, what projects and tasks are involved, and so forth. For example, an advisory topic might be substance abuse. The activities and formats utilized will depend not only on the topic itself, but on whether the expected outcome is awareness of risks or change in behavior. Awareness might be accomplished with readings, speakers, and brief discussions. Changing behavior will involve awareness activities plus skill lessons, reflections, practice, and coaching.

There is an infinite array of options for selecting activities, projects, routines and formats. However, there are some likely starting places, some components included in most advisories, and some formats that fit with those components. These are listed below, followed by questions for design teams to consider. The Implementation chapter includes more ideas for expanding on these basic components.

- **Adjusting to school, making a successful transition**
  Whether students are entering 6th or 7th grade at a middle school or 9th grade at a high school, making the transition to a bigger, more complex, and pressured environment is not easy. There are new rules, new norms, and new expectations. Advisory can help more students make that transition more gracefully.

- **Community-building and promoting a positive school climate**
  Most advisories, no matter the rest of the focus, hold as a goal that students will feel respected and supported, and will feel a sense of belonging in their advisory group. Special attention can be given to students who are new to the school, no matter what grade they enter or when in the year they arrive. Advisory groups can support students to participate positively in the school as a whole as well.

- **Academic advising and coaching**
  Most schools expect advisors to watch out for their advisees and help them succeed, whether that is helping them learn how to keep track of assignments and prioritize tasks, or checking with them during a slump. Some advisory groups make this a function of the peer group as well.

Adjusting to school, making a successful transition

What can advisors do to make sure students find their way physically through the building?

Maps, tours, scavenger hunt activities, or assigned buddies might help students.

What can advisors do to make sure students find their way to various resources?

Students need to learn about what is available at school and be encouraged to take advantage of it. This might mean having upper-class students describe clubs and teams, or arranging group introductions to administrators, counselors, and technology and media staff.

How can advisory help with the places and times that are likely to feel awkward and challenging in the first few months of school, such as the cafeteria, auditions and try-outs, or parent night?

Maybe students can rehearse, do things in pairs, or simply be offered encouragement.

How can advisors help students understand the expectations, the support systems, and the rules and consequences of the new grade level?

Introducing all students, intentionally and thoughtfully, to new responsibilities and standards helps to level the playing field.

Community-building, group maintenance, and promoting a positive school climate

What can advisors do so that their advisees know each other?

Students can participate in fun and quick get-to-know-you activities, longer interviews and discussions, and/or extended studies of who they are, where they live, what their preferences and heritages are. The last option might be a kind of advisory demographic study.

What can advisors do so that their advisees feel safe (emotionally, intellectually, and physically)?

Advisories should include a process for establishing guidelines or group agreements, and a habit of revisiting those agreements when they are not upheld. Discussions about what respect looks and sounds like, or what the effects are of sarcasm and teasing, can encourage reflection on positive norms.

What can advisors do so that their advisees improve skills for participating in a group?

Many practices and activities can be used to improve skills for group participation. To contribute effectively to group discussions, time limits can be used to avoid monopolizing; go-rounds to avoid opting out; and pairs to practice saying something before speaking to the whole group. There are many such practices. Similarly, there are innumerable activities for helping students learn to listen more carefully, encourage each other, and problem-solve collaboratively.

How can advisory groups be used to create a sense of ownership of the school and encourage a positive school climate?

Groups can make proposals for improving conditions in common spaces, identify issues for the student government to undertake, or participate as a group in school-wide efforts.

Academic advising and coaching

How can advisors monitor, support, and influence student achievement?

In order to monitor achievement, advisors will need initial and ongoing data. They can support students with tips for studying, managing stress, or finding resources. Advisors can establish various practices, for example, homework buddies, to support and influence progress. Advisors can be proactive; nagging is not the only option!

What is each student's role in his or her own academic development?

Some schools have students facilitate their own progress conference with teachers and parents. Many have students set goals for themselves, monitor, and reflect on accomplishments.

Routines and formats

What routines will help separate advisory from the rest of the day and encourage a sense of community?

See Activity Formats in Chapter 5 for descriptions of 15 formats that are especially appropriate in advisory. If your advisory time is brief, consider emphasizing small and large group dialogues, personal conferencing, organizing, and journaling. If your block is longer, think about which formats will support your goals and outcomes.

What routines and formats will offer practice at various skills?

Morning goal-setting, end-of-the-day reflections, activity debriefings, listening labs, and many other options give advisees practice and opportunities for coaching from you and their peers.

Food or no food?

This question arises in many advisory programs and affects content decisions. In some schools, students have enhanced their sense of community by choosing to rotate responsibility for bringing snacks. In other schools, food was prohibited as it distracted them from focusing on discussions and activities.

What longer-term practices will encourage group cohesion?

Practices that are established for group discussion or small group check-ins will encourage a positive atmosphere. Journal writing can become an advisory routine to encourage reflecting on group participation and academic progress. What will advisory do around birthdays? What will the group do if a new student joins? What if a student leaves the group? How will the advisory handle closing for the summer, especially if the group won't be together next year?

Questions for identifying additional and long-term focus areas

What are the long-term themes that might give advisory a focus?
Such themes could be career exploration, doing a community study, teaching each other skills, or many others. Having long-term themes will help advisors plan; some advisors complain about punting all the time, scrounging for random activities when they are in a school without themes. Identifying long-term themes will also create an identity for advisory. Without this, students have been known to press advisors to allow advisory time to become study hall or social time.

What can be group projects?
These might include projects in preparation for a holiday, for a school event, for an ill classmate, decorating a part of the school, an out-of-school environmental project, or a service project.

What topics will students naturally gravitate toward? With which topics will they need the most support over the course of the school year?
Advisors can map out a calendar of the topics that will likely be on students' minds. Progress reports, grades reports, holidays, major school events, planning for the summer, and other calendar-related topics naturally lead to certain activities, discussions, or journal writing.

Possible content beyond the basics

Many schools have focus areas beyond adjusting to school, advising, and peer-group connections. A sampling are listed below.

- Learning to have a participatory voice, practicing democracy, talking about local or global issues

- Self and community—conducting interviews, discussing one's relationship to a larger group, giving service

- Sense of self as an adolescent—considering images from music, ads, interviews, self-reflections, reading and discussion of adolescent challenges

- Conflict, cooperation, and communication skills

- Goal-setting, overcoming obstacles, study skills, time management

- Teaching each other origami, knitting, or other crafts (especially before the winter holidays). One advisory group that did this found at least three benefits: students found out they actually had skills to offer each other; they got practice giving encouragement and feedback; and (surprising to the advisor) they discussed personal concerns in a calmer and more reflective manner than they might otherwise have done.

- Gender issues

- Career exploration: sorting through Help Wanted ads to identify job areas and titles, investigating pathways to get to various jobs, interviewing or shadowing someone, having guest speakers

- Service projects

- Supporting the development of students' logical and abstract thinking through exercises, problems, and games

The following icons illustrate four aspects to keep in mind as you make decisions about the kinds of activities that will match your advisory goals and outcomes:

- Advisory content and themes

- Activity scheduling and frequency

- Activity groupings

- Activity formats

The Activities chapter, Chapter 6, is organized around these aspects.

Advisory content and themes:

 Community building, group cohesion, and group maintenance

 Orientation, school citizenship, and school business

 Goal-setting, reflection, and self-assessment

 Tools for school and learning

 Life skills, healthy development, and self-care

 Moving on to high school, college, or career

 Real-world connections and service learning

 Personal passions, hobbies, and interests

 Rituals, celebrations, and closure

 Rainy-day fun stuff

Activity scheduling and frequency

The following icons provide a way to think about different scheduling configurations that will provide the right amount of time and frequency for specific activities. They are not meant to be rigid, but rather to support advisors' planning about various times of the year, regular versus one-time routines, daily versus quarterly exercises, and so on. All of the activities, exercises, and routines in the Activities chapter include recommended scheduling and frequency arrangements using these, similar, or more specific terms.

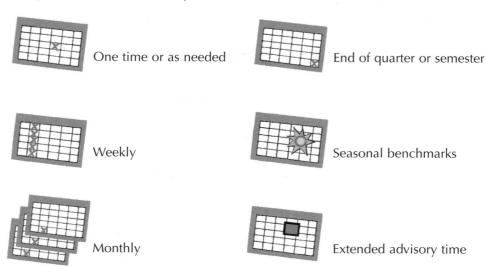

One time or as needed

End of quarter or semester

Weekly

Seasonal benchmarks

Monthly

Extended advisory time

Activity Groupings

 Individual student tasks

 Advisee-advisor tasks

 Pairs and small groups

 Whole advisory

 Mixing it up across groups

 School-wide participation

Who leads activities?

Almost all advisory activities can be led by advisors, the advisor and a student, two students, or one student. Encourage students to think about the kinds of activities they want to lead. Provide coaching for students who volunteer.

Activity Formats

- Gatherings

- Reading & test prep

- Organizing & representing ideas and information

- Journaling & written reflection

- Skill lessons

- Projects

- Assemblies

- Closings

- Announcements (within advisory, not via the public address system)

- Small & large group dialogues

- Personal connections & conferencing

- Class meetings

- Interactive exercises

- Games & team challenges

- Videos, guest, or student presentations

**Advisors' role
& expectations**

If an advisory program is new to your school, we have found that the role description for advisors will be clearest if it articulates what the role of an advisor is and is not. Teachers, counselors, students, and parents have expressed both hope and concern about whether their words show assumptions that the role will be extremely limited or quite expansive.

To accomplish the task of defining the advisor's role, the design team can consider the questions below. Understanding one's role is a personal matter, however, so even if the design team has discussed these questions, advisors should have a chance to explore them as well.

How are advisors different from teachers?
This question has encouraged interesting conversations about the different style and pace of being an advisor as compared to being a teacher. It is important for advisors to realize that their first focus is on their advisees, with far less pressure to cover content area and prepare for tests.

How are advisors different from counselors or school social workers?
This question has generated some of the most important conversations, as teachers consider becoming advisors. Many are relieved to find out that the advisor role is quite different from that of counselor and social worker, who have very specialized training. Advisors will have ten to twenty advisees over a year or more, as compared to a school counselor with several hundred students on her or his caseload. Thus, advisors are often the first person to notice that an advisee needs counseling, and they may monitor a given situation over time. They should not, however, be expected to provide psychological or crisis counseling.

How are advisors different from friends?
Students consistently reported that they were less interested in having an advisor be their friend than having someone who believed in them and could support them. Several students specifically described advisors as insincere when they try to act like a peer. Though the role of advisor is less formal than that of teacher, it is, nonetheless, a professional role.

To what extent are advisors expected to follow a prescribed lesson plan or theme?
Schools can provide detailed lessons each week, expecting every group to use them as written, they can allow for adaptations, they can leave each advisor to find and create lessons within specified themes, from certain resources, or they can give them free reign.

Are there specific outcomes to be achieved?
Depending on your advisory program goals, you might identify certain skills to be learned and practiced, topics to be covered, a style of participation to be encouraged, or specific behaviors to be coached.

What materials can advisors expect?
The answer to this question should be consistent with the responses to the questions above. The more that advisors are expected to follow prescribed lessons, or teach specific skills, the more that explicit materials need to be supplied on a predictable schedule.

When and how will advisors receive training?
The next piece of the design puzzle deals with professional development, and offers an array of questions for designing the training and coaching program for your advisors. The advisor role description should address this topic at least to ensure that there will be sufficient and appropriate support for fulfilling the role.

What will be the advisor's role vis-a-vis parents and guardians?
There is a series of subquestions to consider whose answers might vary depending on whether or not advisors are expected to be the primary school contacts for parents and guardians. If advisors are to be the primary contacts, they will need to be informed of their advisees' progress and their academic program. Staying informed is certainly much easier to accomplish when advisory groups are organized within teams and small learning communities.

If advisors are to be the primary contact for parents/guardians

- How will advisors be kept informed of advisees' academic progress?

- How will advisors learn about course content?

- How might mediating between parents and teachers affect collegial relationships?

- Under what circumstances will parents contact teachers directly?

Whether advisors are the primary contact for parents/guardians or not

- When and how can parents and guardians contact advisors?

- How often are advisors expected to communicate with parents?

- Is there a preferred or arranged time?

- About what are advisors expected to communicate with parents?

- Via what means (in person, phone, email, letters)?

- When a parent contacts an advisor, how fast a response is expected?

- Are advisors to keep a record of contact with parents and guardians?

- Are there guidelines or suggestions for communication with parents—for example, that the first contact contain only a positive message?

What will be the advisor's role related to academics?

Minimally, most advisors are expected to meet with students to review grades and set goals. Many advisors are responsible for monitoring their advisees' progress and, when necessary, making referrals for counseling, tutoring, or other services. Some advisors are expected to teach study or test-taking skills, guide course selection, and make suggestions to teachers as to how to reach a particular student. When advisory includes enough time, advisors can very effectively help students develop portfolios and practice making presentations.

In some schools, advisors distribute report cards and progress reports. In other schools, teachers send progress reports to an advisor, who reads them, looking for patterns, challenges, and accomplishments, sometimes writing a summary progress report that goes to parents/guardians. In any of these cases, will it be teachers' responsibilities to keep advisors informed, vice versa, or both?

What will be the advisor's role related to college and career counseling?

Advisors can be assigned to teach, or to encourage practice of, interview skills. They can encourage college and/or career exploration. Advisors can be responsible for supporting advisees as they prepare personal statement essays. In some schools, guidance counselors take the lead on college and career counseling, with advisors playing a hosting and coaching role. Of course, any of these duties can be time consuming, so it will be important to make sure that this piece of the puzzle is in sync with the advisory schedule.

What will be the advisor's role related to discipline?

Some schools have found that directly involving advisors in disciplinary matters has a detrimental effect on the advisor-advisee relationship. In those cases, advisors are often involved behind the scenes as coaches. In other schools, advisors are more directly involved, accompanying an advisee to a disciplinary hearing or monitoring a behavior plan.

What is the advisor's role related to involvement in extracurricular activities?

Most advisors help their students become informed about extracurricular activities, encourage them to participate, and celebrate their accomplishments.

To accomplish any of the above duties, what data will advisors need?
Some data is likely to be needed by everyone: for example, a list of all advisor groups organized by advisors, and an alphabetical list of all students, with advisors identified. Depending on their role, advisors might need past as well as current academic data.

Several questions should be sorted out:

- What data will advisors need?

- How often will advisors need data? While many schools send data to advisors quarterly, some do so as frequently as daily.

- How and from whom will advisors get data? Some schools have a large gathering for advisors to chat with each other in orchestrated fashion about their students/advisees. In other cases, information is passed to advisors on paper or electronically.

- What information might advisors want to gather from their advisees via questionnaires, interviews, or activities?

- What data are advisors expected to keep, and where are they to keep it?

- What data is confidential and expected to be shared with advisors, and what data is confidential and not to be shared with advisors?

In what ways are advisors supervised and evaluated? By whom?
To what potential effect?
When advisory has significant content and is graded, most schools use the same supervision and evaluation processes that they use for faculty, though it varies as to how much effect being a poor advisor can have on a teacher's performance review. In some schools, there is an advisory supervisor or coordinator who conducts professional development for advisors and coaches them when needed, but may not have evaluative authority. Minimally, these coordinators are watching for ineffective advisors, possibly to assign a co-advisor or replace them if other advisors are available.

Can students become leaders or co-leaders of advisory groups?
If a goal of your program is to develop youth leadership, this might be an effective option. Students can be very successful in running activities and encouraging discussion. Some schools have found that incorporating students as co-leaders helped to overcome student and faculty resistance to advisory.

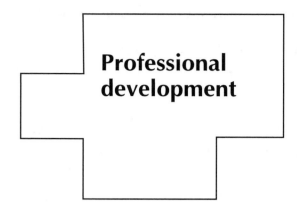

Professional development

When asked what they thought was important to include in this guide, high school students at several schools said unanimously, repeatedly, and sometimes in stronger language, "Make sure people know that advisors have to be trained and prepared. It shows when they're not. Then it's just an empty block and we don't have time to waste. If they're not going to do something real, we could use the time to study."

This is another pitfall to watch for while developing your advisory program—neither assessing the need for professional development and ongoing support, nor providing it. According to a study of advisory programs, training was seen to be the key to success; the success of advisory groups varied widely based on each advisor's experience, training, and attitude.[1]

Unfortunately, there is no prepackaged Advisor Group Professional Development Program that your administrator or design team can call up and order. Each program has to be designed to fit the goals and content of that school's advisory program. Further, it should not be underestimated how different the role of advisor is from other adult roles in schools. The professional development program will need to address the content goals identified and the skills needed to facilitate groups, and to coach and support students.

How experienced and comfortable are the advisors-to-be with facilitating groups?

Have they been involved with experiential education programs or used cooperative games? Are they competent with debriefing skills? If not, then they will need workshops on group dynamics, facilitation, handling sensitive topics, and how to use many different activity formats.

How experienced and comfortable are the advisors-to-be with coaching and supporting individual students?

Do they have effective listening skills? Are they aware of varying learning styles? Are they informed about referral options for specific challenges that might arise? All of these skills and understandings can be learned in a well-designed professional development effort. Such skills and knowledge bases are not acquired quickly, so design a program that involves follow-up sessions.

How experienced and comfortable are the advisors-to-be with the particular content that has been identified for their groups?
On this piece of the puzzle, the design team should consider any and all of the following:

- workshops before advisory begins

- sessions to provide continuing support and practice of skills (especially during the first years of the program or when making major programmatic changes)

- sessions to provide specific information before a topic that is information-heavy and/or sensitive

- brief reviews, tips, and demonstrations during regular faculty meetings

- a coordinator or advisor coach(es)

What other considerations should be thought about in the professional development design?
Try to offer advisors-to-be an experience similar to what students are expected to experience.

In many high schools, teachers have frequent contact with colleagues within their department and nowhere else. Teachers within a department often have, or perceive that they have, more in common than they might with other teachers. A goal of almost all advisor groups is building safe and supportive environments among diverse students. Advisors might find it challenging to facilitate a group to that end if the advisors have not experienced this environment themselves. If advisors participate in a cross-departmental ongoing group for training, they can have a parallel experience to the one they are trying to provide students.

If your school is small, or if your advisor group program is limited (maybe it's just for 9th grade, for example), and there are only ten to twenty advisors, you can organize professional development sessions before the school year starts, followed by biweekly or monthly sessions. Advisors will benefit particularly if this group has the small size, format, and supportive feel of an advisory group.

Most schools, of course, have a large number of advisors. A training for 50 advisors, or 150, will not likely feel like an advisor group. Here is one proposal. Try to arrange a professional development format that contains the most important qualities of advisory—small, consistent, supportive learning teams. Let's say you've got 120 advisors to train. Advisors can be arranged in eight teams of fifteen, mixing departments, roles, amount of experience, gender, race, or other aspects. If those teams work collaboratively within initial large training workshops and in the follow-up sessions, they may provide an advisory experience and still be cost effective. Perhaps the follow-up sessions will meet simultaneously (if a program coordinator or consultant trainer is not involved), or on different days or at different times.

If students are to be leaders or co-leaders, what leadership preparation will they need?
As you read in the Highland Park and Deerfield High School snapshot, student co-leaders will benefit from workshops and ongoing support. Your school could count their educational program as a leadership or service course and credit, or depending on the advisory themes, count their role toward a health credit.

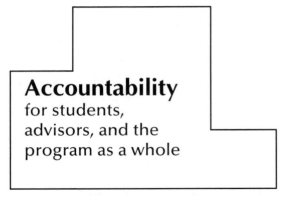

Accountability
for students,
advisors, and the
program as a whole

Will students be held accountable for attending and participating in advisory?

Schools that schedule advisory like an extended homeroom, perhaps ten minutes per day, and use it for personal contact and coaching, make attendance required, but generally do not grade participation. Schools in which advisory involves more time and a content focus can choose to have advisory ungraded, pass/fail, or assign regular grades. By the time students are in middle or high school they have had several years to learn that what counts is graded, so if advisory is not graded (at least pass/fail), advisors will have to compensate to make sure it is taken seriously. For example, East Palo Alto High School in Menlo Park, California, is establishing an on-line system for teachers to send information daily to advisors on students' behavioral and academic progress.

Will students work with an alternative form of assessment, such as a participation rubric?

Whether advisory is graded or not, it may be useful to consider using a participation rubric to promote self-assessment. A corollary advisor's form to assess student participation would provide comparative data for individual conferences. The advisory program at East Palo Alto High School uses a rubric on personal responsibility and social responsibility, two of the school's core standards.

Will advisors be held accountable for conducting effective advisory groups and being good advisors?

Will advisory be part of their supervision and evaluation process? Will advisors work with a self-assessment rubric? Supervision, evaluation, and self-assessment promote seriousness, consistency, and effectiveness across a faculty. Furthermore, advisors who engage in a self-assessment process will likely expand their empathy for students who engage in parallel experiences of self-assessments and reflections.

Having some means to promote accountability is clearly important where advisory involves significant time and content. But even if advisory is only ten minutes per day, it has an important impact on students' experience of school, so efforts should be made to promote effectiveness. The extent to which advisors can or should be held accountable depends on how their role is articulated and what provisions (for professional development, preparation time, and adequate materials) are made to support them in the role.

The steps taken to build accountability for advisor effectiveness should be aligned with the structures that make instruction effective. If a middle school team or a high school small learning community is where faculty are working together on shaping teaching and learning, then being accountable to that team or community for advisory success will be most effective. If a faculty member's department is where he or she is influenced, then it will be important for department meetings and supervision processes to include responsibility for advisory. If faculty are part of critical friends' groups or study groups, then those structures can provide peer support and reflection/improvement opportunities.

There can also be informal pressure to be active advisors, quite different from the formal pressure brought to bear through supervision processes. For example, if advisory groups engage in door decorating about an issue or holiday, it will be obvious if a few doors remain plain.

Will advisors be expected to keep logs of group activities?

If so, how formal or informal? Do records have to be turned in? If so, to whom—a person with evaluation authority or not? For what purpose? Maybe logs are submitted to assure advisor accountability and/or maybe advisors are contributing to a growing resource of advisory ideas.

Where does the buck stop?

If an advisory group is not working, what will happen? Which, if any, administrator has responsibility for advisory? Is there an advisory coordinator who will coach a struggling advisor? Will the team leader or department head be responsible for monitoring and supporting advisors?

How will you know if your school's advisory program is effective?

Some schools have used school climate surveys before implementation and again one or two years later if their goals included having an effect on school climate. Each school will have to determine what outcomes will be a sign of success. Maybe it will be a decrease in dropout rates, greater skill development in certain areas, more successful completion of portfolios, or a decrease in the achievement gap.

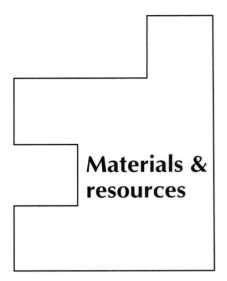

Materials & resources

To accomplish your program's goals and engage in identified focus areas, what materials and resources are needed?

This can vary enormously, so the design committee can consider any and all of the following:

- Curricula for building personal skills – interpersonal skills, goal-setting, etc.

- Curricula dealing with specific issues – health and wellness, harassment, etc.

- Speakers – on careers, health issues, cultural celebrations

- Supplies for projects and activities

- Props for activities

- Newspapers and magazines – if your advisories are meant to help students pay attention to and understand the world around them

- Videos – Imagine, for example, the discussion students could have after watching Frontline's program "Inside the Teenage Brain" or other videos

This advisory guide includes an extensive Activities chapter. Also, see the Resources list for further suggestions.

To what extent will your advisory program have and use a set curriculum?

Many schools interviewed for this guide used multiple resources from which advisors could pick and choose, and other schools had binders of carefully collected material, yet there were no schools that had successfully found or enforced a set lesson-by-lesson curriculum. At Souhegan High School, it is understood that "the curriculum of Advisory is really the experiences, interests, values, skills, hopes, and fears of all the individual members. It boils down to skills and process…Students…develop the ability to function in a heterogeneous group of their peers."[2]

Whatever materials your approach includes, where will they be located and how will they be disseminated?

Whether the design team considers a shelf in the counselors' office, a binder given to all advisors, or a web page to which many people can contribute, some mechanism will need to be identified.

Will your advisory program involve students as gatherers of materials?

Students might see news articles about adolescent or community issues, or poems related to a certain theme that they can bring to advisory.

Linking advisory
to other school programs

Advisory will exist within the context of your school, so it's important to be conscious of that context as you plan. This is one of the many reasons why it will be important for the design team to include people who have varied roles.

Starting with the large view, what is the context for influence and implementation at your school?

An advisory program that is linked well to the school will be connected through the corner-stone structures—departments, teams, whatever the basic units are for meeting, planning, mentoring, and coordinating teaching and learning. An advisory program that is linked well to the community will build support among parents.

Conversely, a program that is designed outside of these central structures will have all the problems of being on the periphery. The program will have to request, even fight for, time on meeting agendas; make special arrangements for mentoring; and work very hard to be in sync with classroom life. Clearly, advisory will develop more easily, become institutionalized more readily, and be better all-around, if it is established through the structures that are already influential.

Has your design team investigated how advisory fits with the programs and services in your school?

Is there already an effective structure for helping students with college essays? Perhaps there is a role for advisory in this area or maybe this role would overlap with another. To what extent are there mentoring programs, peer tutoring, youth leadership opportunities, or career exploration? Advisory could be where these efforts are initiated, or supported if they already exist.

Has your design team investigated how advisory fits with courses?

To what extent are there communication skills classes (maybe in English) or adolescent issue discussions (maybe in health education)? Is there a role for advisory in these areas or would it overlap with other classes?

Will information flow easily, clearly, and in the right directions?
How will counselors find out about students who need referrals? How will advisors find out about students who are struggling in class?

Is there a connection between advisory groups and student government or large school forums?
Advisory groups can take turns assuming certain responsibilities for school-wide "town meetings," assemblies, or school spirit activities. Student government representatives can come from each advisory group.

If counselors do serve as advisors, and let's say they have students from the 11th and 12th grades, will they be less available to the 9th and 10th graders? What will that mean?
Some counselors who have 12th grade advisories have appreciated having more time than they otherwise might with students preparing college applications. Those same counselors felt somewhat torn about not knowing the younger students well, and did not necessarily feel being an advisor was the best use of their time after application season was over.

Refer back to the Design Checklist (p. 41). Are all your puzzle pieces in place? Which ones need fine-tuning, reshaping, or overhauling?

The next chapter offers suggestions for sharing your plan with colleagues, students, and parents.

Endnotes

[1] Gail Boorstein. "A Study of Advisory." ERIC No. ED408544, 1997.
[2] Silva, p. 62.

CHAPTER 4

The Bridge between Designing and Implementing: The PR Campaign

The design team has done the research, analyzed the options, and formulated a plan. Does that mean parents, students, board members, and colleagues will be eager and ready to implement advisory tomorrow? Not usually.

People often demand to be informed and heard. More importantly, they deserve to be informed and heard. So the design team (or a partner PR team) needs to take its outreach and public relations role seriously. Chapter 1 listed some of the benefits of advisory programs and discussed building buy-in; Chapter 2 offered stories to share; and Chapter 3 detailed the design process. In this chapter, we offer suggestions and tips for reaching out to teachers, parents, students, and school leaders to communicate the benefits, stories, and rationales for a chosen design. Also, refer to the Preface for an overview of recent research.

Think creatively about getting your message out. You may need to utilize various media and communication tools—some to reach parents, others to coax faculty, and still others to entice students. The design team and PR team can distribute articles, hold discussions, host speakers, articulate an advisory mission statement, make brochures and buttons, write articles for the school and local newspapers, post highlights on the school's website, send email updates, and/or many other tasks. In addition to getting your message out, the PR process is a chance to let others have input and feel ownership. For example, the design team can involve students in selecting a name for the advisory program, as they did at Westerville (Ohio) South High School. Or the team can send out surveys or hold focus groups of student, parents, and/or teachers to gather ideas for topics.

These tasks need to go hand in hand with implementation steps. Collect positive quotes from teachers after an advisors' workshop, and post them in a faculty newsletter. Collect statements about students' hopes for advisory from surveys and interviews, and post those on the school's website. Remember, people inside a school community have more influence with their peers than any outside consultant or research article.

The keys are to respect the people to whom you're talking and have a clear, worthy, and optimistic message. By this time, everyone on the design team should be able to recite the inspiring rationales that will drive your advisory program. For example, "All students will be supported to do their best"; "Each student will build skills for future learning and work." Know your rationales and represent them enthusiastically. Meanwhile, you may also need some tips for meetings and preparation for the various "Yeah, but…" statements that will be voiced. The next two sections provide such tips.

Just in case your school jumped in a little (or a lot) too fast, the final portion of this chapter is, "Oh no! What do you mean there are nine pieces? We started with only two! What can we do now?" While most of this chapter is about building a bridge between the design stage and the implementation stage through intentional outreach, design teams should also monitor the early stages of implementation. Sometimes, dramatic steps are needed.

Tips for faculty and parent presentations

Get people involved and connected to each other and to the advisor concept.

Start with an exercise that everyone can relate to and that draws people into the conversation in a positive heartfelt way. Reflect and share in small groups, which offer a greater sense of safety for sharing personal statements.

The starting questions might be:

- Describe someone who was an important advisor, formally or informally, to you at some point in your life. How did that relationship affect you?

- Describe a time when you were helpful as an advisor to someone, whether that was in a formal or an informal role. What skills and qualities did you offer your advisee?

After discussing both questions, ask people to tell you the most important qualities they heard in their group. This type of exercise enables people to remember the value of advisors and encourages them to identify with the people who were their role models. It takes the advisor role out of the abstract realm and makes it concrete, personal, important, and successful.

Opening questions, statements, and exercises create momentum—either toward openness and optimism, or toward pessimism and argument. Craft your openings carefully!

Set a positive tone.

If you act defensively, you give people permission to be offensive. "Well, I know you're against advisory, but maybe this design won't be so bad." With this statement, listeners don't have to choose a negative attitude, because you have given it to them from the start. A colleague would have to be oppositional just to be positive! In contrast, "I'm excited about our design. May I tell you about it?!" will likely generate a more positive conversation.

Encourage positive momentum with go-rounds and/or allies.

If you ask a question and open the floor for comments, some of the most negative voices are likely to speak first, creating a defensive and argumentative discussion. Instead, if you ask people to speak in a consecutive order around the room, you enable all voices to be heard. Further, if you can predict that certain negative people will be vocal, ask a few positive people in the group to be ready to speak as well.

Listen, listen, listen.

Listening to people doesn't mean that you are necessarily agreeing with them: it just means you are willing to hear what they are saying. Listening can diffuse strong emotions and can help you understand more of the concerns that you need to consider. Try to listen to the information people are conveying and to their emotions. For instance, a mother might ask, "It is my role to advise my child. Who do you think you are becoming my daughter's advisor?" If you ask this parent to tell you more about her statement, you might hear that she feels frustrated and scared about losing influence with her growing adolescent, or about specific career or financial concerns, or any of many possible issues. Without listening, you could offer a response (maybe a defense) that does not relate to her concern.

Keep the conversation from getting polarized.

All too often controversial topics become polarized, with people entrenched on opposite sides. Teachers in one school heard about a wide range of advisory models, including a formal content-driven graded model. In the conversation afterwards, it sounded like that was the only one they had heard about. Statements such as "They can't give me another course," and "I'm going straight to the union!" abounded. Advisory is complicated and nuanced; protect discussions about it from becoming simplistic or two-sided. Emphasize the goal(s) and the many choices about how to reach those goals.

Yeah, but...

People need to find their own meaning in any new effort. Their need to discuss the potential challenges along with the intended benefits is normal and even helpful. If resistance and concerns are suppressed at the beginning, they can easily show up later in actions and cause greater damage.

Listed below are several commonly voiced comments of resistance. Expect to hear these remarks and many others. Advocates of advisory groups can hear these comments as sabotage and rejection, or as cautionary, clarifying, and concerned. Choosing the latter stance and listening openly will take time, but in the long run will provide a stronger foundation.

"Advisory will take time away from academic areas, preparation for state assessments, and SATs."

Research shows that students who feel greater attachment to school achieve more academically. Additionally, advisory groups can offer students specific coping techniques for dealing with stress, problem-solving, and learning to focus their attention. Some advisor groups focus on learning styles and study skills, directly supporting students' achievement in their academic subjects.

"Teachers shouldn't have to focus on anything other than academics."

Though this statement is rarely, if ever, heard in an elementary or middle school, it is quite common in high schools. Before responding to this "yeah, but," it's important to determine more clearly what it means. Through further conversation, we have understood some faculty to mean they are unfamiliar and thus uncomfortable with assuming a nonacademic role.

Giving some concrete examples of advisory activities and describing the professional development and support system that will be in place for them can ease some of the anxiety. Filling a significantly new role will, however, come with some growing pains, so it may take a year or two for advisors to become comfortable in the role.

In other conversations, teachers have expanded on this "yeah, but," and described an underlying belief that cognitive development can actually be separated from social and emotional development. This belief will need to be addressed during discussions in the planning/building buy-in phase and in the professional development program. Students are whole people, even when they reach adolescence. They cannot leave their social and emotional selves at the school door and push their cognitive and physical selves through the day. The research on emotional intelligence can persuade some faculty that trying to separate these human aspects is futile and counterproductive. All students, even those who are in honors classes, need skills to be successful in high school, college, and work—skills in self-awareness, self-direction, and working with others.

"Helping kids become organized and persistent, feel heard, and helping them plan for their futures—aren't those roles for parents?"
In conversations with teachers, sometimes this question seemed to mean the same thing as the last question; other times, some teachers added, "Isn't it someone else's fault that students are not prepared or successful, not my fault, not my responsibility?" Passing blame around can go on forever. The design team can try to frame the conversation as, "These are the students in our school; these are the families in our community. We have a commitment to teach all students. There's an image of a successful student that we often carry—a student who is in honors classes, shows leadership and caring, seems well-adjusted and future-oriented, whose parents model, coach, and support. To wish that every student fit that profile is to ignore the vast array of assets that all the other students bring and to ignore the complexity of all students."

"I don't like that touchy-feely stuff."
Fine. There are many options for activities, exercises, and projects that will achieve the same goals, whatever those goals are. Effective advisory programs allow for variation in content and style. Some groups may do explicit trust-building exercises with careful debriefings. Others may discuss current issues respectfully or share skills with members of their groups. Still others might do cooperative logic puzzles. In any of these examples, advisors can find their own style of connecting and coaching.

"Facilitating an advisory will be a tremendous amount of extra work."
Facilitating an advisory group will take extra work, though calling that extra time "tremendous" depends on an advisor's experience and perspective, and the design to be implemented. Having a sufficient professional development process, materials, and an advisory coordinator might assuage some people. Professional development credits, stipends, exchanges of other responsibilities, even food at meetings can help gain support from others.

"Aren't advisory groups meant primarily for private schools?"
Independent schools have used advisors and advisory groups for many years, but public schools have been implementing the structure as well, and increasingly so in recent years.

The oldest enduring public school advisor group program is thought to be at New Trier High School in Winnetka, Illinois, started in 1924. However, tragic events, such as the killings at Columbine High School in 1999, as well as research about personalizing the learning environment and about the benefits of small learning communities have provided ample reasons for public middle schools and high schools to consider advisor groups.

"Teachers aren't trained to be counselors."

True, nor should they be. The role of advisor does not replace the guidance counselors or school social workers. There will need to be a clear definition of the boundaries between roles, and it will take time to get used to those boundaries. Advisors are not counselors, and students will still need counselors for specific purposes, but their advisor can give them ongoing mentoring, help them to set goals, explain grade reports, check on progress with difficult projects, coach them about communicating with adults, and so forth.

"Will being an advisor undermine my authority as a teacher?"

Some teachers have worried that they would be taken less seriously by students if they interact with them in less formal ways. Being an advisor can be a less structured role than being a teacher, and it can be a way for students to know their teachers in a more comprehensive way, similar to advising a student club or team. Adolescents are so relationally conscious that this usually leads to greater motivation and respect, rather than less, as they do not want to disappoint a particular teacher.

"What if an advisor doesn't get along with a certain student, or if two students really clash?"

Advisory can be a place where students and advisors get an explicit chance to practice the notion that you don't have to like people to work with them and treat them respectfully, an important life lesson. As a last resort, however, many advisory programs allow for midyear changes (a task for the advisory coordinator or committee).

(from parents) "I don't want faculty prying into private family matters."

Some parents have worried that advisory groups will encourage therapy-like sharing of family issues. While advisors may be helpful to students individually during a crisis, the group time does not need to focus on family challenges. Make sure parents are informed of the goals and sample topics for sessions.

(from parents) "Advising and supporting my kids is my job, not the school's job."

Peer pressure increases greatly during adolescence, making support crucial for healthy social and emotional development. Meanwhile, adolescence is also a time when young people are trying to gain independence from their parents. Invite parents to name the qualities and choices they want reinforced by advisors so that students get consistent messages from all significant adults in their lives. Further, advisory groups can be a vehicle for shaping a healthy peer culture in school.

"Oh, no! What do you mean there are nine pieces? We started with only two! What can we do now?"

What should you do if you started when you only had some of the puzzle in place?

- First, know that you are not alone.
- Second, assess your situation. How much of the puzzle is in place?
- Third, problem-solve, make a plan, and act on it.

Here are some possible scenarios.

Scenario 1: We're close, but ...

A good portion of the puzzle is established at your school, but there's a lot of resistance around _____ (perhaps the parent contact role or the less structured forum) or awkward arrangements with _____ (maybe the materials or the schedule). People are still holding a positive attitude or, at least, a wait-and-see attitude. They haven't declared failure yet.

Organize meetings, feedback forms, and/or interviews to identify what is going well and what remains an obstacle to smooth and successful groups. It will be more effective if many advisors are interviewing each other, collecting and sorting stories from each other, than if only one or two people are collecting and announcing feedback. The more people who are involved in collecting positive stories, the greater ownership there will be of those positive stories.

As advisory program designers, acknowledge that you know things are not perfect or smooth. Let people who have concerns or complaints know they have been heard. After all, if you don't say it out loud, someone else will, and they will put their own spin and tone on it. Solicit input, make a plan, act on the plan, and solicit feedback on the action. Communicate frequently—that you heard people's concerns and their suggestions, that steps to improve the design start next month, that the improvement steps seem to be working for most people, and that remaining kinks will be worked out the following month. Collect student comments and celebrate successes.

Scenario 2: Half the puzzle

You have got half the pieces established, or all the pieces half-established. Complaints and a sense of being overwhelmed are building, but you know that some positive things are happening in at least a few advisories.

Act quickly. You have the challenge of actively reshaping negativity. Once a culture of complaint gets firmly established, it's hard to rise above it—so you'll need to take quick, public action.

What are the pieces that are causing the most frustration? Conduct some assessment through individual or small-group conversation. (Large-group assessment can cement negativity.) Collect positive stories, too. You'll need to commit people, time, and your leadership to address the identified problems. Can you free up time for someone to find and disseminate activities each week? Can you establish a design team and give them dedicated time and authority to work out kinks? Can you pair the vocal, weak, and/or resistant advisors with those who are more skilled and optimistic? Can you share articles or send a few groups of advisors to visit successful advisory programs to build buy-in?

Meanwhile, notice the positive things that are happening, have students and teachers speak about them at the Board meetings, at department meetings, at leadership meetings—wherever you can.

Scenario 3: Disaster
You only had a couple of pieces of the puzzle in place (probably the groupings and schedule). You had not sorted out goals, content, professional development, materials, or anything else!

If advisors and students have positive attitudes despite the chaos, you may be able to reduce the time (such as going from two sessions per week to one) or postpone it for a half-year, while you quickly establish a design team with time and authority to accomplish its task. Take these steps while offering apologies for starting without enough preparation, gratefulness for everyone's positive attitudes, continuous communications about progress, and an ice cream party.

If advisors do not have a positive attitude and/or there aren't people or time to redesign the program, you have a hard choice to make. You can keep pushing while everyone feels (and is) set up to fail, but we do not recommend this strategy. Results often include: evaporation of trust in administrators; passive sabotage (such as letting the group watch TV); direct sabotage (constant vocal venting); alienation of the advisory proponents, undermining their credibility on many levels; and a label of failure on the advisory concept that will last years. It is very hard to recover from this scenario.

Alternatively, you can thank everyone for the time and energy spent, apologize for the chaos, give advisory a graceful rest for a couple years. And give everyone an ice cream party!

CHAPTER 5

Facilitation and Formats

Effective advisors pay attention to *how* their advisory group *is* together, not just *what* the group *does* together. This chapter offers tips for implementing and facilitating advisory groups, as well as formats that will sustain connection, participation, and learning.

How you facilitate advisory and what formats you use will teach just as much, if not more, than the actual activities you use. For example, a lesson on listening will teach far less than frequent use of formats that offer regular practice in various forms of listening. As you plan what will occur in advisory sessions, think about formats just as carefully as activities. Some advisors may be surprised that there is no specific activity on listening in this guide—this crucial skill is woven throughout the formats. Likewise, professional development for advisors should focus on facilitation of groups and formats, in addition to activities.

We have created four sets of icons to encourage creative thinking about scheduling activities, formats, groupings within advisory, and the actual content itself. There are many possible activities to use. See the Activities Chapter and the Resources List for suggestions of entire volumes of get-to-know-you activities, cooperative games, communication exercises, and more.

Depending on your focus, you may need to find resources on adolescent health issues and risk prevention, on college preparation, on community or world events, on so many different possible aspects. This guide would have to be hundreds of pages longer to include a year's worth of activities on each focus area. Instead, we offer a structure and samples to build the range of experiences that will best suit your students.

Thus, the Facilitation and Formats chapter includes:

- Facilitation tips for building and maintaining group cohesion
- Facilitation tips for discussing tough topics
- Tips for developing interpersonal and intrapersonal skills
- School – home connections
- Formats—15 ways of structuring activities, discussions, tasks, and projects

The Activities Chapter includes sample activities for each theme that demonstrate various scheduling, frequency, format, and grouping options.

Facilitation tips for building and maintaining group cohesion

No matter what the focus of your advisory program—career development, academic coaching, interpersonal skills, or any other focus—the students in the group will need to feel comfortable with each other. We have listed some basic tips for encouraging and sustaining a sense of community. It is crucial that this kind of group development happen before you have to deal with tough or sensitive topics. For many more suggestions, see Facilitation tips for discussing tough topics you have.

Further, some of the significant learning available through advisory will be about group membership and group dynamics. Advisory can be a lab for understanding how people initiate and develop a sense of community, how they join and leave groups, and how they lead or dominate, participate or distract. The tips below offer many strategies for group development, feedback, reflection, and debriefing practices. The formats and several activities encourage this aspect of advisory as well.

- **Spend time in the first few sessions making absolutely sure that students know each other's name.** Build from exercises that are easy and safe (name games, group bingo-type games, sharing summer stories) to exercises that encourage more bonding (peer interviews, sharing stories of family culture and heritage, compiling hopes and goals for the year). Everyone wants to be known and feel welcome, so the initial too-cool-to-play attitude usually subsides quickly. If the group has 15 or more students, these experiences will be especially important for curtailing cliques and isolation.

- **Encourage students to assist each other at the beginning of and throughout the year.** Attend to basic needs, such as knowing where the bathrooms and cafeteria are for students who are new to the school. Assign buddies to help students find classes and get over the first awkward lunches. Advisees can be homework partners, study buddies, or peer reviewers.

- **Have the group identify a few guidelines or agreements for how they want to interact.** "What guidelines will promote the most comfortable atmosphere in our advisory group?" Another approach is "Describe a group or team in which you participated that met everyone's needs and functioned really well. How did the members treat each other? What were their norms? What should our norms be?" Also, talk about who is responsible for maintaining the agreements. Do not let the group name you, the advisor, as the sole enforcer. Advisory is the students' community; these are their agreements. Establishing in the first few weeks that they want to be treated with respect, for example, and what that looks and sounds like, will prevent some challenging behaviors and give you and the students a mutually agreed upon guideline to talk about. When referring to the agreements, don't treat them like institutional rules, as in, "You've broken our rule about respect. Please live up to it." Refer to the value of the group. "Wow, that comment didn't sound respectful to me. Do you want to change your wording? Should we alter the agreement? How do others feel about it?"

- **Expect your advisory group to go through typical stages of group development**—forming, storming, norming, and performing—and avoid blaming statements when storming begins. Small and large groups go through these stages, friendships and full faculties do as well, sometimes gracefully, sometimes clumsily, sometimes hurtfully. Brief descriptions of the stages may help you recognize them, and the facilitation tips will help you get through these stages more productively. During "forming," group members are eager and optimistic, though not necessarily feeling committed or open yet. The group enters "storming" when people vie for leadership or reveal differing perspectives or abilities. During "norming," the group readjusts its tasks and roles and (re)commits to improved norms. Finally, in "performing," the group members balance each others' strengths and weaknesses and work toward a common goal.

- **Comfort and familiarity develop more easily in small groups than large ones, and rarely develop within the timing of one simple exercise.** Start the year with various activities and tasks to be done in pairs or small groups. Have each small group work together on a few tasks, and have students work with different partners for the next few tasks. Continue the pattern.

- **Picking partners for activities can create awkward moments for advisees.** Early in the year, and as needed, use techniques for assigning partners, rather than having students choose. Formats such as concentric circles give students quick introductions to each other in a nonintimidating way. Use partner-matching techniques, especially if you suspect that race, class, gender, clique, or other differences will likely limit advisees' easy interaction with each other. Such techniques can include matching candy, birthday month, middle initial, or playing cards.

- **Advisory groups need some playful moments.** Groups that bond well, like friendships, do a mix of serious and light activities, always with respect, gradually building a sense of community.

- **Set specific habits for small-group work.** For example, have students greet their partners, sort out the task, include everyone, and then reflect on whether everyone was welcomed, included, and participated. Even brief reflections or feedback, such as two ways the group worked well together and one way to improve, will help. Peer pressure used positively can have an impact on participation and attitude.

- **Establish positive habits for small-and large-group work, making those habits routine, not just for a particularly challenging activity or the least productive group.** Implementing inclusion expectations, reflection, feedback, and debriefing practices frequently in the first several weeks and intermittently thereafter establishes expectations and prevents many problems. When difficulties do arise, students will have more practice at how to understand and communicate about group interactions.

- **Groups benefit from debriefing in depth, with more specific reflection questions after some activities.** To what extent did everyone participate? Did the group accomplish its task? Did anybody have ideas that were ignored? How did ignoring their ideas impact the group? Did anybody try to lead the group's task? In what ways did that leadership help or not? Did anyone try to withdraw? What was the effect of that behavior? Can each person explain the group's process and result? What could each person have done to improve the group's functioning? What could the group try next time to be more effective?

- **Establish some rituals so students encourage and celebrate each other's accomplishments.** The rituals can include giving energizing fruit and munchies to the 10th graders about to take the state assessments, or offering a group cheer to the 11th graders after their PSATs or the actors and musicians in a recent play. Some advisory groups note birthdays—another way to celebrate every member.

- **Identify personal goals for group participation.** Using a reflection journal and advisor-advisee conferencing, advisees can set goals for what they personally hope to gain from advisory and identify how they need to participate to achieve those goals.

- **Encourage students to help choose and lead activities, individually or in pairs.** Coach them ahead of time so they are not set up for embarrassment.

- **If new students join your advisory group during the year, take the time to invite them into advisory rituals and projects explicitly.** Use new exercises, letting everyone feel a bit shaky and unprepared again.

- **If a student leaves your advisory group, or becomes ill for an extended time, note the loss or absence with a send-off, gift, card, visit, or other supportive gesture.** As a group bonds, the loss or absence of a group member decreases the sense of cohesion. If it goes unnoted, it can feel like a secret that cannot be discussed.

- **Check on the group agreements, habits, and rituals and make adjustments at the second and third month of school and again midyear.** Discussing how the group operates need not occur only when there is a problem; make it a normal topic. "We've had these agreements and practices for a month. Are there any we could improve or need to add? Are we operating at our best?" Cohesion and a sense of ownership support each other.

- **Use questions that build on group members' specific, positive, and direct experience.** The questions you ask powerfully shape the conversation that follows. You can promote guilt, blame, and resistance, or commitment, understanding, and openness by the questions that frame an upcoming topic. The question, "What problems have we been having as a group?" asks everyone to focus on the negative and point fingers at each other. Who would want to be part of that group after such a discussion?! The question, "How does a fabulous group operate?" is positive, but abstract. Advisees could name norms without believing they had in the past, or could in the future, live up to them. "In what recent experiences (discussions, projects, tasks) have we been at our best? How did we act toward each other? How can we do more of that?" These questions build from experiences that were successful, concrete, and personal; they encourage optimism about the group and belief in one's own efficacy. They are energizing rather than depleting. Apply this principal to dialogues, class meetings, and even individual conferencing.

- **Reflect the dynamics of the group back to the group for consideration in order to model and encourage conscious participation.** Ask the advisory group questions about its own behavior and style. These questions help them articulate their own group dynamics, and give them responsibility for describing the dynamic they want. "We seem stuck. Does it seem like that to you?" "I think about half the group has spoken. Is that enough?" With the last question, advisees have to say, "No, I want to hear from Tara and Carlos," rather than the advisor's having to say it.

- **Watch for advisees who dominate, distract, rebel, or withdraw.** Reach out to them privately to find out how they perceive the group and their own role in it, what they need from the group, and offer feedback.

- **Encourage full and reasonably equal participation.** This includes watching for discussion patterns that get in a rut, advisees who are excluded, those who frequently accommodate others, those who always seem to be the leaders or the attention-seekers. Group members operate in relationship to each other. For example, the presence of dominators probably assumes the presence of accommodators, etc. Talk privately with these advisees and their counterbalancers. Ask how they perceive their role and their effect on others, what they might like to change, and then offer them feedback. Also, see the Formats section (p. 92) for many techniques that help everyone participate.

- **Initiate a conversation with the group about challenging dynamics if dominating, withdrawing, unequal participation, or other challenging behavior persists.** Although private interventions will hopefully succeed, the challenging behavior did not just happen to one individual, it happened to the whole group. If one student has been especially difficult, help her/him figure out what to say to the group to get a head start on diffusing some of the tension. "I don't think our group has felt as comfortable or been as effective as we could have been lately. I've spoken with Alex about it. I think he and all of you probably have some important views on what's been happening."

Facilitation tips for discussing tough topics[1]

Tough topics will arise. Maybe it will be about cliques in the advisory group, or a drinking and driving collision involving students, or a national event like a terrorist attack or going to war. Students know what is happening and their concerns can easily show up in their behavior or mood. Advisory is ideal as a forum to clarify information, name emotions, and receive support. If advisors have spent time building a sense of community and establishing positive norms, most of the groundwork will have been laid. Here are a few more specific tips for tough conversations. Please see Small-and large-group dialogues in the Formats section for additional suggestions.

- Be available; show that you are paying attention. Particularly during crises, whether they are personal, local, or global, students need to know that adults are available to talk to them and are watching out for them.

- Listen to students and invite their thoughts. When students are concerned or upset, it is helpful for them to know they are not alone. Feeling a sense of connection is more reassuring than hearing a sophisticated analysis.

- Encourage students to generate an array of questions and consider different perspectives. If complex events are handled as if they are simple, they can quickly lead to polarized debates.

- Facilitate the group so that it models the reassuring community that students are sensing has been shaken. Many techniques can help, such as:

  - Go-rounds, so that everyone, not just the loudest voices, can speak if they so choose;

  - Wait time between speakers or maybe even paper for jotting down thoughts, so more students will be able to contribute ideas, and those ideas will be clearer; and

  - A talking stick or other object (if students are nervous speaking publicly, holding something can help).

- Quickly intervene or defuse verbal attacking. Students who already feel anxious about a recent occurrence might express things strongly, but it won't do them or their peers any good if those strong expressions are personal.

- Check specifically with students who are especially quiet or acting in uncharacteristic ways. Some students will seek you out if they need to talk; others need proactive encouragement.

- As an advisor, you are a support, not necessarily an expert. Use the group as a resource; they can compare perceptions and find information. The advisory coordinators can supply a list of information or referral resources.

- Reflect on your own views and beliefs, and consider to what extent those are appropriate to contribute to the conversation. What is most important is showing students that you are listening, not lecturing.

Tips for developing interpersonal and intrapersonal skills

Your advisory program may have an explicit goal of teaching interpersonal skills, such as communicating and collaborating, and intrapersonal skills, such as managing anger, motivating oneself, and setting and reflecting on goals. Or your program may not have these as explicit goals. These skills will be part of the implicit life of your advisory group either way, however, so here are a few tips to keep in mind.

- Think of how you learned to read, play a musical instrument, or play a sport. It probably took instruction and coaching, exploring and practicing, observing and reflecting, all over time. The same will be true for developing interpersonal and intrapersonal skills. One skill lesson won't do it.

- Students will benefit from demonstrations, role plays, giving as well as receiving peer feedback, individual coaching, and frequent practice in small-and large-group tasks. Discussing perseverance, for example, may introduce this character trait, but students are more likely to develop that trait through identifying a historical role model who persevered, showing perseverance to accomplish a service project or improve a grade, and reflecting on it in a journal, pair/share, and/or a conference with you.

- Take advantage of teachable moments. They are likely to arise during small-group exercises, large-group discussions, individual conferencing about goals and grades, and during many other moments.

- Acknowledge students' use of skills when you notice them. Encourage them to notice their own and peers' use of skills as well. "Thanks for being patient while I was finishing my thought. That was hard to get out." "That was a difficult task that you accomplished. What inner strengths did you use to succeed?"

- Connect the skills to things that matter—to school climate, to future work life, to world events.

School-Home Connections

If advisors in your school are the primary contact for parents/guardians, they will need to contact each advisee's parent or guardian early in the year and periodically during the year. It will help advisors and parents if the advisory coordinating committee sets some clear expectations for when and how this will take place. Some schools have the first parent conference of the year with advisors; in other schools, advisors visit parents before school opens; in others, advisors contact them by phone in the first few weeks of the academic year and later by e-mail.

Your first contact with parents and guardians sets the stage for communication for the rest of the year. Kids do better in school when parents are informed and involved in their children's education—parents' influence with their teenage children is far greater than they often imagine.

Therefore, it is important for parents and guardians to know what's happening in advisory and how much their support and encouragement can influence both their child's motivation to learn as well as his/her academic success.

No matter how the contact takes place, this is a chance to develop a supportive relationship on behalf of individual students. Do not make the first contact a conversation about a discipline problem or an academic failure. The first contact will be well spent by finding out the parents' perspective on the student's growth and development, letting them tell you their hopes and dreams, as well as clarifying what your role is—how and when they can contact you and viceversa.

If advisory is new, send a brief letter home to describe the purpose, benefits, and activities that are at the heart of your school advisory program. This is important, whether the scope of your advisory program is fairly limited or more comprehensive. If advisory has been in place for years, parents will still appreciate knowing the current goals and focus as well as hearing you, as their child's advisor, describe your role and expectations.

If one of your primary responsibilities is to be the adult liaison between home and school for your advisee regarding discipline and academic progress, here are some ideas for how to integrate parent connections into your weekly routine, as well as a few suggestions for how to conference with parents and guardians:

- Be proactive when it comes to kids with challenging behaviors or kids encountering academic difficulties. Pace your "problem calls" so you don't feel overloaded. In many middle schools that have daily team planning time, one session per week is devoted to contacting parents. These are the critical calls that inform parents about behavior or academic problems; behavioral plans or academic contracts; follow-up consequences; updates regarding a student's progress or lack of it; and arrangements for a parent-student-teacher conference.

- Do a couple of "sunshine calls" per week to parents. The goal is to talk to every parent at some point during the semester, sharing something their child has done well and something you appreciate about their child. "Sunshine calls" can be a powerful connector between you and the parent, the parent and the student, and you and the student. Prioritize your calls, making sure you first call the parents of students who don't get the spotlight, students who have made a turnaround, and students for whom a positive call home is probably rare.

- "Sunshine notes" serve the same purpose and take much less time. Try to do a few every week and send them home with the student.

- Parent phone calls are never easy. One strategy that can make phone calls more productive is to conference with the student beforehand, so that you can share what the student intends to do to rectify a given situation. Having a script sometimes helps. Here are some suggestions:

1. Introduce yourself. Ask the parent if it is a convenient time to talk for a few minutes.

2. Indicate that you know something about the student—a positive quality that she or he brings to the advisory group, something that he or she does well, or something unusual with which she or he is familiar.

3. Share the reason you are calling by stating the problem simply. For example, you might say, "I'm calling about an incident that occurred yesterday. Here's what happened." Or, "We have a procedure in class about _____. I'm calling because your daughter/son has/has not _____." Or, "I'm concerned about _____'s academic progress. Here's what I've observed over the last couple of weeks." Or, "I've been concerned about a couple of behaviors that have become more frequent in the past few weeks. Your son/daughter has been _____."

4. Share why you are concerned about the particular behavior and explain how you think the behavior is affecting their child, other students, or the classroom learning environment.

5. Ask the parent if they have any thoughts or questions about the situation. If the parent is upset, acknowledge their feelings and try to find a common concern or hope that you share about their daughter/son.

6. Explain that you have already discussed the issue with the student, who has made a commitment to _____. Inform the parent of any other consequences.

7. Share how much you would appreciate it if the parent would talk to their son/daughter about this. Reassure the parent that this is not the end of the world. You're calling now because you have confidence that the student can turn this situation around. Thank them for their support.

8. Let parents know that you make a specific period available for parent phone calls at the same time every week.

Post Advisory information on your school web site

Use your school web site to post advisory-related information, such as

- Description of advisory

- Goals, objectives, and benefits of advisory

- Calendar of events, themes, and/or sequence of topics and activities

- Roles and expectations of advisors

- Expectations for students in advisory

- Frequently asked questions about advisory

- What parents can do to make advisory a positive experience for their child

Advisory Formats

Effective teachers use many different formats to structure teaching and learning—lectures, discussions, simulations, research, and experiments, to name just a few—and they think carefully about them. Similarly, advisory can involve various formats. The professional development program that you provide advisors should help them build skillfulness in the formats you will use the most.

The fifteen formats described below shape the way a group interacts or even if members interact. Some formats are short, others long; some are mostly verbal; others more experiential. Think about your advisory program goals, time allotments, and content as you identify which formats will be the most suitable for your program. For example, daily short advisories will likely find gatherings, brief small-and large-group dialogues, personal conferencing, and journaling that fit best. Interactive exercises and team challenges take time, and can backfire if rushed.

Gatherings

Gatherings are short exercises that bring everyone together at the beginning of an advisory group session and mark the transition from the rest of the day to advisory time. They provide a structure for listening and speaking in ways that demonstrate and offer practice in respect, understanding, and empathy. Everyone is acknowledged and invited to share stories, responses to interesting questions, appreciations, or reflections about what's happening in their lives. This format creates a powerful opportunity to know others and be known.

The invitation to express one's thoughts and feelings strengthens the perception that everyone is important and everyone has something important to say. Two guidelines for gatherings include (1) respecting the "right to pass"—the choice to only listen is as powerful as the choice to speak, and (2) using topics and questions that all students can address without feeling vulnerable, embarrassed, or defensive. Gatherings usually take five to ten minutes.

Some examples:

- Reading aloud a quote, poem, or passage, perhaps followed by short reactions

- Warm-up exercises that set the stage for a skill lesson or discussion

- Physical energizers like a deep breath or group stretch that help change the pace, mark a transition, or shift the energy

- Quick go-rounds about the past weekend, today's mood, a hot topic of the day, or a question for the week:

    What's something new and good in your life right now?

    What's something you'd like to learn about or learn how to do that's currently not offered here at school?

    What is the most meaningful present you've ever received? Why was it special?

    What's one school-wide rule that you would change to make school a better place for everyone?

    What's something in which you excel that ends with "-ing"?

    Name a word that describes how you feel today and why.

Announcements

Announcements within your advisory group (not the public address system announcements) involve opportunities to:

- Review and clarify school, house, grade level, and team rules, procedures, policies, and routines

- Recognize individuals and the group for various contributions, achievements or successes

- Preview upcoming events, deadlines, applications, and opportunities within the advisory, team, grade level, house, or whole school

- Note newsworthy events and activities happening in the larger school community or the communities surrounding the school

✐ Small and large group dialogues

Small-and large-group dialogue on a wide range of topics and issues is the dominant advisory format. This extended section includes a variety of structures and guidelines that help turn group talk into good talk and enable students to practice active listening and thoughtful speaking. These dialogue formats range widely in time usage, so select the formats that suit your topic and your advisory schedule. The guiding principle in all of the structures is to build understanding rather than win debate points. The following list[2] highlights this distinction.

Dialogue	Debate
Dialogue is collaborative: the sides work together.	Debate is a type of fight: two sides oppose each other to prove each other wrong.
Dialogue builds a learning relationship between people.	Debate builds a competitive relationship between people.
Dialogue encourages the participants to identify questions and goals they could share.	Debate encourages each side to articulate its own questions and goals.
In a dialogue the goals are finding common ideas and new ideas.	In a debate the goal is winning with your own ideas.
In a dialogue everyone contributes to solving a problem.	In a debate one person and viewpoint wins, the other is dismissed.
In a dialogue you believe that many solutions might exist, and that different people have parts of the best solutions.	In a debate you believe that there is one solution, that you have it, and other solutions are not considered.
In a dialogue you are sensitive to each other's feelings, hopes, and ideas.	In a debate you do not care about the feelings, hopes, and ideas of others.
In a dialogue you contribute your best ideas to be improved upon.	In a debate you contribute your ideas and defend them against challenges.
In a dialogue you listen to each other to understand and build agreement.	In a debate you listen to each other to find flaws and disagree.
In a dialogue you search for the good parts of other people's ideas.	In a debate you search for weaknesses in other people's ideas.

Dialogue

In a dialogue you may consider new ideas and even change your mind completely.

Dialogue encourages you to evaluate yourself.

Dialogue promotes open-mindedness, including an openness to being wrong.

Dialogue encourages you to see all sides of an issue.

Dialogue invites keeping the topic open even after the discussion formally ends.

Debate

In a debate you do not admit you are considering new ideas and you must not change your mind, or you lose.

Debate encourages you to criticize others.

Debate creates a close-minded attitude, a determination to be right.

Debate encourages you to see only two different sides of an issue.

Debate, by creating a winner and a loser, discourages further discussion.

The structures below can be used separately or in conjunction with each other. A quick tour of dialogue formats:

- **Pair/Share** – Create opportunities for multiple conversations at the same time. Pairs can respond to a question by (1) giving each partner one minute to share while the other partner listens, or (2) giving pairs two minutes to converse with each other with the purpose of agreeing on a response that they will share with the whole group. Some questions might warrant longer times.

- **Brainstorming** – Brainstorming is a process for generating ideas that fosters creative thinking and problem solving. The advisor or an advisee facilitates the brainstorm, and another person records students' responses. Some guidelines for good brainstorming include:

  1. All ideas are accepted; every idea will be written down.

  2. Try to avoid commenting, positively or negatively, on ideas presented.

  3. Say what you're thinking even if it seems odd; unexpected ideas may be useful and can generate creative thinking.

  4. Consider what others have suggested and use those ideas to spur new thinking and adaptations.

  5. Push for quantity.

- **Listening Labs** – In groups of three to five, students take turns responding to questions about a particular issue or topic. Each person has a specified amount of time (45 – 90 seconds) to respond. When one student speaks, other students are expected to give that student their full attention and interested silence. Listening labs are not time for back and forth conversation, but rather provide each student with an opportunity to share her/his perspectives and experiences without being interrupted. Remind students that what's said in the group stays in the group.

- **Paraphrasing Circles** – This is a variation of the listening lab format. The goal is to use paraphrasing (accurately restating a person's thoughts in one's own words) to ensure that everyone who speaks is understood. Each group of four or five students sits in a circle facing each other. You might want all groups to discuss the same issue or questions, or you can invite groups to choose which two to three questions they want to discuss from a larger list of questions.

  In paraphrasing circles, the first student in the group responds to the chosen question without being interrupted. Then the second student paraphrases what the previous student said and checks for accuracy of understanding. The first person can correct or clarify the restatement at this time. Then the second student responds to the same question without being interrupted. The third person paraphrases the second person, checks for accuracy, and shares her/his perspective on the question. This process is repeated until everyone has a turn.

  You might want to add one more part to each round. Invite one student from each small group to summarize students' perspectives by reporting to the larger group. Or you might invite one student to record any questions that arise after everyone in the small group has spoken.

- **Council** – For topics that generate highly charged emotions, polarized opinions, or intensely personal responses, sit in a circle and invite each person to take one or two minutes to respond to the issue. Some advisors convey a difference in tone and encourage supportive, respectful listening by using a "talking stick" or special object that students pass to each other. The person who holds the object is the only person who can speak.

- **Connections** – Set a timer for three to five minutes and invite group members to share final thoughts and feelings after an intense discussion, a video, a journal exercise, a guest presentation, a skills workshop, etc.

- **Structured Discussions and Dialogues** – Structured discussions help students pay close attention to the conversation. These structures help slow down thinking, thus improving listening and encouraging participants to choose more carefully what they say and how they say it. Experiment with these process suggestions to determine what structures and guidelines work best for different topics and types of discussions:

1. Limit the size of the group involved in a dialogue. If you can divide the group in half using two facilitators, there are more opportunities for each person to participate.

2. Sit in a circle or horseshoe shape so that everyone can see each other.

3. Explore what factors contribute to a discussion in which people feel comfortable and encouraged to speak, and what contributes to a discussion where people feel shut down and afraid to speak.

4. Discuss the differences between dialogue and debate. Many students keep silent because they often feel like they are in the middle of somebody else's contest! Brainstorm a list of the differences between dialogue and debate. Think about how the goals differ, how people attend and respond differently, and the strengths and limitations of each type of discourse.

5. Prepare a set of questions beforehand that students have helped to generate. Craft questions that are open-ended so they encourage an exchange of ideas, rather than quick polarization. You might want to prioritize questions or identify two or three that students are eager to discuss.

6. Do at least one go-round with an open-ended question, where everyone who wants to respond gets to speak, before the group raises questions or shifts to back and forth dialogue.

7. Increase wait time before inviting students to speak. Silence encourages deliberative thinking. Use index cards or create a dialogue form that students can use to compose their thoughts before they speak, jot down follow-up questions, and reflect on the dialogue when it's over.

8. Encourage self-monitoring so a few people don't dominate the conversation. You might want to introduce constraints that support sharing the air time. For example, limiting comments to one minute so students don't speechify, limiting the number of times each person can speak during a dialogue, or inviting different subgroups to respond to questions—boys, girls, certain letters of the alphabet, sides of the room, etc.

9. Ask participants to paraphrase what the previous speaker has said before sharing their own thoughts.

10. Before students rush to argue, ask them first to identify something they agree with that a previous speaker has said. "I agree with _____ and I'd like to add/ask _____."

11. Emphasize that changing positions or shifting opinions isn't about backing down, but rather is about reassessing their views after taking in more data and perspectives.

12. Encourage students to clarify whether they are speaking from their own experience or making observations about what they have read, heard, or seen.

13. Remind students that respectful listening isn't about agreeing or disagreeing with the speaker—it's about taking in what someone says and communicating that you have understood them. Respectful speaking is about communicating your own thoughts and feelings in ways that your audience will hear and understand. Keep exploring how people can disagree and still be respectful listeners and speakers.

14. Summarize important points before the conversation goes in a new direction. Or take a two-minute time-out to pair/share, write about, or reflect as a group on these questions: What issues are clearer for you? What's still vague or confusing? What two or three things have been said that have helped to deepen your understanding of _____? Was there any question or comment that really grabbed your attention and made you stop and think, reevaluate, or want to find out more? Are there any important questions that haven't been asked yet? Are there any points of view that we've left out?

15. If the dialogue starts to feel combative or emotionally intense, stop for a minute and do a feelings/perspectives check. Ask how people are feeling about what's being said. How do others see this issue? Who else wants to respond before we move on? Is there anyone who has another opinion? Is there anyone who agrees?

16. Loaded, provocative, or negative language heats up tensions and drains positive energy from the room. Encourage the group to think about how they can respectfully call attention to language being used. For example, a student might say, "I'm not sure that language helps us better understand _____. Could you use language that doesn't _____?" Or say, "It's easier for me to hear you if you could say that in another way, so it doesn't sound so judgmental/negative/offputting."

- **Moving Opinion Polls** – Moving opinion polls are a way to get students up and moving as they place themselves along a STRONGLY AGREE to STRONGLY DISAGREE continuum according to their opinions about specific statements. The most powerful aspect of this exercise is the insight, new to many students, that people can disagree without fighting—in fact, people can listen to various points of view respectfully and even rethink their own opinions upon hearing the views of others. This format of large-group dialogue allows all participants to show where they stand, without pressuring everyone to speak.

Create a space in your room, from one side to the other side, that is long enough and wide enough to accommodate your whole group. If you can make a horseshoe shape, students will be able to see each other during the comments time. Make two large signs and post them on opposite sides of the room:

Strongly Agree   **Strongly Disagree**

Explain to students: "You will be participating in a moving opinion poll. Each time you hear a statement you are to move to the place along the imaginary line between "strongly agree" and "strongly disagree" that most closely reflects your opinion. If you strongly disagree, you will move all the way to that side of the room. If you strongly agree, you will move all the way to the other side of the room. You can also place yourself anywhere in the middle, especially if you have mixed feelings about the question. "After you have placed yourselves along the continuum, I will invite people to share why they are standing where they are. This is not a time to debate or grill each other. Rather, this is a way to hear what people are thinking and get a sense of the different ways people perceive the issue."

When you do this activity, begin with a statement that indicates noncontroversial preferences such as, "Chocolate is the best ice cream flavor in the world." Or, "Basketball is the best spectator sport." Then introduce statements related to a topic you're exploring in your advisory.

Personal connections and conferencing

Use these formats (whether it's a 30-second check-in or formal appointment) to connect with individual advisees and their families. A primary advisory role is becoming an advisee's advocate by

- monitoring and supporting students' academic progress, year by year academic planning, and high school, college, and career planning;

- strengthening connections between home and school;

- helping students get the services that they need when they are experiencing academic and behavioral difficulties;

- providing positive doses of attention and support and providing opportunities to listen and problem solve; and

- "red flagging" a student's particular needs or circumstances to other faculty or administrators when necessary and appropriate.

These functions are difficult to do successfully unless you create ways to get to know each student and make meaningful connections. You will need to decide how and when you make these opportunities happen during advisory (while the rest of the students are engaged in individual student tasks) and during nonadvisory time. What's desirable and what's possible will depend upon your school's advisory goals and advisor expectations, the number of students in your advisory, the amount of time per session, and frequency of the advisory period. Here's a quick checklist of possibilities for making connections with individual advisees:

During Advisory Periods

- Two-minute check-ins rotating students over time. If you have one long period a week, you can do this for ten minutes at the beginning of advisory when students are writing or journaling

- Ten-second "hits" – personal comments and questions directed to individual students before and after advisory and while the group is engaged in an activity that you're not facilitating

- academic assessment, grade report, and goal-setting conferences at the beginning, middle, and/or end of a quarter

- observing, listening, and providing feedback to students during interactive exercises, skill lessons, and small-group dialogues

During Non-Advisory Times

- the "lunch bunch" – inviting two or three advisees to have lunch with you

- providing an advisory "conference hour" on the same day every week before or after school

- sunshine calls – calling each advisee's parent/guardian once a semester to communicate something positive about their child

- quarterly grade conferences with the advisee and the advisee's parent/guardian

- once-per-quarter or semester extended in-school or out-of-school activity where you can have informal chat time with each student (i.e. skating, bowling, boat ride, picnic, pot luck and a movie, fitness work-out, etc.)

Reading and test prep

These activities can include the following:

- silent reading for pleasure

- reading activities with a skill development focus

- test review and preparation for current course work

- standardized test preparation and practice

Every state and district has its own tests and practice materials; use any that are appropriate. If your advisory meets twice per week or more, you can designate one session every week or two for one-to-one help with any of an advisee's teachers, student-led study groups, and academic and special education support services. These tasks can happen within your advisory group or across groups. Also note the many activities, coaching suggestions, and goal-setting and reflection questions to help students handle stress, improve study habits, and enhance skills.

Organizing and representing ideas and information

These activities can include:

- writing, recording, charting, drawing, or mapping your ideas, feelings, opinions, observations, and questions, individually or in a group

- completing surveys, forms, and polls

- planning tasks involving assignment notebooks, subject notebooks, and organizing course material

- portfolio, project, and exhibition organizing and planning tasks

- preparation for report card conferences

- written responses related to academic and behavioral contracts

- career and college organizing and planning tasks

Journaling and written reflections

These activities can include:

- writing with a focus on developing writing skills

- written responses to a specific reading

- peer review and editing of written assignments

- written feedback about advisory activities

- written reflections and assessments related to academic goals and course work

- written reports and status updates related to internships, service learning, and independent projects

- letters to oneself (to be opened next term or next year), to the advisor, other advisees, parents

- journaling about personal growth, that is, reflections on self-management, getting along with others, leadership, and/or making good decisions

⟋ Class meetings

Class meetings offer an ideal structure for negotiating group decisions, discussing problems as they arise, and dealing with all things that affect how the group functions. Several core features set class meetings apart from other learning structures:

- Students take primary responsibility for generating the agenda and facilitating activities for class meetings.

- Students are expected to practice effective communication and problem solving skills as participants and facilitators.

- Students play a primary role in solving problems and making decisions about issues addressed.

Class meetings serve many purposes. One of the most important is creating a special time and space to confront and solve problems that impact the group—whether they are issues identified by one advisory group member, problems that emerge within the group, concerns about the larger school culture, or the wider world outside of school. Equally important, however, class meetings provide opportunities for students to do things that strengthen their desire and capacity to be a high-functioning group. The purpose of class meetings can shift given the specific needs of the group. Sample purposes include:

- **Open Dialogue:** The goal of this meeting is to provide a safe space to air concerns, share feelings and perspectives, and gain deeper understanding of issues raised by students or the advisor.

- **Planning and Problem Solving:** The goal of these meetings is to use negotiating, planning, and problem solving strategies to make decisions and resolve issues that affect advisory, the grade-level team, or the larger learning environment. These meetings help the group plan special activities and projects or resolve concerns around procedures, habits, and routines, cliques and exclusion, testing protocols, etc.

- **Hypothetical Discussions:** The goal of this class meeting is to discuss hypothetical situations or case studies as a way to anticipate and generate solutions to problems before they happen. ("If this happens, then _____." "In a situation such as _____, what would you do—or hope you would do?")

- **Group Reflection, Feedback, and Assessment:** The goal of this meeting is to provide maintenance and support for the group. These activities usually involve group goal setting, check-ins, and assessment of group goals and behaviors.

- **Crisis Meetings:** The goal of this meeting is to address situations that require an immediate intervention and attention in a serious, sensitive, and supportive way. Crisis meetings are an important vehicle for reducing tension, restoring order, dealing with a critical concern, or providing care and support for students impacted by a school, personal, or family crisis.

Set the stage for class meeting by developing specific, positive guidelines for facilitating and participating in class meeting: meet in a circle or square where everyone can see everyone else; create an agenda that becomes a routine; review the agenda and identify specific goals; solicit feedback about the meeting when it's over; and invite students to take various roles as they become more comfortable (class meeting facilitator, summarizer, note taker, time keeper, feedbacker, activity leader, etc.) Group problem solving is more effective when you follow these tips:

- Carefully craft how to frame the topic or use an introductory exercise so students can build from strengths, rather than starting from weaknesses. (See Facilitating Tips for more on this.)

- Ask several people to help describe the problem or topic and share perspectives on why it's a problem.

- Encourage active listening by inviting students to paraphrase and summarize each others' ideas.

- Explore different points of view, making sure there is room for respectful disagreement.

- Point out commonalities and encourage advisees to do the same.

- Listen and respond to others empathically.

- Share the air time and ensure that everyone's voice is heard.

- Identify goals for solving the problem or addressing the topic, i.e., what do you hope will change as a result of working it out?

- Develop several desirable solutions from which to choose.

- Ask open-ended questions to gain a deeper understanding of various suggestions.

- Evaluate advantages and disadvantages of various solutions—does this solution work for some people at the expense of others? Does everyone get something they need so it feels like it will work for them?

- Encourage as many students as possible to speak, even if their comments are in agreement with others who have already spoken. This is the way you begin to get a good read on the direction the group seems to want to go.

- Summarize the discussion and state what the group seems to think are the most important things to incorporate in the best solution.

- Use straw polls and a consensus process to reach your decision.

- Have the advisory or a small group plan precisely how the solution will be implemented. The group should also be able to suggest ways to evaluate how effectively the solution achieves the goal of the meeting.

It will help the group if you facilitate the first few meetings, modeling how to do it while communicating your expectation that students will take on the role of facilitating class meetings over time. You may want to invite three or four volunteers who are interested in facilitating meetings to be part of a planning group that prepares for class meetings.

It's important to appreciate that facilitating regular class meetings can feel a bit risky to many teachers. It's an open-ended process. You can't invite students to discuss an issue thoughtfully if you already assume that you have the right solution at hand before you even begin. Teachers who have taken this risk share how their advisories were transformed by making class meetings a regular activity. As one teacher put it, "I was anxious about this. I knew that if I was doing it 'right,' I wouldn't be in charge of the outcome. I had to tell myself that I was already a good problem solver. My job was to help my advisees become better problem solvers. After using class meetings for a month, I noticed that the climate shifted. The more students felt this was their process, the more attuned they became to working out issues that got in the way of making our advisory a good place to be."

Skill lessons

Many advisory programs develop a sequence of academic, health education, social development, and/or life skills lessons for each grade level in middle or high school. Some middle schools develop a three-year cycle of skill lessons where all advisory groups at every grade level receive the same set of skill lessons in the first year, a different lesson set in each successive year, then the cycle repeats itself. A sampling of skill lessons is included in the Activities Chapter under the theme Life Skills, Healthy Development, and Self-Care. If your advisory includes a focus on health education and/or social skill development, the following tips can lead to more effective lessons:

- Develop a sequence of organized, coherent, and developmentally appropriate lessons in which student learning at one level builds upon what has come before and prepares students for what comes later.

- Provide multiple years of direct skill instruction throughout the school experience versus one "dose" for one year only. Prevention research suggests that developing a specific skill competency requires six to eight hits—in other words, a one time experience will not produce a change in behavior or help students become comfortable practicing and using a skill.

- Incorporate exposure to and instruction of a new skill with continued practice in different contexts, coaching and feedback, and opportunities for students to demonstrate competency and mastery. Students will achieve far more if they are learning and practicing a few skills in depth, rather than trying out many skills superficially. Be choosy!

- Communicate explicitly to students the skill they are learning, why they are learning it, the activities they will be doing to learn and practice the skill, and how they will be assessed on their use of the skill.

- Be sure that lessons, role plays, and case studies have a cultural and social context that feels real to your students. Teaching a social skill lesson that appears unrelated to students' lives is likely to flop or even backfire.

- Teach by example—your capacity to model effective self-management skills, interpersonal communication skills, and conflict management skills will send a more powerful message than most lessons.

Interactive exercises

This category includes activities that involve a high level of active participation from every group member and the use of multiple intelligences and different ways of knowing and learning. Examples include:

- role plays, skits, and improvisation exercises

- simulations and experiential exercises

- "adventure-based" learning activities

See the Activities Chapter and Additional Resources for a listing of additional books that feature interactive exercises.

Games and team challenges

The spirit of play is as essential for adolescents, who need healthy outlets for physical, sexual, and emotional energy as it is for younger children. Games and team challenges involve invention, rule-making, role-playing, social organizing, problem solving, physical or intellectual challenges, and the harnessing and release of positive emotions. In its purest sense, play is kid-driven—they are in charge of what happens. Students' choices for how to play go a long way in shaping both positive and negative social norms in the larger school culture. Games and team challenges provide opportunities for students to think strategically, negotiate differences constructively, regulate peer behavior, and fine-tune their abilities to "read" and lead a group. Team challenges are a laboratory for practicing cooperation and leadership skills.

If you frame any activity as a game that involves cooperation and competition, you've doubled the fun and interest level. Add a problem to the activity that the whole group or small groups have to solve and you've hit the trifecta! The shortcoming of these activities is the time crunch. Some advisory programs create an extended advisory session for team building activities and group challenges in the beginning of the year and mid-winter. See the Activities Chapter and Additional Resources for additional games and team challenges.

Projects
Projects include:

- planning an activity that the advisory carries out as a whole group or in small groups (for example, planning and participating in an outdoor adventure day, an urban excursion, designing and facilitating an activity for International Day, or preparing for a visit to an eldercare center)

- planning, developing, and completing a product or presentation over an extended period of time (for example, the management of an advisory-run store at lunch time, the development and analysis of a student survey, or a presentation to the school leadership team about new courses and credit options)

- internships, in-school service and stewardship activities, and service learning in the larger community

- independent student projects (variously called "I" projects," "passion projects," or "orbital studies" because the student makes a deeply felt personal choice to study and become an expert on something that matters to her/him. Independent studies may or may not be directly related to the rest of a student's academic course work)

- hands-on projects where individuals or groups of students work with materials, designing, creating, and making a product that's all their own. These might range from a couple of advisory sessions to a whole term.

Videos and guest or student presentations
Videos and guest or student presentations offer important ways to bring a topic to life and experience a wider range of perspectives about a particular issue. It's helpful to have students take the lead in making suggestions about the kinds of guests they would like to invite to advisory and the kinds of student presentations or student-led discussions they would find interesting.

Assemblies

Advisories can be effective ways to prepare for and followup on assemblies; they can be the organizing force behind assemblies, or simply determine the seating. There are good reasons to gather as a whole group and experience a collective sense of belonging, purpose, and celebration. Yet assemblies are awful when they're too long, too boring, or become the setting for "bad behavior" lectures. And assemblies are terrible places to practice good "public space" behaviors when the real concern is about a very small group of students. Instead, try convening brief assemblies that give most students and faculty something important to know and use, to celebrate, to anticipate, to raise awareness of and ponder, or feel good about.

There are some useful guidelines for making assemblies work:

1. Make assemblies brief—20 minutes—or include varying forms of presentation (speakers, demonstration, video).

2. Don't use assemblies for the "bad behavior" lecture — use advisories or town meetings to communicate concerns about discipline, serious incidents, etc.

3. Ensure that adults and students jointly facilitate assemblies.

4. Focus the assembly on one thing.

5. Make assemblies "upbeat" with a dose of humor if possible, or make them meaningful; give people a reason to say they were glad they came.

6. Utilize advisories to plan, organize, and facilitate assemblies.

7. If the assembly is about a sensitive topic, remember that large groups can be forums for raising awareness, but they do not provide the comfort or time for students to ask important questions, to reflect, or to internalize new understandings. Advisory groups are, however, ideal for that purpose.

Closings

Closing activities provide a way to conclude the time the group has spent together and send them off at the end of advisory, the end of the week, or the end of the semester. Like gatherings, closings create opportunities for every student to be heard. Where gatherings focus mostly on sharing personal stories and reflections, closings provide an excellent vehicle for students to give feedback on what they've experienced during the session or week, communicate what they've been learning, and assess their progress and personal development. The advisor can get a quick sense from the group that helps shape advisory topics and activities and even guides connections and conferencing with individual advisees. A few examples include:

- Tell us in five words or less what's the most important thing you learned this week.

- What's a banner headline of five words or less that would best summarize the progress you're making in your challenge course?

- Share a story about someone who helped you this week, or someone you helped this week.

- When you feel discouraged or frustrated with an assignment or topic, what do you say to yourself to keep going?

- What's the best thing that happened to you this week?

- What's one thing you're looking forward to doing this weekend?

- What's something you've accomplished this week that you're proud of?

Endnotes

[1] Rachel A. Poliner. "Tips for Challenging Times and Tough Topics" (Needham, MA: Needham High School, 2003).

[2] Reprinted, with permission, from *Dialogue: Turning Controversy into Community*, by Rachel A. Poliner and Jeffrey Benson, (Cambridge, MA: Educators for Social Responsibility, 1997).

CHAPTER 6

Activities

Okay, now you're ready to plan what you will do in advisory from week to week. This chapter offers a sampling of activities on ten themes related to the goals most frequently cited in advisory programs. The themes include the following:

- Community-building, group cohesion, and group maintenance

- Orientation, school citizenship, and school business

- Personal goal-setting, reflection, and assessment

- Tools for school and learning

- Life skills, healthy development, and self-care

- Moving on to high school, college, or career

- Real-world connections and service-learning

- Personal passions, hobbies, and interests

- Rituals, celebrations, and closure

- Rainy-day fun stuff

No successful advisory program we have found uses a stock curriculum or requires advisors to implement activities exactly as written. Our experience tells us that advisors bring a range of needs and preferences to facilitating effective advisory sessions. Some advisors are perfectly happy finding and designing their own activities, given their advisory program's goals and themes for a particular session, week, month, or season of the year. Other advisors are more comfortable with a prescribed set of activities and detailed instructions. Most advisors are somewhere in between. They appreciate having a sequence of suggested activities and want the flexibility to adapt and alter activities in ways that serve the needs of their group. Thus, the activities described in this chapter are not designed to be used as a set curriculum.

Our intention is twofold. First, these are activities that you can use with your advisory group. Second, the activities demonstrate a range of topics in each theme and model how to apply format, grouping, and frequency decisions. There are numerous other sources of activities on the market to draw from as you shape your specific advisory content. We hope this schema gives you a language and structure that will help you develop the right array of activities for your students and school.

The facilitation tips and formats in Chapter 5 and the activities in this chapter support each other. Many of the activities refer to specific formats that will enhance the activity. Also, keep in mind that some formats like "test-prep" and "class meeting," serve as the activity itself. Other activities in this chapter call for attention to group facilitation skills.

Each activity also includes suggestions for scheduling and frequency. For example, there are several activities that help build a sense of community and establish positive norms that are best implemented early in the year, while other activities for later use support ongoing group cohesion and help the group revisit norms when necessary.

Some activities are simple to implement; others are more complex. Either way, it is the overall facilitation of the group and the relationships you develop that make advisory groups supportive to students. Schools can offer professional development so advisors learn how to conduct complicated activities and learn to facilitate advisories through the normal, sometimes smooth and sometimes rocky, stages of development. Formal training sessions will be useful, as will modeling the formats and facilitation tips in department meetings and faculty study groups.

Some activities offer a dozen discussion and reflection questions, any two of which might generate a rich advisory dialogue. We wrote the activities with middle school and high school students in mind, so choose the activities and prompts that best serve your students' needs, ages, and interests, and your advisory program goals and design. There will likely be a few themes that fit strongly with your goals and others that are not within your parameters. Don't try to do everything—it is important to offer advisees an experience with depth and integrity.

In some cases, activities will not be necessary. Advisees may need time for discussing issues that arise within the group or generating and sustaining their own ongoing conversation. Moments when the group is steering itself are important. If your advisors are very experienced, the program is well established, and the goals are fairly broad, organized activities will be less important. Having coherent themes and a logical progression of activities will be very important if you are still building buy-in, developing advisors' skills, or are committed to learning outcomes such as building interpersonal skills, enhancing academic skills, or developing personal educational plans.

To help guide your selection of activities, see the appropriate grid, which is organized by theme and format.

Grid of activities by theme and format

Community-Building, Group Cohesion, and Group Maintenance

Activity by format	Page	Gatherings	Announcements	Group Dialogue– sm. and lg.	Conferencing, Connections	Reading, Test Prep	Org. and Rep. Ideas, Info	Journaling, Written Refl.	Class Meetings	Skill Lessons	Interactive Exercises	Games, Team Challenges	Projects	Videos, Speakers	Assemblies	Closings
Paired Introductions	116	•														
Advisor Interview	117	•														
Name-Matching Exercise	117										•					
60-Second Interviews	118										•					
Find Someone Who…	119										•					
What Do We Have in Common?	119										•					
You Like, I Like …	120	•														
Making Advisory … Welcoming	120									•						
Silent Squares Puzzle Problem	121											•				
Chocolate River	123											•				
Who's Going to the Concert?	126										•					
Synectic Connections	127										•					
Cultural Sharing	129	•														
Family Banners	129										•					
Personal Identity Cards	130												•			
Personal History Museum	130												•			
Metaphor Toy Bag	131	•														•
Make Connections in 10 Secs.	131				•											
Group Resolutions	133								•							
Group Member Reflections	134				•			•								
Adding or Subtracting…?	134			•	•			•								

Orientation, School Citizenship, and School Business

Activity by format	Page	Gatherings	Announcements	Group Dialogue– sm. and lg.	Conferencing, Connections	Reading, Test Prep	Org. and Rep. Ideas, Info	Journaling, Written Refl.	Class Meetings	Skill Lessons	Interactive Exercises	Games, Team Challenges	Projects	Videos, speakers	Assemblies	Closings
First Day of Advisory	137			•												
First-Week Student Profile	138				•											
This Is How We Do School Here	138														•	
All-School Advisory Team Chall.	139											•				
The Game of School	140											•				
Passport to School	142												•			
Previewing the Week … Events	143		•													
School Spirit	143												•			
School Climate Check	144			•	•			•								
Town Meeting	146								•							
Boys in the Bathroom, Girls in…	147			•												
Adopt a Space	150												•			
School Climate … Surveys	150			•				•								

Personal Goal-Setting, Reflection, and Self-Assessment

Activity by format

Activity	Page	Gatherings	Announcements	Group Dialogue– sm. and lg.	Conferencing, Connections	Reading, Test Prep	Org. and Rep. Ideas, Info	Journaling, Written Refl.	Class Meetings	Skill Lessons	Interactive Exercises	Games, Team Challenges	Projects	Videos, Speakers	Assemblies	Closings
Mapping ... Personal Pathway	151						•									
Reflections about Me	151							•								
Postcard and Picture Check-ins	152	•														•
Quarterly Goal-Setting	153				•			•								
Acknowledging Your Assets	155				•			•								
Speaking of Character	155			•				•								
If I Had a Wish	157	•														
Reflecting ... the Week That Was	157														•	
Assessing Learning	158	•						•								
Grade-Report Conferencing	161			•	•		•	•								
Make Time to ONLY Listen	164			•	•											
Guidelines for Conferencing ...	165			•												

Tools for School and Learning

Activity by format

Activity	Page	Gatherings	Announcements	Group Dialogue– sm. and lg.	Conferencing, Connections	Reading, Test Prep	Org. and Rep. Ideas, Info	Journaling, Written Refl.	Class Meetings	Skill Lessons	Interactive Exercises	Games, Team Challenges	Projects	Videos, Speakers	Assemblies	Closings
Perspectives on School,...	167	•		•												
Calendars and Assignment Books	168			•	•		•					•				
Drop Everything and Read	171					•										
Writing, Writing, Writing	171				•			•		•						
Finding Your Voice	172			•	•					•						
Time and Task Management I	173	•						•			•					
Time and Task Management II	174	•						•			•					
Remembering...Things on Tray	175						•									
Portfolio Review and Selection	177						•									
Discussing, Solving Problems...	178								•							
...School-Smart Strategies	178			•	•											
...Match Behaviors to Setting	181										•					
Academic Networking and Enrich.	182			•	•											

Life Skills, Healthy Development, and Self-Care

Activity by format

Activity by format	Page	Gatherings	Announcements	Group Dialogue– sm. and lg.	Conferencing, Connections	Reading, Test Prep	Org. and Rep. Ideas, Info	Journaling, Written Refl.	Class Meetings	Skill Lessons	Interactive Exercises	Games, Team Challenges	Projects	Videos, Speakers	Assemblies	Closings
This Issue of Respect	184									•						
Friendship Questions	186	•		•				•								•
Making Things Right	187							•		•						
Peer Pressure	189			•			•	•			•					
Drawing a House	191										•					
Teach Win-Win Basics	194									•	•					
Negotiating	196									•						
Group Problem-Solving	200									•						
Making Good Decisions	202			•				•					•			
All about Conflict	203									•	•					
Questions about Conflict	205	•		•				•								•
Managing Your Feelings…	206	•		•	•			•		•						
Assertive, Passive, Aggressive	210									•						
Guidelines for Giving Feedback	212			•												
Stress Management	215			•						•						
Wellness Week or Month	216			•						•			•		•	
Self-Care Check-up	217			•				•								
Giving and Getting Support	218			•				•								
The Violence Continuum	218			•				•								
Thinking…about Harassment I	219			•				•		•						
Thinking…about Harassment II	221									•						
Harassment Survey	222						•						•			
Counter Harassment and Bullying	222										•					

Moving on to High School, College, or Career

Activity by format

Activity by format	Page	Gatherings	Announcements	Group Dialogue– sm. and lg.	Conferencing, Connections	Reading, Test Prep	Org. and Rep. Ideas, Info	Journaling, Written Refl.	Class Meetings	Skill Lessons	Interactive Exercises	Games, Team Challenges	Projects	Videos, Speakers	Assemblies	Closings
Imagining the Future	224	•		•				•								
Quotations about Moving On	225	•		•				•								
Personal Statements	225													•		
Career Exploration I	226	•					•	•								
Career Exploration II	227												•			
… Planning for College, Career	228						•									
Practice Interviews	229			•										•		

Real-World Connections and Service Learning

Activity by format

Activity	Page	Gatherings	Announcements	Group Dialogue– sm. and lg.	Conferencing, Connections	Reading, Test Prep	Org. and Rep. Ideas, Info	Journaling, Written Refl.	Class Meetings	Skill Lessons	Interactive Exercises	Games, Team Challenges	Projects	Videos, Speakers	Assemblies	Closings
Checking Out (their) World ...	230	•														•
Introducing My Neighborhood	231						•				•		•			
Teens and Freedom I	232			•				•								
Teens and Freedom II	232								•					•		
Growing Up Then and Now	233							•			•					
What's Doing around Town?	234		•			•										
Rant and Rave about Real World	234							•								
Quotations about the Real World	235	•		•				•								•
Explore and Map Your Community	237						•						•			
Service-Learning Projects	241												•			
Discussing World Events, Crises	244	•		•				•								

Personal Passions, Hobbies, and Interests

Activity by format

Activity	Page	Gatherings	Announcements	Group Dialogue– sm. and lg.	Conferencing, Connections	Reading, Test Prep	Org. and Rep. Ideas, Info	Journaling, Written Refl.	Class Meetings	Skill Lessons	Interactive Exercises	Games, Team Challenges	Projects	Videos, Speakers	Assemblies	Closings
How Do You Like to Learn? ...	247					•	•									
Personal Interest Inventory	248							•								
Passionate Presenters	249													•		
Wall of Fame	249		•													
Teen Trading Bin	250												•			
Exploratorium	250											•	•			
Passion Project	251												•			
Did You Know?	251		•													

Rituals, Celebrations, and Closure

Activity by format

Activity	Page	Gatherings	Announcements	Group Dialogue– sm. and lg.	Conferencing, Connections	Reading, Test Prep	Org. and Rep. Ideas, Info	Journaling, Written Refl.	Class Meetings	Skill Lessons	Interactive Exercises	Games, Team Challenges	Projects	Videos, Speakers	Assemblies	Closings
Thought or Story of the Week	252		•													
Team Congratulations	252		•													
... Something to Cheer About	253														•	
Recognize Accomplishments...	254	•		•				•								
Transitions to Holidays	254	•		•				•								
Preparing (to) End ... Year	255	•			•			•								•
10 End-of-the-Year Rituals	257	•			•			•								•

Rainy-Day Fun Stuff Activity by format	Page	Gatherings	Announcements	Group Dialogue – sm. and lg.	Conferencing, Connections	Reading, Test Prep	Org. and Rep. Ideas, Info	Journaling, Written Refl.	Class Meetings	Skill Lessons	Interactive Exercises	Games, Team Challenges	Projects	Videos, Speakers	Assemblies	Closings
Time Out for Games	259											•				
Story Time	260					•										
Let's Eat	260	•														
Afternoon … at the Movies	260												•			
Cafeteria Birthday Party	261	•														
Stand Out in the Crowd	261												•			
Rainstorm	262	•														

Community-Building, Group Cohesion, Group Maintenance

 ## Activity: Paired Introductions

Format: **Gathering**
Grouping: **Whole advisory**
Scheduling: **Beginning of the school year**

Directions:
During the first advisory meeting at the beginning of the school year, invite students to introduce each other to the whole group. Brainstorm and post questions that students would like to ask each other. Then pair students randomly by using any of the following:

- Two decks of playing cards (students with the same card are partners)

- Counting off (if you have 20 students, have students count off one to ten twice and find the person with the same number)

- Drawing names out of a hat (half of your advisees draw the names of the other half of your advisees)

Give advisory pairs five minutes to ask each other three or four questions and prepare their introductions. Then gather in a circle and ask each pair of advisees to introduce each other.

 ## Activity: Advisor Interview

Format:	**Gathering**
Grouping:	**Whole advisory**
Scheduling:	**Beginning of the school year**

Directions:

Students like to know about the adults who spend a lot of time with them. After you communicate to students what's within the boundaries of appropriateness and what's off limits, invite advisees to interview you, using any of the following formats:

- **Take Three:** Answer any three questions that advisees would like you to answer.

- **"Rainy Day" Interview Questions:** Invite students to write their questions on note cards and put them in a basket. When you've got a couple of minutes left in advisory or want to change the pace during advisory, pull one of the questions from the basket and share your response to it with the group.

- **Seven Questions (Not 20!!!):** Think of something you've done or something unusual about yourself, your family, your younger years that students would probably never guess. Then invite the group to figure out what it is by asking seven questions.

 ## Activity: Name-Matching Exercise

Format:	**Interactive exercise**
Grouping:	**Whole advisory**
Scheduling:	**Beginning of the school year**

Directions:

On a 5"x 8" note card, ask everyone to write one word that begins with the first letter (or sound) of their first name that reflects something about themselves (e.g., Chris-creative, Cindy-smiling). In a circle, ask everyone to say their name, the word, and the connection they have to the word they chose. Then ask everyone to toss their card into the circle. Using a timer, ask for a volunteer to see how fast they can return the correct card to the person who wrote it. Do this a number of times to see if successive advisees can beat the previous time.

Activity: 60-Second Interviews

Format: **Interactive exercise**
Grouping: **Whole advisory**
Scheduling: **Beginning of school year**

Directions:

Create an interview sheet with any of the following questions. Ask students to find a partner and choose one question that interests both of them. Have them interview each other and jot down their partner's name and something they want to remember that their partner said. Give pairs 60 seconds and then have them each find a new partner. You could end this activity by asking students to share something new that they learned about their advisory team members.

An alternative way to structure the pairings is to use concentric circles. Have half of the students arrange themselves in a circle facing out; the other half form an outer circle facing in. After each interview question, rearrange the pairing by rotating one or the other circle, such as "For the next question, the inner circle will move two steps clockwise." This format makes finding partners less self-conscious.

- Describe your family. What is something funny, weird, unusual, or special about one person in your family?

- What's one place you would like to visit in your lifetime? Why do you want to go there?

- What's your favorite TV show and why do you like to watch this show?

- If you had to eat the same meal everyday for a month, what would it be?

- What's one thing you would like to change about your neighborhood that would make it a better place to live?

- What worries you the most about the world you live in today?

- Name one thing you could teach someone how to make or how to do.

- What's your favorite holiday of the year? What makes this holiday your favorite?

- What's one thing that you would like to change about your school that would make it a better place for you?

Activity: Find Someone Who ...

Format: **Interactive exercise**
Grouping: **Whole advisory**
Scheduling: **Beginning of school year**

Directions:
Create a Bingo sheet using the information you collected from the First-Day Student Profile, **Handout 4**, so that each box asks for a piece of information that is unique to one advisee. For example, "Find someone whose birthday is on _____; find someone who was born in _____; find someone who knows how to _____; find someone who speaks _____; find someone who has _____."

 ## Activity: What Do We Have in Common?

Format: **Interactive exercise**
Grouping: **Whole advisory**
Scheduling: **Beginning of the school year**

Directions:
Give each student a sheet that has three columns and a place for three students' names. Then ask students to pair up with someone they don't know well or use grouping cards to place people in pairs. Give each pair two minutes to write down all the similarities they can think of (physical characteristics, family stuff, things they both do, possessions they both own, etc.). Then ask students to pair up two more times, repeating the process.

At the end of the activity, ask: "What surprised you about what you discovered you had in common with someone else?" "How many similarities did you find the first time? the last time?" "Did it get easier for anyone?" "Why might that be?"

Point out that when we are having a disagreement or having trouble working together, it's especially important to remember what we have in common.

Activity: You Like, I Like...

Format:	**Gathering**
Grouping:	**Whole advisory**
Scheduling:	**Beginning of school year**

Directions:

This is an activity that meets two goals: (1) hearing everyone's names repeatedly and (2) finding out something interesting about each person. Call out a question that invites students to name something they like or like to do. Going around the circle, each person must repeat the names of the five previous students and what they like. For example, if the question is, "What are your two favorite things to wear?" and the first person who speaks says, "My name is Marisa. I like to wear jeans and hoop earrings," the next person would say, "Marisa likes to wear jeans and hoop earrings. My name is John and I like to wear patched overalls and leather jackets." Continue around the circle until everyone has had a turn to both share and repeat what five others liked.

 ## Activity: Making Advisory a Safe, Friendly, and Welcoming Place for Everyone

Format:	**Skill lesson**
Grouping:	**Whole advisory**
Scheduling:	**Beginning of school year**

Directions:

1. Do a two-minute quick write on index cards, using the following question: What are the qualities of a good friend?

2. Share responses with the whole group and invite students to brainstorm the differences between being **"friends"** and being **"friendly."** For example:

   Being friends is an ongoing relationship that you have with someone.

   • You talk to each other a lot.

   • You see each other outside of class.

   • You choose to spend social time together.

Being friendly is a way of treating all classmates with kindness, respect, and courtesy whether they are your friends or not.

- It's being willing to work with everyone in your group.

- It's being willing to help when someone asks.

- It's responding when someone asks you something.

- It's saying "hello" first and saying "hello" back.

- It's showing appreciation for everyone's efforts.

- It's saying "please" and "thank you."

- It's asking for permission or asking whether something's okay with another student.

- It's showing interest in what others have to say.

- It's showing appreciation for everyone's efforts.

Explain that no one expects everyone in advisory to become "fast friends," although some of you might become good friends over time. What we do expect is that everyone makes an effort to be respectful and friendly, so students feel safe to share and discuss what's important to them.

 ## Activity: Silent Squares Puzzle Problem

Format: **Team challenge**
Grouping: **Whole advisory in groups of five**
Scheduling: **One time**

Directions:
This activity can be used to explore problem-solving tools and group member roles and responsibilities. Divide your advisory into groups of five students each. If the numbers are uneven, several students can be observers. Explain to the group that this is a PUZZLE PROBLEM that they will solve without speaking. You will need to use **Handout 1** as a guide for making sets of puzzle pieces for each group.

1. Create an envelope for each group, each filled with all of the puzzle pieces. Give each group their envelope. Ask for a volunteer per group to give three pieces to each group member. When everyone has received the pieces, ask students to leave their pieces on the table without touching them.

2. Explain the goal of the activity: "At the end of this exercise, your group goal is to have five completed puzzles on your table. Each completed puzzle should be exactly the same size and each completed puzzle should have three pieces."

3. Here are the rules:

    - You may not speak.

    - You may only give pieces away to another member of your group.

    - You may not take pieces from any member of the group.

    - No finger pointing, grabbing, grunting, or groaning!

4. You will have about seven minutes to solve the problem.

5. If groups get stuck, ask the group if they would like one clue. If they communicate a YES to you nonverbally, take one piece that is placed in the wrong puzzle and place it in the correct position in the puzzle where it fits.

6. Debriefing:

    - What did you notice about yourself and your group as you worked on this puzzle problem?

    - What feelings came up for you — at the beginning of the exercise, during the exercise, and at the end of the exercise? (This is a good opportunity to name the different comfort levels, experiences, and feelings we bring to specific learning experiences. Check out students' reactions when they heard the word PUZZLE or saw the puzzle pieces. Some students may have shut down immediately, while others couldn't wait to begin. How we approach a new learning experience is often shaped by the feelings associated with prior similar experiences. Emotions drive our readiness and motivation to learn; we bring various kinds of comfort and competencies to different learning tasks.)

    - What are the tools, skills, and attitudes that helped you solve the puzzle? (Students will probably say things like: cooperation; trusting that if I gave you a piece, you would give me a piece; letting go of my original plan; observing what others were doing to see if one of my pieces fit in someone else's puzzle; give and take; negotiation; experimenting; patience and perseverance; thinking about the whole group and not just about me and what I needed.) Chart advisees' responses to use for the next two questions.

- In what ways are these same skills and tools useful to you as a student, a friend, and a family member?

- In what course or activities does it feel particularly important to apply and use these skills regularly?

 ## Activity: Chocolate River

Format: **Games and team challenges**
Grouping: **Whole advisory**
Scheduling: **Beginning of the year and as needed**

Directions:
Whether they take 15 minutes or an extended time period, teambuilding activities help students strengthen the skills of cooperation, communication, leadership, strategic thinking, and problem-solving. A key objective of effective teambuilding activities is that no one wins unless everyone wins.

However much fun these challenges are to do, it is the debriefing and reflection questions afterwards that make them important learning experiences. The Additional Resources at the end of the guide include many teambuilding activity resources. This team challenge example can be modified for groups from 20 to 80 participants.

1. Explain to students that they are going to participate in a team challenge and a discussion about it afterwards.

2. Set two ropes (or make two masking tape lines) parallel to each other about 25 feet apart and divide the group in half, with each group on opposite sides of the ropes or lines. For very large groups, place four ropes (or make four masking tape lines) into the shape of a square at least 30 feet on each side and divide the group into fourths, with each group on one side of the square.

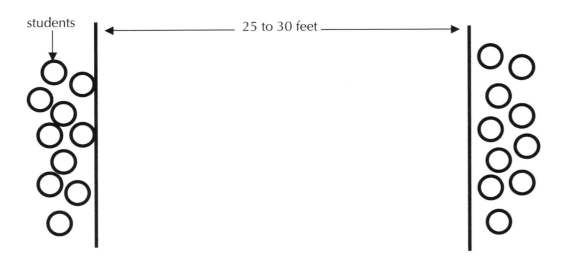

students

25 to 30 feet

3. Give each group cardboard or carpet squares about 12″ x 12″ in size, using this ratio:

    •   15 students on opposite sides = about 8 squares for each group

    •   20 students on opposite sides = about 12 squares for each group

    •   20 students on each of four sides = about 10 squares for each group

    Explain to the group, "The space between the ropes is a chocolate river. The problem is that it's boiling hot, so falling in it would be a disaster. Your goal here is to get every-one across the river, from one side to the other. The squares you have are marshmal-lows; they will float on top of the river, so if you use them to step on, you can get across safely. However, there is a problem. If you fall off a marshmallow or touch the river at any point, you have to go back and start over. And there's one more thing. I'm a monster in the river, and I love marshmallows. If I see a marshmallow in the river that no one is standing on, I will snatch it up and eat it. You will have about five min-utes to strategize with your group and then you will have about 15 minutes or so to solve the problem."

    You might want to suggest three guidelines for this kind of physically active experi-ence: PLAY HARD, PLAY FAIR, PLAY SAFE. Discuss with the group how they think each of these guidelines applies to this particular team challenge.

    Let students know that you'll answer three questions before they begin. If anyone asks whether they can talk to the other group, you can say that each group can identify one person to negotiate with the other side. It's likely that both groups will figure out that if they share their resources and work together it will be much easier to get everyone across. Give the groups about five minutes to strategize, and then give them about 15 minutes to solve the problem.

Facilitator's Note: During the activity, if the groups are having a lot of difficulty listening to each other or working cooperatively, stop the play, asking everyone to freeze. Take three comments from the group, saying: "I'm open to hearing three observations from the group that help describe what's not working." Then say, "I'll take three suggestions from the group about strategies that you think will help you achieve the goal of getting everyone across Chocolate River."

4.   Use any of these questions for postactivity discussion:

   •   What happened? How did you feel about doing this activity? What did you like or dislike?

   •   How did your group decide what strategy to use? Was everyone listened to or included in the decision? How do you know?

   •   What did you observe about how your group worked together? What did your teammates do or say that helped your team be successful? Is there anything you could have done that would have helped your group to be more effective as a team?

   •   How would you describe the role you played? How did it feel to be a leader or a follower? What would you personally do differently next time if you were involved in a similar activity?

   •   What learning can you take from this experience that you can apply to our work as a group in the advisory?

5.   Close the activity by saying: "We're not born with the skills to work together effectively in a group. We learn these skills by watching other people work together and by practicing these skills ourselves."

Activity: Who's Going to the Concert

Format: Interactive exercise
Grouping: Whole advisory
Scheduling: Beginning of the school year

Directions:
This activity is an excellent way to put a problem in the hands of your advisory and see what they do with it. Using **Handout 2**, cut the statements into individual strips and give each student one statement. The directions are fairly simple:

"Each of you has a strip of paper with information on it. You can read your statement out loud, but you can't show it to one another and you can't trade it. As a group, decide what the problem is, and then solve it."

You may also want to ask for two volunteers to be observers who take notes and indicate what they heard and what they observed during the activity. After the activity, invite the volunteers to give their observations and then ask the whole group to comment on these questions:

- What strategies did you use to solve the problem?

- What behaviors helped or hindered you as you were solving the problem?

- Can you describe a turning point when you figured out a process to solve the problem? When did it happen?

- How did leadership emerge in the group? What roles emerged that were particularly helpful?

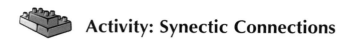

Activity: Synectic Connections

Format: **Interactive exercise**
Grouping: **Whole advisory**
Scheduling: **Monthly**

Directions:

These activities are a wonderful way to help students move easily between abstract and concrete thinking by connecting concepts and ideas to objects in the three activities below.

1. **Synectic Cards** – Create a group of object cards that depict one object on each card. An easy way to do this is using online clip art, copying four images to each page, then cutting the pages. Invite each student to choose a card. Then pair students and give the following instructions:

   Name a concept or idea that advisees are to connect to their image.

   Using the object on their cards, advisees are to finish this sentence:

   _____ is like _____, because

   _____.

   For example, "Negotiation is like a canoe because both people have to paddle in sync with each other to get where they want to go," or, "Friendship is like a Slinky because each person needs to bend a little and be able to bounce back when you get mad at each other."

2. **Simile Synectics** - Think of a word that advisees will work with, but don't tell them the word yet. You can start with almost any word, such as *family, learning, winter, 10th grade,* or *history.* We'll call this the starter word.

   Next divide advisees into pairs or trios. Ask them to use a blank sheet of paper, leaving a space at the top. Then as you read aloud the following categories, they will agree on and list one item per category. We'll call these the category words.

   • Write down the name of any machine, appliance, or electronic equipment.

   • Write down the name of any living plant or animal.

- Write down the name of any household object.

- Write down the name of any geographical or environmental feature.

Now tell advisees the starter word, have them brainstorm similes and have them use each category word. Give the pairs five minutes and then have them share, one category at a time, with the whole group.

For example:
A FAMILY is like a TOASTER because …

A FAMILY is like an OAK TREE because …

A FAMILY is like a CHAIR because …

A FAMILY is like a RIVER because …

3. **Synectic Sculptures** – Divide students into groups of five or six and give the following directions: "Using your bodies and three chairs (allowing three signs with up to three words on each sign can be optional), create a sculpture that communicates _____. You have five minutes to discuss your ideas and create your sculpture. When you present your sculpture to the rest of the group, the audience will make observations about what they see, and then you will get a chance to interpret your sculpture." At the end, take a few minutes for anyone to share final comments and connections.

Here are some ideas you might want to try:
- Create a sculpture that communicates in-groups and out-groups at school.

- Create a sculpture that communicates how the adults in your community perceive teenagers.

- Create a sculpture that communicates your idea of a fair and just discipline system.

- Create a sculpture that communicates what it will take for every student to pass your high school exit exam.

- Create a sculpture that communicates the kinds of negative peer pressure that students experience.

Activity: Cultural Sharing

Format: **Gathering**
Grouping: **Whole advisory**
Scheduling: **One time**

Directions:
Use any of these questions for journaling, pair-shares, and listening labs of three or four students.

- Where was your family born? Where did people in your family grow up?

- Share something that's a tradition or an important event in your family.

- Share two values or beliefs that are really important in your family.

- What is something you're proud of that's part of your family or cultural heritage?

- Describe one way that you have felt different from everyone else, either in the past or in the present.

 ## Activity: Family Banners

Format: **Interactive exercise**
Grouping: **Individual student task and small groups**
Scheduling: **One time**

Directions:
The day before doing this activity, give each student a large piece of paper and say, "We're going to create family banners. Write your full name on your paper, adding words, symbols, and drawings that symbolize something about yourself, your family heritage, your cultural background, your community, and/or important events in your life and your family's life. We will be sharing them tomorrow."

At the next class, divide the students into groups of four and give them at least three minutes each to share their family banners.

Activity: Personal Identity Cards

Format: **Project**
Grouping: **Individual student task and whole group**
Scheduling: **One time**

Directions:
Every student wants her/his identity affirmed and appreciated. Invite students to create an ID card in which they can self-identify using various descriptors: country of origin, race and ethnicity, gender, groups, organizations, pop culture icons, products, music, media/sports stars with whom they identify. Have advisees share their cards with the whole group. Pay attention to what advisees say about themselves so you can make connections throughout the year.

 Activity: Personal History Museum

Format: **Project**
Grouping: **Whole advisory**
Scheduling: **One time**

Directions:
Invite students to create a display of at least five artifacts with accompanying descriptions that communicate who they are, who their family is, what's important to them, and what their hopes and dreams are for themselves and their families.

Activity: Metaphor Toy Bag

Format: **Gatherings or closings**
Grouping: **Whole advisory**
Scheduling: **Monthly**

Directions:
Collect a bag of toys, magnets, and small objects. Invite students to pick a toy or object that represents any of the following (advisor names an aspect of group membership):

- The best thing I bring to a group

- A personal strength or skill that I bring to working out problems

- A contribution I've made to advisory during the last month

- An attitude that helps me get through difficult situations

- Something I've learned how to do that has made it easier to participate in group activities

- One way I've helped someone this week

 ## Activity: Make Connections through Ten-second "Hits"

Format: **Personal connections and conferencing**
Grouping: **Advisee-Advisor**
Scheduling: **Weekly**

Directions:
Imagine for a minute that every student is a web site, receiving "hits" everyday. Some students get deluged with positive social and academic hits all day long from peers and adults. Others may get more negative than positive hits. And some of your advisees might belong to the "invisible middle"—these are the kids who might go through a whole day with few or no hits at all from peers or adults. Everyone wants to feel noticed, important, and respected. When teachers take the time to direct specific comments to individual students, kids feel that someone cares about them personally.

Some Sample Ten-second "Hits"

Before, during, or after advisory make comments to individual students that let them know that you notice who they are:

- Ask or comment about things that advisees are doing: sports events, extracurricular activities, or events and projects in which students participate inside and outside of school.

- Say something about their appearance—a new hairdo, a cool t-shirt, unusual earrings, a different color fingernail polish, a jacket you like, etc.

- Give students positive feedback about something they've done well in advisory recently.

- When you are summarizing a discussion or linking ideas, mention students' names and the comments they made earlier that contributed to a better understanding of the topic.

- Check in with advisees who look tired, upset, worried, or rambunctious by reflecting what you see to them. The samples below give you a way to acknowledge what you see and learn more. They also give students a way to name what they're feeling and to get ready to focus.

  "You look kind of tired; it's been a long day, huh?"

  "Wow, you look like you've got energy to spare. We can sure use your energy in the activity we're doing today."

  "So _____, you look like this has not been your best day. Need a minute to get it together?"

 **Activity: Group Resolutions**

Format: **Class meeting**
Grouping: **Whole advisory**
Scheduling: **Beginning of a new term or early January**

Directions:
At the beginning of a new term or the new year, when students are setting goals and making personal resolutions, advisors can engage advisees in a parallel exercise regarding the group. This process models that active shaping of group dynamics is everyone's responsibility, and that a focus on the group need not happen only when there is a problem to address. Discussing the questions below in pairs and then in the whole group will encourage more students to contribute a wider array of ideas.

- Think of a time in the last month or two when you experienced our advisory group as being at its best. What were we doing? What do you think made us function so well? How did you feel about the group?

- What gets in the way of functioning that way all the time?

- What could each of us do individually or as a group to keep us humming?

Help the group identify just a few very concrete steps to put into action.

Note that the above questions did not start with, "What problems have we had lately as a group? How can we fix them?" Starting by asking about problems puts everyone on the defensive, focuses on the negative, and presents a pessimistic mood. The goal of this class meeting is to have everyone feel more committed and optimistic about the group, not less!

Activity: Group Member Reflections

Format: **Journaling, personal conferencing**
Grouping: **Individual student tasks and advisor-advisee tasks**
Scheduling: **Quarterly**

Directions:

Use the following questions to have advisees reflect on and build responsibility for the way they participate in the group via journals and/or individual conferences.

- When have I been at my best in advisory lately? How was I participating during those times?

- When I'm not at my best, what am I doing? At those times, how am I affecting others?

- What two activities could I do more of to help me contribute positively to advisory relationships and activities?

- For advisory to be a better place for me and others, what do I wish would change?

- What could I do to bring about that change?

Activity: Adding or Subtracting — What's My Impact?

Format: **Journaling and written reflections, small-group dialogues, personal conferencing**
Grouping: **Individual student task, small groups, advisor-advisee tasks**
Scheduling: **Mid- to late fall, with follow-ups later**

Directions:

Once advisees have been together two or three months, some of their helpful and not so helpful behaviors will have surfaced. Take advantage of this timing to introduce students to language for identifying skills and behaviors that may add to or subtract from the effectiveness of a group. If your advisory group meets twice per week or more often, this activity can be used after a month together. The important thing is to introduce group behavior terms and this type of reflection before negative behaviors become entrenched.

Give advisees **Handout 3**, "Adding or Subtracting — What's My Impact?" Have students fill it out individually, encouraging them to take their time and to think about how they interact in group activities, discussions, and tasks.

The positive and negative behaviors apply to small and large groups, to advisory and classes, to school and outside activities. With early adolescents, focus on recent tasks in advisory; with mid- or late adolescents, ask them to compare settings. The questions below can be used for journaling, pair/shares, or personal conferencing immediately following the handout reflections, and/or later as follow-up.

Help advisees understand the following concepts:

- It takes many skills for groups to be effective; organizing is not the only one.

- How we behave in a group helps or hurts the group. We can add ideas, enthusiasm, order, and harmony; or we can subtract ideas, enthusiasm, order, and harmony.

- We can help the groups we're involved in by increasing what we add, and by decreasing what we subtract. So, even if we aren't ready to be the main initiator, we could perhaps cut down on distracting behaviors.

- It's OK to admit that we demonstrate the negative behaviors at times. Noting that we sometimes use behaviors that have a negative impact on others does not mean we're bad people; it means we're honest with ourselves, and we can be responsible for changing.

- Depending on the developmental readiness of your advisees, encourage them to consider how others perceive their behavior, in addition to how they perceive themselves. For example, some students might think they are coordinating, while others see them as dominating.

Questions related to "The Positives"

- Which of the positive skills do you enjoy using and use well? Describe an experience.

- Which of the positive skills feel difficult or uncomfortable?

- What might you do to add more to the advisory group?

- How do you think other people would score your skills for effective group work? What are they seeing that gives them the impressions they have?

- How does your use of the positive skills vary from small to large groups, from advisory to classes, or from inside to outside of school? How do you feel about those variations? What could you do about them?

- Describe the people you identified as good models of the positive skills.

- What actions showed you they were adding to their group's efforts?

- How do you feel when you're in a group with these people?

Questions related to "The Negatives"

- Describe one of the times when you "subtracted" from the group. What did you do? How did you feel? What else might you have done or said?

- What can you do to decrease your use of these behaviors?

- What can members of your group or your advisor do that would help you?

- What can you do for others to help them avoid these behaviors?

- Do you think other people perceive you as using the negative behaviors more or less than you see yourself using them? What are they seeing that gives them the impressions they have?

- How does your use of the negative behaviors vary from small to large groups, from advisory to classes, or from inside to outside of school? How do you feel about those variations? What could you do about them?

Orientation, School Citizenship, and School Business

 ## Activity: First Day of Advisory

Format: **Large group dialogue**
Grouping: **Whole advisory**
Scheduling: **The first day of advisory**

Directions:
Give students an opportunity to share what they think advisory is about and give yourself an opportunity to answer their questions and clarify their misconceptions or information gaps. Begin the discussion by inviting students to share their understanding of

- the purpose and goals of advisory;

- the advisory schedule;

- the role of the advisor;

- expectations for advisees — as individuals and as an advisory group; and

- types of activities that advisees will be doing throughout the year.

After you have responded to students' questions, it's a good idea to preview the first month of advisory activities. You may also want to give each student a basic one-page advisory information sheet.

Activity: First-Week Student Profile

Format:	**Written reflection**
Grouping:	**Individual student task**
Scheduling:	**Beginning of school year**

Directions:

Gathering data and key information about your advisees the first day and the first few weeks can help you develop a more complete picture of each student. This kind of information comes in handy for several reasons:

- It helps you make connections between individual students and what is being learned in your advisory.

- It provides a starting point for personal conversations.

- It gives you warning about issues that might affect a student's progress and learning.

- It provides a bridge for parental/guardian contacts.

Trust builds slowly, so information collected in the first weeks should not be very personal. Collect information that will give you the basics that you need at the beginning, and build from there. **Handout 4** is a sample student profile.

 Activity: This Is How We Do School Here

Format:	**Assembly**
Grouping:	**School-wide participation**
Scheduling:	**Beginning of the school year**

Directions:

Convene a student and staff-facilitated assembly by grade level, team, or house that communicates do's and don't's, what's in and what's out, what's old and what's new, and/or the ten things every kid needs to know to stay out of trouble and keep on track. Create skits and other creative presentations that utilize humor to get across critical information that helps everyone get off to the right start. Encouraging teachers to play the roles of students and students to play the roles of faculty makes this type of assembly memorable.

Activity: All-School Advisory Team Challenge

Format: **Games and team challenges**
Grouping: **School-wide participation**
Scheduling: **Beginning of the school year**

Directions:

Depending on the size of the student population and number of large physical spaces inside and outside the school building, suspend regular classes and implement an all-school, all-house, or all-grade-level Advisory Team Challenge afternoon during the first week of school. An hour and a half to two hours seems to be the ideal amount of time to carry out four or five activities that promote team building, group problem solving, and friendly competition.

Entire school events can go a long way to communicating core school values and setting a positive tone. School-wide events like this generate stories that become part of your advisory history. Although a Team Challenge Afternoon requires a lot of coordinating, communicating, and organizing, the advisory structure makes it much easier.

Create a planning group of students and faculty who prepare a packet of instructions and materials for every advisory. Pair up advisors with adults in the school who do not serve as advisors and pair up advisories for some of the planned activities. Here are a few suggestions that can help create a successful event:

- Review the instructions in a meeting with all advisors before the big event.

- Choose two volunteers from your advisory who will help facilitate activities, pass out and collect materials, and give instructions.

- Choose a group of activities that involve a combination of kinesthetic, verbal, spatial, and visual modes of learning.

- Choose some short warm-up or ice-breaker activities and at least one longer, team problem-solving activity.

- Emphasize that the goal of problem-solving activities is for everyone to succeed— "nobody wins unless everybody wins."

- Review expectations about how the group will work together. Three good guidelines, courtesy of Project Adventure, are

Play HARD, Play FAIR, Play SAFE.

Introduce the principle of Occasional Observer. This means that students have the option to be an observer rather than an active participant during a particular activity. If a student expresses genuine resistance to or discomfort with a certain activity, forcing participation can dampen the positive energy you're trying to generate.

- Include one activity in which your advisory group has to submit its solution to a problem. Several advisories with the most creative solutions can be announced the next day. For activity suggestions, see Additional Resources at the back of the book.

 ### Activity: The Game of School

Format: **Team Challenge**
Grouping: **Whole advisory or mix it up with two advisories**
Scheduling: **Beginning of school year**

Directions:
Advisory provides the perfect opportunity to discuss and review school rules, consequences, where to go for _____, when you can and can't _____, what you can do when _____ happens, who can help you _____, etc. Make the review more interactive by structuring it as a game. Create questions related to these topics:

- School-wide rules, procedures, and consequences

- Grade-level team, house, or academy procedures

- The quickest way to get from _____ to _____

- Schedule information

- Procedures and expectations regarding homework

- Hall pass procedures

- What to do and where to go when _____

- "Need to know" locations

- School-wide student expectations, rights, and responsibilities

- Core values or qualities of character that the whole school promotes

- The mission of the school

- Major school events

- Extracurricular and co-curricular activities

- School history and rituals

- Key people

Divide your advisory into four teams and explain that when each team has a turn, the whole team can consult before they respond to the question. Ask for a volunteer to be the scorekeeper. Try one of these Jeopardy game-show formats and modify the rules to meet the needs and competitiveness of your group.

- **Jeopardy (question format)** – Make a deck of cards with the "answer" on one side and the "question" on the other side. Clarify the rotation you'll use to call on teams. Then call out an answer to the first team and give them 45 seconds to call out the question that matches the answer. If their response is correct, their team gets ten points. If their response is incorrect, they lose five points. The next team can choose to respond to the same "answer" item and receive ten points if their question is correct, pass and miss their turn, or respond to a new "answer" item for five points. Throw in some "jackpot" answers that are worth 20 points.

- **Jeopardy (answer format)** – Post five to eight categories of questions on the board, and beneath each category tape a series of note cards with one question on each card. Rotate from team to team, inviting each team to select a category and point value of the question. Teams receive 5 to 50 points for correct answers (depending upon the question's difficulty, from the mundane to the arcane). If the team's answer is incorrect, the teams gets the same number of points subtracted from their total score and the question goes back on the board. The next team gets to choose a question from any category for any point total.

School Rules and Expectations	What do you do when___?	Scheduling Courses and Credits	Location, Location, Location	Team, House, or Academy Procedures	People You Should Know	School History and Rituals	School Events and Activities
#1 (5 points)	#1 (5 points)	#1 (5 points)	#1 (5 points)	#1 (5 points)	#1 (5 points)	#1 (5 points)	#1 (5 points)
#2 (5 points)	#2 (5 points)	#2 (5 points)	#2 (5 points)	#2 (5 points)	#2 (5 points)	#2 (5 points)	#2 (5 points)
#3 (5 points)	#3 (5 points)	#3 (5 points)	#3 (5 points)	#3 (5 points)	#3 (5 points)	#3 (5 points)	#3 (5 points)
#4 (10 points)	#4 (10 points)	#4 (10 points)	#4 (10 points)	#4 (10 points)	#4 (10 points)	#4 (10 points)	#4 (10 points)
#5 (10 points)	#5 (10 points)	#5 (10 points)	#5 (10 points)	#5 (10 points)	#5 (10 points)	#5 (10 points)	#5 (10 points)
#6 (10 points)	#6 (10 points)	#6 (10 points)	#6 (10 points)	#6 (10 points)	#6 (10 points)	#6 (10 points)	#6 (10 points)
#7 (20 points)	#7 (20 points)	#7 (20 points)	#7 (20 points)	#7 (20 points)	#7 (20 points)	#7 (20 points)	#7 (20 points)
#8 (50 points)	#8 (50 points)	#8 (50 points)	#8 (50 points)	#8 (50 points)	#8 (50 points)	#8 (50 points)	#8 (50 points)

 Activity: Passport to School

Format:	**Project**
Grouping:	**Individual student task**
Scheduling:	**Each semester or quarter**

Directions:

This is an excellent orientation activity for incoming 6th, 7th, or 9th grade students. If you work on grade-level teams, create a passport that everyone on your team receives. During the first quarter, students are expected to collect items that they attach to pages in their passport, get their passport stamped by various staff, and provide evidence through signatures and notes that they participated in various activities or found out specific information about the school, its graduates, its programs, the building and grounds, etc. Provide enough options so students can make choices about the items they complete. You might want to set a goal of a specific percentage or number of items that every student completes by the end of the first quarter.

At the end of the first quarter, take some time to share what students did and what they found out. Also invite students to give feedback about the ways this project helped them get connected to more people and become more familiar with their new school environment.

This project was designed by the 9th-grade planning team of Westerville (Ohio) North HS.

Activity: Previewing the Week and Upcoming Events

Format: **Announcements**
Grouping: **Whole group**
Scheduling: **Weekly**

Directions:

When advisory groups are organized by grade level, academy, or house, Monday is a great time to

- preview key assignments and deadlines;

- review any scheduling changes for the week

- clarify school-wide and team rules, procedures, and routines; and

- provide information and invite discussion about upcoming school-wide events that impact everyone in the school.

Activity: School Spirit

Format: **Project**
Grouping: **Whole advisory**
Scheduling: **Special weeks during the year**

Directions:

Encourage advisories to generate and implement ideas that boost school spirit, make all students feel welcome, generate pride in the school, its students, and faculty. Or, invite everyone to bring and share something, or share in the same activity during a day at school. Try to go beyond the sports team pep rally to pep rallies for lesser-known teams and groups that compete with other schools or put on a major event. Brainstorm a list of ideas for

- announcements that let everyone know the good things that are happening at school;

- a day of service in the community;

- silly-dress days;

- teacher appreciation day;

- specific contributions (food, books, clothes, toys, soap and other personal items) that students can bring to support various local, national, and international efforts to reduce hunger, increase literacy, provide resources for the homeless, the elderly, and needy children and families;

- special "meet and greets" where volunteers welcome all students and faculty in the morning at every entrance to the school building;

- civic activities that can happen on school grounds (voter registration, blood bank, letter writing to support a public effort or law that will benefit young people and the school district, a volunteer sign-up matching students with people and projects that serve the community and reach out to people who may be isolated or excluded;

- a "DID YOU KNOW...." campaign to create posters that let the school community know success stories around reducing absences, tardies, failure rates, and/or suspensions; the completion of monumental tasks that involve massive numbers of students; new improvements in the physical environment; new courses, programs, and opportunities available to students; interesting demographics that describe your student and faculty populations; or other highlights.

 Activity: School Climate Check

Format: **Connections, listening labs, or journaling**
Grouping: **Whole advisory**
Scheduling: **Beginning of school year**

Directions:
Here are some questions that can help you get a sense of your advisees' perceptions of school. Some of these questions might become a starting point for further exploration with other advisories, or students might choose to take issues of concern to a student/faculty forum, student government, or other school task force or committee. These questions can be used for journaling. You can invite the group to prioritize the questions they find most interesting to discuss, or you can divide your advisory into three or four groups, with each group choosing to discuss and chart two or three questions.

If you discuss any of these questions as a whole group, remind students that this is an opportunity to hear different perspectives—it is not the time to begin a debate, but to really listen to each person's take on the question.

1. What do you like best about going to school here?

2. What do you like least about going to school here?

3. On a scale of 1 to 10, how respectful do you see the staff being to students? How about students being respectful to staff? students to students? staff to staff? Say a little about the number you chose.

4. On a scale of 1 to 10, how safe do you think students feel here at school? What kinds of things make a school feel safe for students? What kinds of things make school feel unsafe to students?

5. Are there some groups of students here who seem to get more attention, more resources, more privileges than other groups? If so, why do you think that is?

6. Are there some groups of students you think feel left out at school? Who gets less attention? Who gets targeted or harassed more? Who can't seem to find a place to belong? Why do you think that is?

7. If you could make changes in scheduling or the curriculum, what would you recommend? How would these changes benefit students?

8. Are there any ways that you feel some students are treated unfairly?

9. When you talk to your friends, what do they complain about the most?

10. What worries students the most about going to this school?

Activity: Town Meeting

Format: **Class meeting**
Grouping: **Mixing it up across groups or school-wide participation**
Scheduling: **Occasionally**

Directions:

Town Meetings with all students and faculty within a team, a grade level, or a house can serve many purposes, including

- discussion of issues when it's critical for everyone to hear and discuss the same information at the same time (for example, when rumors about what did or didn't happen in a serious incident need to be addressed, when there is a significant change in school personnel or policies, or when an external event in the community impacts the life of the school);

- clarification of rules, procedures, and policies (from the mundane—where students can and cannot park their cars—to the serious—what will happen if students engage in bullying and harassment);

- clarification of course registration procedures, quarterly elective sign-ups, graduation requirements, report card conferences;

- airing grievances and concerns about problems that impact large numbers of students and faculty and then providing time to generate possible solutions to the problem;

- gathering perspectives and information that will help the school leadership team make effective decisions about rules, policies, courses, programs, and requirements.

Town Meetings can be facilitated by administrators, faculty, and/or students, depending upon the purpose. If the meeting is about an important change that affects what students should or should not do, put the explanation in writing and provide copies for everyone. If a town meeting goal is to solicit information, opinions, and suggestions, provide a structured format in which small groups of students and faculty can discuss, record, and report their ideas.

Activity: Boys in the Bathroom and Girls in Tank Tops: Adolescent Issues that Never Go Away

Format: **Large-group dialogue**
Grouping: **Whole advisory or cross-advisory GIRLS ONLY and BOYS ONLY groups**
Scheduling: **As needed**

Directions:

There are times during every school year when adults need to engage students in "The Talk" about basic issues of public decorum, restraint, civility, and safety. Here are several issues that never seem to go away:

- The condition of the boys' bathrooms

- Provocative clothing, not enough clothing, clothing so oversized it's falling down, clothing with messages you shouldn't read in school, and clothing associated with gang or criminal behavior

- Profanity and disrespectful speech in classrooms and public spaces

- Graffiti, low-level vandalism, littering, and the state of the cafeteria at the end of lunch

- The classroom and cafeteria as beauty salon

- Public displays of affection and sexualized behavior and speech that has no place in public settings

- Boys touching girls and girls touching boys that looks an awful lot like harassment to adults, but for kids the behavior is "just fooling around"

- Male posturing and supersized physical gesturing (for example, "wind-milling" down hallways with arms flailing) that are overtly aggressive, hostile, and unsafe

- Play-fighting and verbal jousting among and between boys and girls that has the appearance of public brawling

- Post-sports event vandalism and public trash talk directed toward another school, an opposing team, or individuals on an opposing team

- "Player hating," bullying, or hazing behaviors in which one group of students is being targeted, excluded, isolated, or ridiculed by another group of students

- E-mail harassment

- Prom night and graduation party rules and decorum

- Serious incidents of off-campus binge drinking, drug use, physical fighting, or criminal behavior that everyone knows about, but students won't talk about or don't know how to talk about

The worst place to have "The Talk" is in the auditorium—these are real-life issues that require more than a lecture about school rules and policies. Kids already know the rules and can tell you the rules verbatim. Repeating the rules in an assembly isn't going to help students understand the rules any better or follow them more often. What's needed here is genuine conversation that enriches, deepens, and complicates students' thinking about critical issues or incidents that impact the safety and wellbeing of any, some, or all students or staff members.

These topics are "direct hits" on the DO NOT ENTER universe that adolescents create for themselves and want to protect at all costs. Adults' efforts to tackle these topics can feel like a frontal attack on students' personal identity, cultural affinity and affiliation, and peer-group norms.

Given the incendiary potential surrounding "The Talk," the best place to have it is in advisory, where the size of the group and the invitation to speak openly and listen respectfully can help reduce the inevitable "us vs. them" tenor and tone of the conversation. It will, of course, go far more smoothly if constructive and respectful dialogue practices are already firmly established.

The principal, counselors, or student support staff may suggest specific guidelines for these discussions. Additionally, here are a few tips that can make various versions of "The Talk" feel more productive and less adversarial:

1. Acknowledge that this is not the easiest topic to discuss, and share why the whole school staff felt it was important to address.

2. Your capacity to remain low-key, curious, interested, and concerned; your patience to listen nonjudgmentally; your clearness about consequences; and your plainspoken explanations about what is unacceptable and why—are all tools you'll need to communicate to students that this conversation is happening because everyone has the right to feel safe and respected, and everyone has a responsibility to maintain a civil culture and a safe, orderly, and clean learning environment.

3. Name the issue and invite students to discuss how they think adults see the issue; how students see the issue; whether all students see the issue the same way or differently; why they think adults might perceive this as a problem; how they think the issue impacts the whole school community or the school's reputation; and/or what their parents and

other adults might have to say about the issue. The bottom line here is to let students talk about it. Listening to students does not mean that you agree with everything that's being said. Listening to students does mean that you're interested in what they have to say. Your job is to work with students to establish guidelines for respectful speech and productive conversation. Your advisees' job is to hold each other accountable to the guidelines you've created together.

4. Elicit evidence and data from the group that confirms that this is a problem for some people in the school, even if it doesn't impact some of your advisees directly.

5. Explore the messages that this particular behavior might communicate to others. How might different groups or individuals view a particular behavior or particular words? How might someone view a person who does _____ or says _____? How do you want to be thought of? What assumptions (however inaccurate) might be associated with this behavior? Does the action have unintended consequences? This is a version of the "What were you thinking?" conversation and becomes a teachable moment to clarify the differences between intention and impact.

6. These discussions offer yet another opportunity to explore the differences between what's private and what's public. Schools are public places where you live out your life in the public view of others. Students need to be reminded that public norms of conduct and civility are different from, not better or worse than, private codes of behavior, which are student's personal business or their family's business.

7. Some of these topics easily lead to questions of personal and social responsibility. What does it really mean to be accountable for one's actions? Accountable for what to whom? What makes one behavior socially responsible and another socially irresponsible? Are there situations where what feels like a private action has very public consequences? When and how does a personal choice impact the larger community? Ask students to consider the public consequences if everyone engaged in _____ behavior. How would you feel about school? What's the ripple effect if no one does anything about it?

8. In matters that involve personal safety, explore the differences between "narc-ing" and sharing information confidentially with an adult about an incident that has already happened or about a situation that is potentially dangerous or destructive. Talk about why this can feel like a betrayal and when it's the only right thing to do.

9. The issue may require a school-wide campaign, task force, or committee involving students, faculty, and parents. Solicit ideas and suggestions for how to tackle the problem, peer to peer, adult to student, and as a whole school community.

10. Finally, it's your job to communicate to your advisees, quietly and firmly, "Here's what I need you to know. If this continues, the consequence for _____ is ...; If we see this happening again, the faculty is committed to ...; Here's what we expect every student to do so that we can ..."

Activity: Adopt a Space

Format: **Project**
Grouping: **School-wide participation**
Scheduling: **Once a quarter**

Directions:

Students learn what it means to take care of an environment when they participate in activities that make the concept of stewardship feel real. Create a school-wide stewardship committee of students and adults that includes building and grounds staff, custodians, and other personnel who know your school building and grounds inside-out, including the areas that are hardest to keep clean or that require some extra care, attention, and sprucing up.

"Adopt a space" possibilities can include everything from the library, hallways, bathrooms, book closets, labs, storage rooms, offices, classrooms, and locker areas to landscaped grounds, athletic fields, parking lots, and other outdoor domains. After the school has created a menu of choices, each advisory can submit their top three choices for the space they want to adopt. The advisory program can schedule a special hour every quarter for advisories to take care of their space.

Activity: School Climate and Learning Surveys and Discussions

Format: **Written reflection and dialogue**
Grouping: **Whole advisory**
Scheduling: **As needed**

Directions:

Advisory is an ideal place to administer school-wide climate and learning surveys, team-generated surveys, and student-generated surveys because:

- You can discuss students' responses in a safe setting.

- You can collect ideas for future advisory discussion topics.

- You can surface issues that students may want to address with the student council, the school leadership team, or other committees and task forces.

Personal goal-setting, reflection, and assessment

 ## Activity: Mapping Your Personal Pathway

Format: **Representing ideas and information**
Grouping: **Individual student task**
Scheduling: **Beginning of school year or a new term**

Directions:
Copy the Personal Pathway, **Handout 5**, for students to map out where they've been and where they want to go. Do this activity near the beginning of the school year as a way for students to reflect on their past and set goals for the current year, or use it for midyear reflections and adjustments. Encourage students to take their time, possibly drawing or writing at home. Students may be interested in sharing their maps with each other and/or with you—these conversations can become genuine community builders.

 ## Activity: Reflections about Me

Format: **Written reflection**
Grouping: **Individual student task**
Scheduling: **Beginning of school year**

Directions:
Develop a personal inventory to find out more about your advisees, including what they care about, what interests them, and what they are concerned about. Students often assume that most teachers only care about their academic performance. Surveys or questionnaires can be a first step in making personal connections with each student. While you are developing this survey, think about what might be fun, interesting, and helpful to know about students that you think they would be willing to share. Depending on your students, before they fill out the inventory, you might want to humor them by acknowledging that sex is a possible response to

many of the questions. You could say, "Since I already know that, I'd prefer that you not get that personal. Stretch your thinking a bit." Here are some starters:

1. Something I think about all the time is

2. Something I worry about is

3. The most boring thing in my life right now is

4. The most exciting thing in my life right now is

5. What do you like most about being a student? What's the best thing for you?

6. What do you like least about being a student? What's the worst thing for you?

7. As your advisor, what should I know about you that will help you learn and be at your best in advisory?

8. I make my family proud when I

9. One thing my family expects of me is to

10. One thing that makes my family special/different/fun is

11. The worst thing about being a teenager is

12. The best thing about being a teenager is

Activity: Postcard and Picture Check-In

Format: **Gathering or closing**
Grouping: **Whole advisory**
Scheduling: **Monthly**

Directions:
Collect a set of photographs, postcards, or greeting cards with compelling, funny, weird, interesting images of people, animals, or elements of nature. Spread your pictures on the floor or on a large table and ask advisees to choose a photograph that reflects (advisor names one):

- How you've been feeling about the day or the week

- A good choice you've made this week

- A study or organizing skill you want to improve this quarter

- Something you've done that is helping you achieve your goals

- Something that's been keeping you from achieving your goals

- How you're feeling about exam week

- Something you need that will help you stay focused on your goals

- Something you do for yourself that will provide a needed break or treat

 ## Activity: Quarterly Goal-Setting

Format: **Written reflection and personal conferencing**
Grouping: **Individual student task and advisee-advisor**
Scheduling: **Quarterly**

Directions:
Setting aside time for students to write and reflect about personal goals accomplishes three things:

1. Goals provide a way to focus attention and effort and create opportunities to predict and plan.

2. Students can monitor their progress and explore how to modify or alter their goals when they feel the need.

3. Goals can be a regular topic for an advisee-advisor check-in or a three-minute conference.

Help students choose and frame their goals using any of these guidelines:

- Choose an academic goal linked to a particular academic course—a quarterly grade you want to earn; specific skills you want to use and improve; or something you want to learn well, learn how to do, or know more about.

- Choose a work habit that you want to improve and use on a regular basis.

- Choose a social behavior (See **Handout 6**: Life Skills Checklist) that you want to improve and use regularly.

- Choose a goal related to school participation and leadership.

- Choose a personal goal for yourself that is not related specifically to school.

Make sure that students' written goals are specific enough so that they are able to answer the following:

- What exactly are you proposing to do? By the end of this term, I want to ….

- What steps will help you accomplish your goal?

- How long do you think it will take to complete each step?

- What resources will you need to accomplish your goal?

- How can others help you work on your goal?

- What indicators will show you that you're making progress in meeting your goal?

- How will you know when you are halfway there?

- What evidence will show you that you've accomplished your goal?

Use **Handouts 7A, 7B,** and **7C** to formalize quarterly goal-setting. This provides a way for you and your advisees to check in and assess their progress during the quarter.

Activity: Acknowledging Your Assets

Format: **Written reflection and personal conferencing**
Grouping: **Individual student task and advisor-advisee**
Scheduling: **One time or as needed**

Directions:

Prior to a round of short individual conferences with advisees, ask them to prepare by doing the following: "Write down something that you are very good at that has nothing to do with school, and then write down the personal skills and qualities that help you to do this well." During your check-in, invite them to share what they wrote. Then explore one way students might use those skills and attitudes at school to get more interested in something, get better at something, do something new or differently in their courses, or take a different approach to something that's not working.

Activity: Speaking of Character

Format: **Journaling, small-group and large-group dialogues**
Grouping: **Individual student task, small groups, whole advisory**
Scheduling: **One time**

Directions:

For many students, it's a challenge to identify the internal strengths and qualities of character that help them complete a task, achieve a goal, change a behavior, develop a new habit, or connect with other people. Using **Handout 8**: Personal Assets and Qualities of Character, here are a few ideas for advisory group explorations about character. Formats include journaling, written reflection, pair/shares, and small- and large-group dialogues. Use any or all of these.

1. **Written reflection and pair/share:** Write the five words from the list that you think most clearly describe who you are to yourself. Write five words from the page that you think your mom, your dad, your best friend, and your favorite teacher would each use to describe who you are. Share your lists with a partner and discuss why you chose the words you selected to describe yourself. If your written reflection of others' views of you were different from each other, talk a little about the reasons you imagine different people would describe you differently.

2. **Written reflection and pair/share:** Pair up with someone you know fairly well. Name three qualities that you most closely associate with your partner. Write the three qualities and explain why you think each quality fits your partner. Then share with your partner what you wrote on your card.

3. **Whole-group dialogue:** Toss out any of these phrases to the whole group to get their perspectives on what they think these phrases mean:

   • a person of character

   • So-and-so has no character.

   • character witness

   • defamation of character

   • What a character!

   • character education

   • character assassination

   • character reference

   • character trait

4. **Whole-group dialogue:** You might want to follow up with these questions to the whole group: Are people born with good character or bad character? What might be differences between someone's character and someone's personality? When someone says, "This builds a person's character," what kind of experience do you think they're talking about?

5. **Journaling:** Choose five words from the list that you think best sum up your character. For each word, write a paragraph that provides personal examples and experiences that illustrate ways you live out this quality in your everyday life.

6. **Journaling:** Choose one quality that is absolutely YOU and everyone knows it. What experiences in your life helped you develop this quality of character? What makes you think the important people in your life would pick this same word to describe you?

7. **Journaling:** What character word on the list is least like you? Is it a quality you would like to see yourself as having? Why or why not? If you wanted to see yourself as having this quality, what would you need to change in your life?

8. **Journaling:** What quality of character on the list do you and your mom share? What about you and your dad? You and a grandparent? You and a sibling? Explain why you think this quality "runs in the family."

9. **Quick write:** After students have completed a major project, finished a particularly grueling week, mastered a difficult skill, or achieved an important goal, ask them to write on an index card two or three qualities of character that helped them to be successful.

Activity: If I Had a Wish

Format: **Gathering**
Grouping: **Whole advisory**
Scheduling: **One time**

Directions:
This circle activity gives students a chance to express their wishes, dreams, and hopes to their peers. Invite students to think about how they would complete the following sentence: "If I had a wish that would be granted, it would be …"

Activity: Reflecting on the Week That Was

Format: **Closings**
Grouping: **Whole group**
Scheduling: **Regularly scheduled**

Directions:
Reflect on the week that was by sharing responses to these sentence stems:

*   One good thing that happened this week …

*   One bad thing that happened this week …

*   One goal I accomplished this week …

*   My best class experience this week was …

- I was really happy this week when …

- I got really frustrated this week when …

Share something

- you learned that felt really important this week;

- you want to remember from the week;

- you learned this week that you want to know more about;

- you learned about yourself that surprised you or made you think about yourself differently this week;

- you admired that someone else did this week;

- you did to help someone else this week;

- you feel thankful for this week.

Activity: Assessing Learning

Format: **Journaling, gatherings, and closings**
Grouping: **Individual task or whole advisory**
Scheduling: **Regularly scheduled**

Directions:

There are several ways that you can use the assessment questions below with advisees:

1. Choose some of these questions for journal writing.

2. Choose some of these questions for closings at the end of the week, the quarter, or semester.

3. Invite students to select a few questions they want to discuss out loud or write about in their journals.

Assessing a specific advisory activity:

- What worked best for you today?

- What about the activity did you like the most? The least?

- Any new insights or ideas?

- Are there any questions or issues you want to make sure get addressed in the next advisory session?

- How can you use what you've learned this week?

- Any other comments or suggestions?

Looking-ahead questions prior to a test, performance, or demonstration:

- What topics are you confident you know and understand?

- What topics are you less sure you understand well?

- How are you going to learn the concepts that you have yet to master?

Looking-back questions after a test, performance, or demonstration:

- What strategies did you use to prepare for the test?

- Which strategies were the most helpful in preparing for the test?

- Did you do as well as you felt you should have based on your preparation?

- What did you do or not do to earn the grade you got?

- What will you do next time?

- If your friend were taking this test tomorrow, how would you tell him or her to prepare?

At the End of the Quarter, Semester, or Course

Advisory may be the only opportunity that students have to reflect on what they've learned and experienced in their courses. One way to frame this kind of reflection is to ask students to compare their experiences in two different courses (their most favorite and least favorite courses, or the course where they performed the best and a course where their effort and performance were nothing to write home about). Invite students to select five questions they will use to reflect on both courses. After students write their reflections, it may be helpful to compare notes in groups of three during advisory.

- What are three things you want to remember most from the course(s)?

- What are two of the most important things you've learned in the course(s)?

- What's a skill you've learned and used that you're sure you will use again?

- Give one example of how you knew yourself better as a learner at the end of the course(s).

- When in the course(s) did you feel really self-disciplined (did what you needed to do without being nagged or getting it together at the last minute)?

- When in the course(s) did you overcome feelings of frustration or anger successfully? When was it difficult to overcome feelings of frustration or anger?

- When in the course(s) did you feel self-motivated? When was it hard to feel motivated at all?

- When in the course(s) did you go the extra mile to complete a project or assignment successfully? Why did this feel important for you to do?

- Describe one thing you've learned about yourself that surprised you.

- What questions do you have at the end of the course(s) that you'd like to think more about?

- Describe two or three activities you liked best and two or three activities you liked least. Why?

- In thinking back on the course(s), what images and experiences stand out most for you? Why?

- What did you do that most impressed your teacher?

Activity: Preparation, Rehearsal, and Suggestions for Grade Report Conferencing

Format: **Journaling, organizing ideas and information, small-group dialogue, and personal conferencing**

Grouping: **Whole advisory and advisor-advisee**

Scheduling: **Mid-term, quarter, trimester, or semester grading periods**

Directions:

Many advisors have responsibility for monitoring their advisees' academic progress and planning throughout the year. In some cases, the advisor is the one adult at school who holds the big picture of a student's academic performance across courses within a semester and across semesters from one grade level to the next. The range of grade report activities you implement will vary, given your school's expectations of your role as an academic advisor. At the very least, students will appreciate a grade report check-in with their advisor. On the other end of the continuum, your school may expect you to prepare advisees for student-led grade report conferences that involve you, the student, and their parents/guardian. Included is a short list of the benefits of advisor-advisee and student-led grade report conferences.

Grade report conferences do the following:

1. Validate student's successes, accomplishments, effort, and expertise

2. Help students assess their progress, proficiencies, and learning challenges as they work to meet and exceed learning standards and benchmarks

3. Help students reflect on their work and their attributes as learners

4. Provide an opportunity for advisees to revisit quarterly goals

5. Create a road map for future academic support and follow-up

6. Provide opportunities to share insights, observations, and information that can inform future course selection, career and college exploration, and planning for life after high school

7. Illuminate where a change in behavior or work habits might have the greatest impact academically

8. Build common expectations among student, parents, and staff

Choose the activity suggestions and question prompts that best fit your goals for academic advisement.

Preparation for advisor-advisee conferences or student-led conferences that involve advisor, advisee, parents/guardians

Journal prompts that students can write about before they receive their grade reports:

- Predict the grade that you think you will earn in each course.

- Next to your grade predictions, share a couple of things that support your reasons for assigning yourself these grades.

- For each course, what stood out as the most important thing you learned or experienced? Explain what made this particularly important to you?

- For each course, what are you most proud of accomplishing?

- For each course, when were you at your best as a group member and active participant in the class?

- For each course, what proved to be most difficult for you this quarter?

- Overall, in what course do you think you made the most progress or improvement? How do you know this?

- Overall, is there any course where you wished you had made a greater effort? What exactly might you have done, or done more often, that would have made the biggest difference in your performance?

- Overall, what's getting easier to learn and do, and what's still really hard for you?

- Review the goals that you created for this quarter. Assess how you did by answering the questions on the bottom of your quarterly goal-setting forms.

- What personal qualities helped you to complete assignments and homework successfully? Or, conversely, what got in the way of completing assignments and homework successfully?

You can also use question prompts from the previous activity, **Assessing Learning**.

Other ways to prepare for grade report conferencing:

- Invite students to choose a sample of their work from each course that represents their best effort and/or met or exceeded standards of high quality and completion. Ask students to be prepared to explain why they chose these work samples to discuss at the conference.

- Invite students to share two work samples that illustrate a quality product and a weak, shoddy, or incomplete product, and ask them to discuss how they decide which one is which. How would they describe the differences between the two products? How was their effort, approach, and attitude similar or different regarding each assignment?

- Invite students to jot down any skill gaps they want to discuss that make it particularly difficult to produce quality work in a particular course.

- Ask students to choose three of their journal responses to share at the grade report conference.

- Prepare a suggested outline ahead of time for the conference so students can review and rehearse.

Rehearsal

Take time in advisory for advisees to rehearse what they want to say and share at their conference, using your conference outline. Students can rehearse in pairs and give feedback to each other afterwards. (Use the feedback form from the activity **Guidelines for Giving Feeback**.)

Grade Report Conference:

- Students bring their journal reflections and work selections to the conference.

- Invite students to begin the conference with the journal response they have chosen to share.

- Discuss advisees' grade predictions. Did they earn grades they expected? If their predictions were way off, explore why that might have happened and brainstorm questions and concerns the student might want to raise with the teacher.

- If this is an advisor-advisee conference, save a little time to share your congratulations, affirmations, encouragement, observations, and comments; invite students to respond to what you have said.

- If this is an advisee/advisor/parent conference, save time for you and parents/guardians to share your congratulations, affirmations, encouragement, observations, and comments; invite students to respond to what you and their parents/guardians have said.

- Close the conference by inviting each person to share something positive about the conference and something that will be useful to remember for next semester.

Activity: Make Time to ONLY Listen

Format: **Large-group dialogue or personal conferencing**
Grouping: **Whole advisory or advisor-advisee**
Scheduling: **As needed**

Directions:
Sometimes teachers are first-rate talkers and second-rate listeners. It's easy for us to interrupt, over-explain, finish a student's ideas, give advice, correct someone too quickly, or make sure we have the last word, especially if it's clever or funny. It takes a conscious effort to only listen without responding. This simple gesture surprises students when we do it. Here are a couple of ways to try it out:

Large-group dialogue — Check yourself during discussions. When you really want to listen to what students have to say, let them know you'll set a timer for five or ten minutes, and invite students to respond to an open-ended question that is likely to generate strong feelings and many different viewpoints. Commit yourself to silent, attentive listening during this time.

Personal advisor-advisee conferencing — When you have made a choice to conference with students one-on-one (especially when you've discovered that there's a concern or a problem), use your favorite opener to invite someone to talk. For example, "So what's going on?" or "You don't seem your usual self. Anything going on that's getting in the way?" Then stop. Don't fill the space with conversation. Sit with the silence and only listen.

Activity: Guidelines for Conferencing and Encouraging Words That Communicate Support and Invite Conversation

Format: **Personal conferencing**
Grouping: **Advisee-advisor**
Scheduling: **As needed**

Directions:

Students need to know that you're not on call all the time. They also need to know when you are available for personal conferencing outside of advisory period. Try to set aside one lunch period and one hour before or after school per week to conference with individual advisees or small groups. This is a good time to check in around quarterly goals, academic plans, academic and discipline contracts, and specific issues that require an extended conference time.

When you need to bring an issue to an advisee's attention or have advisees bring a problem to you:

- Tell them that you appreciate their willingness to talk about it.

- Say little and let the student talk it through.

- Ask the student if he or she wants to problem-solve. Sometimes just listening to a student's story is enough. If a student does want to problem-solve, you might ask, "Where would you like to go from here?" "What would a good solution look like?" "What might be one step you can take toward resolving this today?"

- Try to identify sources of the problem and explore ways to meet that need. For example, was the behavior a way to gain attention, exercise power, protect one's identity and dignity, seek revenge, or convey inadequacy?

- When young people use absolutes or they overgeneralize, help them to clarify their thinking and speak more precisely about their own situation. You can respond by saying, "Always? That never happens? Everyone does that? Are you sure that you're the only person who...?"

- With students who are really struggling, choose to work on one behavior at a time. Limit negative feedback. Ask the student what you as an advisor can do to help. Create a daily check-in with the student. Give encouraging feedback when you see the student engaging in the desired behavior.

When students feel discouraged, blue, angry, frustrated, or disconnected, the words you choose will influence their comfort and trust in your capacity to listen and be supportive. No one phrase or question is magic. The trick is knowing your advisees well enough to use the right opener that invites reflective conversation. Here's a list of openers that experienced advisors have found to be useful tools in their connecting and conferencing repertoire.

"Take a deep breath and a minute to gather your thoughts. I'm here to listen."

"I learned a lot from you today."

"What was that about yesterday?"

"A lot's been going on. Tell me what you're feeling right now."

"You really sounded upset earlier. Is that right?"

"So tell me what I should know about what happened."

"How can I help you?"

"I hear _____. Can you tell me more?"

"Remember when you _____ and you felt really good about yourself."

"Name one thing you've done well today."

"Let's break this down into easier chunks."

"Is there another way to _____?"

"I'm glad you're here today because _____."

"Can you help me with _____? I like the way you _____."

"I know this is difficult AND I think you can do it."

"Let's just focus on one thing. I know you can get through this."

"Let's work this through together."

"What did I do that prompted _____?"

"Are you okay?"

"Let's start over."

"What choices do you have right now?"

"Do you need some time to think about this before we talk?"

Tools for School and Learning

 ## Activity: Perspectives on School, Teaching, and Learning

Format: Gatherings, small- and large-group dialogues
Grouping: Whole advisory
Scheduling: Beginning of the school year

Directions:
Invite students to talk about their experience of school, their ideas about what it takes to be a good student and a good teacher, and their ideas about what makes a good class.

Personal Perspectives:

1. What things can I do as a student to be successful in school?

2. What can my teachers do to support my success in school?

3. What makes a classroom a safe space where I can be honest and open, where I can say what's on my mind?

4. What kinds of learning tasks, activities, and homework are easiest for me to do?

5. What kinds of learning tasks, activities, and homework are hardest for me to do?

6. What do kids do and say that annoys me the most? What happens in class that I feel angry about?

7. In what ways do I like to be challenged?

8. When I'm having difficulty or get stuck, how do I let a teacher know that I'd like some help?

Classroom Perspectives:

1. What are the most important qualities of a good teacher?

2. What are the most important qualities of a good student?

3. What can I do to support other students to do their best in class?

4. What makes learning fun in class?

5. What things do I hope a teacher will never say or do?

6. What things do I hope students will never say or do?

7. What kinds of pressures and obstacles do some students face that make it tough to be a successful student?

School Perspectives:

1. One thing about this school that I feel really angry about is …

2. One thing about this school that I'm proud of is …

3. I think this school would be a better and more caring place to learn if more of us …

4. I want to help make this school a place where people …

Activity: Using Planning Calendars and Assignment Books

Format: **Organizing and representing ideas and information, small- and large-group dialogues, games, personal connections**

Grouping: **Individual student tasks, pairs, whole advisory, and advisor-advisee**

Scheduling: **As needed**

Directions:

Many schools require middle and high school students to use planning calendars or assignment notebooks, and rely on advisors to introduce and support the practice. Some organizationally savvy students already use calendars or task lists. However, those who are organizationally challenged (this includes many adults and most adolescents) can benefit from exercises, discussions, and writing prompts that help make this practice a tool for success.

Try any of the following ideas to introduce assignment notebooks in a lively way and support their ongoing use.

1. Create a "Top Ten" list of reasons for using an assignment notebook. Encourage students to sprinkle the list with serious, thoughtful rationales, as well as goofy, David Letterman-style responses.

2. Make a game of finding information in the agenda book. Many agenda books include inspiring quotations, historical and scientific information, maps, punctuation rules, mathematical formulas, study tips, and career information. The game can be structured as an information hunt (as is done at Boston Community Leadership Academy), in a Jeopardy game structure, or as a team activity, with groups of advisees writing questions for other groups to answer.

3. Discuss the benefits of making lists, recording tasks, and keeping a calendar. In pairs or with the whole group, invite students to share their responses to any of these questions:

   • For those of you who keep a calendar, what do you like about this habit? What does it do for you?

   • For those of you who don't keep a calendar regularly, what gets in the way of making this a regular habit?

   • Academically, what are the benefits of writing tasks down?

   • What kinds of tasks are you most likely to keep track of without reminders? Why is it easy to remember and do these tasks?

   • What kinds of tasks or assignments are you most likely to delay or avoid? Discuss the reasons for your procrastination. What are three things you can tell yourself that will help you shift from delaying to doing?

   • What's your worst nightmare about forgetting an important event or task?

   • Share an experience in the past when you regretted not being prepared or on time. What happened? How did it affect your performance or other people's perception of you?

4. Try these ideas for making assignment notebooks a meaningful tool for goal-setting, planning, reflection, and assessment.

   • Provide time for writing and reflecting on weekly or quarterly goals, making task lists, and creating timelines for long projects. Coach advisees so their lists and goals are clear, specific, and realistic.

- Have students create symbols, color coding, or graphics that help them plan ahead and look back on individual tasks on their weekly calendar.

The following suggestions can help students become more aware of themselves as learners.

- After a week of using assignment notebooks, ask students to share how this effort has helped them.

- Take time in advisory for students to review, edit, and supplement the notes and reminders they have recorded in their assignment notebooks.

- Ask students to predict how long it will take them to complete various assignments. The next day, ask students to report whether their predictions were accurate or off the mark.

- Give each student a Post-it note to stick next to an important assignment or project that they have not yet started or completed. Ask students to write down a deadline date for completion and three specific steps that will help them complete the task.

- Encourage parents to sign assignment notebooks on a weekly basis and write little notes that congratulate and encourage their children.

- If you are in the habit of checking all or some of your advisee's assignment notebooks, jot down your own comments, kudos, and questions in their notebooks. Simple statements can be very supportive. "Tell me how this project turned out when you've completed it." "Wow, this looks like a heavy-duty week for you. Let me know how it's going." "Is it getting any easier to keep up with your reading in AP History?"

- At the beginning of a week, ask students to pair up and assess how they did the previous week and share their goals for the week ahead.

- At the end of the week, ask students to review the week and share the one thing they were most proud of accomplishing during the week.

- During personal check-ins and individual academic conferencing, invite students to refer to their assignment notebooks as they assess what's going well and what needs improvement.

- Offer an incentive when everyone has noted all of their assignments sufficiently for the entire week.

Activity: Drop Everything and Read!!!

Format: **Reading**
Grouping: **Individual student task**
Scheduling: **Weekly**

Directions:

Many schools designate a specific time every week all year when every person in the building "drops everything and reads." One way to support this experience is to set aside a space in your advisory room where you and students can record what you're currently reading, and then upon completion of your novel, article, or other reading material assign it a one- to five-star recommendation.

Activity: Writing, Writing, Writing

Format: **Written reflection, skill lesson, and personal conferencing**
Grouping: **Whole advisory, individual student tasks, and advisee-advisor**
Scheduling: **As needed**

Directions:

Many of the activities in this guide include a writing component because advisory groups can help advisees improve their writing skills by

- making reflective writing a habit;

- writing frequently for varied purposes;

- writing about topics that feel important and personal;

- engaging in writing tasks with peers;

- engaging in peer editing before turning in work for other classes;

- getting feedback and encouragement from their trusted advisor, sometimes even in writing; and

- offering a nonthreatening environment and low-pressure tasks.

Look for opportunities to clarify a story, produce a polished survey, or craft an elegant question. Through consistent encouragement and gentle coaching you will help advisees to internalize high standards and the habit of writing as a lifelong medium for organizing their thoughts.

 ## Activity: Finding Your Voice

Format: **Skill lesson, small and large group dialogues, and personal conferencing**
Grouping: **Whole advisory, individual student tasks, and advisee-advisor**
Scheduling: **As needed**

Directions:
Advisory can help students develop crucial speaking skills that will serve them well in classes, presentations and exhibitions, jobs, interviews, and an infinite number of other interactions with peers and adults. The activities that use dialogue, class meeting, announcement, and presentation formats are especially good opportunities to practice sorting one's thoughts and saying them clearly.

A few tips that can help are as follows:

- Encourage students to practice or jot notes prior to making an announcement or presentation

- Ensure that advisees share the role of reporting from small groups, and share the role of facilitating gatherings, closings, and discussions

- Establish the practice of pausing or passing until ready

- Practice assertion skills, coaching advisees away from withdrawing or aggressively exaggerating, attacking, or dominating

- When needed, coach students on leaving the spotlight and showing restraint

- Demonstrate phrases that draw others into conversation, as in, "My reaction was … . Is that how you saw it?" By speaking, we can express our own ideas and show interest in others' views

Activity: Time and Task Management I

Format: **Gathering, interactive exercise, written reflection**
Grouping: **Whole advisory and individual student tasks**
Scheduling: **As needed**

Directions:
Gathering go-round: What do you always make time to do every week that's really important to you?

Time Log: Using **Handout 9**, ask students to keep a log of how they spend their time for one week from Sunday through Saturday. Students will use their completed time logs in Time and Task Management II.

Task Log: Ask students to write down their To Do list for the week on **Handout 10**. Introduce the PREP tips for task management to help students get things done. Encourage advisees to review and rework their To Do lists.

> **Prioritize** — Sort the tasks into three groups – 1s are absolutely essential for having a productive, successful week at school, 2s are important for your physical and mental health and your relationships with family and friends, 3s are everything else.

> **Reorganize** — Predict how much time the most important tasks will take. Write in a day of the week next to each #1 task and each #2 task. These are the two things each day that you will make sure you do. If you have multiple tasks that will take significant amounts of time, spread them out.

> **Eliminate** — Cross out two things from your list that are either unrealistic expectations for this week or things that won't have a negative impact on your life if they don't get done.

> **Plan ahead** — Forecast three important To Do's that you know you will need to schedule time for next week.

Close by inviting students to share some of their top priorities for the coming week.

Activity: Time and Task Management II

Format: **Gathering, interactive exercise, written reflection**
Grouping: **Small groups or individual student tasks**
Scheduling: **As needed**

Directions:

Time and Task Log Check-in: Form trios and take five minutes for students to share what they learned from their time and task logs. What stood out for them when they looked at how they spent their time and reviewed To Do tasks that they completed. What To Do's got completed? What didn't? Were there any surprises about how they spent their time? Any patterns that emerged?

Rotation Stations: Post six or seven of the questions below on chart paper around the room. Ask trios from the previous activity to place themselves by one of the questions posted. Pass out markers to each group and give trios two minutes to write down at least three responses to the question. Then ask trios to rotate clockwise to the next question, again taking two minutes to record their responses. Keep rotating so trios get an opportunity to respond to at least four or five questions.

- How do you keep track of assignments and responsibilities?

- What tasks generally take longer than you expect?

- What are your best tips for completing projects and papers?

- What are the final steps you take before knowing you're done with a task or project? How long do those steps take?

- What are things that keep you from completing homework or projects?

- What are your best tips for preparing for a test or exam?

- What are your best tips for recording, reviewing, and using class notes effectively?

- Why keep a daily and weekly calendar?

- What do you do to keep all of your school papers and materials organized so you can find and use them when you need them?

- How can you use these three (or other) tools to make your life easier as a student?

  Sticky Notes   Note Cards   Colored pens and markers

- If you devoted one hour on Sunday to getting ready for the week ahead, what would you do?

  Make a list of...   Organize...   Schedule in advance...

- What do you give up during "crunch weeks" when there are high-pressure academic demands that require more of your time and effort?

- Managing your time and tasks effectively helps you to reduce ..., increase ..., eliminate ..., and develop ...

- Effort creates ability – what specific efforts are good indicators that you take your academic responsibilities seriously?

Silent Gallery Walk: When you are finished, give everyone three minutes to take a look at the responses, in silence, with these instructions: Write down three tips that you want to try out or use more regularly that you think will help you manage time and tasks more effectively.

Revisit Time Logs: Looking at the upcoming week, review your time log with the following tasks in mind. Looking at the total number of hours in different categories, circle the category where you want to spend more time and write in the number of hours. Write down why this is a good idea for you and write down three things you will do to make this happen. Circle categories where you will need to spend less time. Write down three things you will not do or do less often in these categories. Your total number of hours will still be the same.

Activity: Remembering What You Need to Know / Twenty Things on a Tray

Format: **Organizing and representing information**
Grouping: **Whole group**
Scheduling: **One time**

Directions:
In order to learn, we must be able to focus and access our memory. This activity helps students to explore how they make meaning of information through categorization, grouping, and other memory devices in order to retain data, make connections between data, and use it now and later. This activity also provides an opportunity to introduce and discuss two important ideas: 1) There isn't one right way to learn; 2) Everyone learns a little differently because each of us

brings a different set of perceptions, interests, and experiences to any learning situation.

1. Introduce the activity by saying that you are going to explore differences and similarities in how we remember and learn. Place 20 things you have collected on a table or on the floor where everyone can gather around and look at them. The objects should be covered at the start of this activity.

2. Explain to the group: "You will have two minutes to look at the 20 objects I have placed on the table. Your goal is to use any strategies you can to remember all 20 objects. Then you will have two minutes to write down as many objects as you can remember when you go back to your desks. This is not a contest. You won't be required to share out loud which objects and the number of objects you remembered. When you view the objects, try to put yourself in a state of relaxed alertness so that you can focus your attention. When everyone has found a place where you can see, I will uncover the objects and ask everyone to be silent for two minutes as you look. Ready?"

3. Set the timer for two minutes and uncover the objects.

4. Call time, cover the objects, and give students two minutes to write down the objects that they remember. This is a silent task to be done alone.

5. Discuss and post the strategies people used to remember the objects. The sharing will be rich. It is amazing to hear the different ways people organize data (i.e. numbering; alphabetizing; categorizing by color, shape, size, kinds of objects, male/female; making up a story using all of the objects; repeating the names of objects over and over; creating a picture where you walk through the scene touching the objects; studying their placement; dividing objects in rows).

6. Here are more discussion points:

   • What objects were hard to remember? Why was that? (The easy-to-remember objects are usually linked to personal experiences. The hard-to-remember objects are usually ones unfamiliar to students or ones students are unable to name.) This is an opportunity to explore how we link new learning to prior experiences.

   • Invite students to think why people used different strategies to meet the same goal in remembering the objects.

   • Look at the strategies that you posted, and discuss how students use these strategies in different subject areas to study and retain information. Add other strategies that students use to the list.

- Give each student a notecard to put in an assignment notebook or planner. Complete it using this format:

Strategies for Retaining and Using Information

In general the three best ways for me to retain information are:

1. _____

2. _____

3. _____

My two best strategies for understanding and remembering what I read are:

1. _____

2. _____

My two best strategies for remembering math formulas, models, and problem solving processes are:

1. _____

2. _____

My best strategy for "cramming" right before a test is:

_____

- As a followup activity, ask students to bring a reading assignment to advisory from English, social studies, science, or world language. After they have finished reading, give students time in advisory to apply their chosen strategies to their reading assignment.

Thanks to Rachel Kessler for this activity.

 ## Activity: Portfolio Review and Selection

Format: **Organizing and representing ideas and information**
Grouping: **Individual student task, small groups, and personal conferencing**
Scheduling: **Every quarter or grading period**

Directions:

Advisory can be a place where students prepare their portfolios for submission and exhibition, or review and select work samples that they will present during grade report conferences with their advisor and their parents. Arrange time to spend a few minutes with each of your advisees alone or in groups of three to share a piece of work that reflects a best effort and high standard of quality.

Activity: Discussing and Solving Problems That Impact Students, Learning, and the Environment

Format: **Class meeting**
Grouping: **Whole advisory**
Scheduling: **Monthly or as needed**

Directions:
Surface problems and issues that students want to discuss by:

- Inviting students to make a list of problem issues that they are fairly certain will arise at various points during the year

- Creating a suggestion box where students can submit problems and issues

- Discussing topics that have emerged from your personal conferences with students—issues that you recommend the whole advisory discuss

- Providing a menu of possible topics and inviting students to prioritize the issues they think are most compelling to discuss

- Identifying problems and issues in team, house, or school-wide staff meetings that all advisories are asked to discuss by sharing student perceptions of the issue, gathering more information, talking about how the issue impacts students, learning, and the environment, and generating possible solutions and recommendations

See Class Meetings in Chapter 5, Facilitation and Formats, for meeting facilitation tips.

Activity: Have a Conversation about School-Smart Strategies

Format: **Group dialogues and personal conferencing**
Grouping: **Whole advisory and advisee-advisor**
Scheduling: **As needed**

Directions:
Most of us would like to think that middle and high schools provide the opportunity for all kids to learn and achieve a modicum of success. Sadly, the gap between achieving and non-achieving students actually increases between 9th and 12th grades, with already advantaged

students becoming more so and disadvantaged students forming an even larger pool of the unsuccessful. Secondary schools tend to reward students who already know how to be smart in school. These kids come to class with norms, habits, resources, and values that mirror what teachers prize and expect from "good students."

Although all teachers are pretty good at spelling out what will get students in trouble, fewer recognize the importance of discussing and teaching specific behaviors and strategies that will help kids become "school smart." Instead, young people who don't fit the ideal student norm are likely to hear a litany of frustrations and complaints about what they should have learned or known before they arrived. This "sink or swim" attitude is not a big motivator for kids who come to school feeling different, alienated, or discouraged.

One option is making time to discuss this topic in advisory. Acknowledging that middle or high school is not always a student-friendly environment for lots of kids goes a long way toward building trust with students who can't imagine that any adult knows what school is like for them. Equally important is explaining to students that people aren't born with "school smarts." Anyone can learn what it takes to maneuver successfully through school. We do need to be mindful, however, that students who grow up in white, middle class, educated families, get more practice at this before they ever enter 6th or 9th grade. Less advantaged students should be able to count on some adults in their lives who will help them decode what middle and high school is all about.

Explain to advisees that even though they have countless occasions outside of school to show they are capable, competent, and responsible, it's the satisfactory completion of high school that remains the gatekeeper to a young person's future. So helping students learn how to succeed at middle or high school is a good thing. Being "school smart" doesn't have to remain a mystery, and it doesn't mean students have to give up who they are.

The composition of students in your advisory will influence whether your conversations occur with the whole group, in small groups, or one-on-one. If most of your advisees could benefit from becoming more "school smart," talking about this openly in advisory can be positive and supportive. On the other hand, if most kids are already savvy about how to make school work, you may want to share some information with the whole group and discuss other issues privately with specific students or a smaller group of students.

How might you begin a conversation about "school smarts"?

1. You can begin by discussing different kinds of "smarts" that students need to survive and succeed. For example, exploring what students need to know to be "street smart" or "work smart" can help them appreciate the need for behaving differently and holding different attitudes in different settings.

2. Brainstorm the benefits of moving successfully from one setting to another, pointing out that people who can do this well usually have more choices and more opportunities in life. How does this ability to move from setting to setting give students more power?

3.   Give students information and teach them strategies that help them become more "school smart."

Some specific school-smart strategies are listed here with suggestions for how you might help students develop these strategies and use them more often.

I know how to "read" what really matters from teacher to teacher. For example, I can figure out the bottom-line rules that I need to pay attention to in each class and I know what to avoid to stay out of trouble.

A Way to Help: Give students a quiz on schoolwide rules and consequences, on boundaries, none-gotiables, and consequences in classes. And be sure they know that it counts toward their grade.

I know what to do and say that will get a teacher's positive attention without "brown-nosing" or "sucking up."

A Way to Help: Let students know five things they can do to get teachers' positive attention. To lighten things up have a bag of mini-candy bars or funky prizes to toss out intermittently when you catch students doing the right thing.

I can adjust to different norms from class to class. For example, I know for one teacher tardy means "not in your seat when the bell rings" and for another teacher tardy means "you've got a minute or two before you will be marked late."

A Way to Help: This is a good thing to discuss with students for all kinds of reasons. Are norms consistent or inconsistent from one class to another? Ask students how they navigate this. You might want to explore what's good and what's bad about having different norms.

I know how to become invisible when I'm not prepared or when I'm distracted by something else going on outside of class.

A Way to Help: This is probably a private conversation. The idea that there are things you can do to disappear or to avoid drawing attention to yourself is big news for some kids. In the same vein, the idea of pretending to pay attention actually helps some kids to focus.

I know how to talk with teachers privately when I've got a problem learning something, completing an assignment, or meeting a deadline. I also know that if I do this sooner rather than later, it will probably be easier to deal with it.

A Way to Help: This is so important that it deserves to be addressed with the whole class. A good way to introduce this skill is to ask students to present two different role plays, showing ineffective and effective ways to get help and understanding. Be sure to do the ineffective role play first so students can discuss what made it ineffective and what they might do and say differently to make it a more effective request. Keep in mind that students who don't have the words might not have the confidence to do this, so rehearsal is extremely helpful.

I can buddy up with other students when I think it will help me study or complete an assignment.

A Way to Help: This may merit a discussion about the difference between cheating, copying, and working collaboratively. You might want to establish study-buddy groups so advisees will automatically have peers with whom they can work throughout the year. Or you and your advisees can discuss possible partners with whom they might want to work.

I can identify the students in class who can help explain or show me how to do something when I don't understand.

A Way to Help: Students ultimately feel more personally powerful when they use strategies that don't always involve going to the teacher for help. One idea is to have students identify two peers they feel comfortable asking for help. Have students write the names down for you and for themselves. This way you have the information to suggest when it's timely.

4. Use **Handout 11** for starting points when you conference privately with students. Together, you can identify habits and strategies that a student already uses effectively and discuss other strategies that a student might want to try or use more frequently. Encourage a student to try one new strategy for a week and then check back to reflect on how it made a difference.

 Activity: Teach Students to Match Their Behaviors to the Setting

Format:	**Skill lesson**
Grouping:	**Whole advisory**
Scheduling:	**As needed**

Directions:
We all behave differently in different settings. For example, we behave more formally at official ceremonies. Talk about how people act differently in their home, school, and community settings. Asking students to think in terms of "What's public? What's private?" can help them identify appropriate behaviors for each context. You might discuss differences between conversations that students have with friends at home and conversations that they have with adults and peers at school or work. How are their behaviors different in each setting? What are the advantages of being able to "code switch"? While some students adjust their behavior automatically, others must be taught and provided with ample opportunities to practice. Involving families and the community can help students recognize the benefits of adapting to different settings.

Activity: School-Wide Academic Networking and Enrichment

Format: **Reading and Test Prep**
Grouping: **Small groups, one-to-one conferencing**
Scheduling: **Regularly scheduled**

Directions:

Personalization is most often associated with efforts to forge positive relationships between students and adults, strengthen students' attachment to school, and promote healthy social and emotional development. Yet efforts to personalize academic support are equally important if the ultimate goal is to help more young people become more successful at school. When students are asked, "What kind of support do you want and need when you're experiencing difficulties in a class?" the response is always the same. Overwhelmingly, kids say they want personal encouragement and one-on-one help from their teachers.

The challenge is designing an academic support system that meets the needs of high-achieving, low-performing, and underperforming students at the same time. The structure of advisory can make such a system possible. If your advisory meets more than once a week or every day, consider setting aside one or two weekly periods for academic support, enrichment, coaching, and networking. Here's how it works:

1. Communicate to all advisors and advisees that time for academic networking and enrichment counts as "instructional minutes." During this time, all students and all advisors are expected to engage in learning activities that support and enhance academic achievement and literacy. The goal is to provide enough flexibility to accommodate a variety of academic purposes and grouping configurations.

2. Set up a process and create the necessary printed forms that will enable teachers to request time to work with individuals or small groups and enable students to request time to work with individual teachers, meet with mentors or student-led study groups, or work in the library, special labs, or studios. Teachers and students sign academic network requests at least 24 hours in advance. After attendance is taken in advisory, students may "travel" to another location in the building as long as they have their signed NETWORK PASS.

3. Develop clear choices for what students can do during academic networking and enrichment periods. This should include "traveling" options as well as specific activities for students who choose to remain in your advisory during this time. Here's a list of sample activities:

"Traveling" Options	"Stay Put" Options
• Individual tutorial and homework help with a specific teacher • Small-group tutorials with a specific teacher • Check-ins with special education staff who supervise students' IEPs • Meeting with a mentor from the community • Meetings between senior mentors and their freshmen mentees • Student-led study groups organized around work for a specific course • Academic support groups that focus on specific skill deficits • Mentoring groups led by community members that provide support and encouragement to specific cultural groups of students or students who are taking advanced courses for the first time • Meetings with sponsors and coaches of individual and team academic competitions, contests, and special projects • Library, lab, and studio time	• "Study Buddies" who sign up to work together on specific tasks related to a specific course • Independent reading – Many schools create an expectation that students read a specific number of books not assigned in class during the year. The more students read, the better readers they become. • Independent learning project – Many schools require students to complete at least one long-term project or exhibition of their own design every year. See "Passion Projects" activity in the Activity section, Personal Passions, Hobbies, and Interests

Life skills, Healthy Development, and Self-Care

 ## Activity: This Issue of Respect

Format: **Skill Lesson**
Grouping: **Whole advisory**
Scheduling: **One time**

Directions:
Whom Do You Respect?

Ask students to write down (very quickly) three to five names of people (living or dead, young or old, personal acquaintances or people in the larger world) whom they respect. Then ask students to identify two or three qualities that all the people on their personal lists have in common. Ask students to close their writing by explaining why they associate these qualities of character with people whom they respect.

What Is Respect?

Invite students to share what they wrote. Record the qualities on newsprint and follow up with a few questions that deepen the dialogue:

1. Is the way you show respect toward some individuals or groups different from the way you show respect to other individuals and groups?

2. Is respect different from admiration, appreciation, and popularity? How so? Can you respect people and not like them? Why or why not? If you disagree with someone can you still show respect toward them? How?

3. Is everyone entitled to be treated respectfully, regardless of what they do? Are there people you automatically respect? Does everyone have to earn your respect, regardless of age, position, and status? Or does everyone start out getting your respect, but earn the privilege of keeping it? Please explain your answer.

More Questions for Journaling, Gatherings, or Listening Labs

1. What are three ways that teachers can show respect toward students?

2. What are three ways that students can show respect toward teachers?

3. What are three ways that students can show respect toward each other?

4. Make a list of Do's and Don'ts about self-respect (If you have self-respect, you … and you don't …).

5. What does "Give respect to get respect" mean to you?

6. What does "What comes around, goes around" mean to you?

7. Can you teach respect? Why or why not? If you can, how do people learn to be respectful?

8. If teachers can't demand your respect, what can they do to gain it?

9. Are respect and civility the same thing? If they're the same, how do you know that? If they're different, explain the differences?

10. In what situations is it hardest for you to be respectful?

11. When kids say "You're 'dissing me," what do they mean exactly?

12. What might be three good reasons to be respectful to people you don't like or who don't like you?

13. When I'm with people I don't know well or at all, I show respect by …

14. When I'm with people who are culturally different from me, I show respect by…

15. When I'm with elders, I show respect by …

Activity: Friendship Questions

Format: Gatherings, closings, small- and large-group dialogues, or journaling
Grouping: Whole advisory, individual student tasks
Scheduling: Regularly scheduled

Directions:
Use these questions or sentence stems for gathering go-rounds, small-group listening labs, large-group structured dialogues, or individual journaling. You might try posting several questions that students can choose from.

Questions about Friendship

1. I believe a real friend should …

2. I've been a good friend when I …

3. Friendships include having differences and arguments. Agree or disagree? How do good friends deal with big differences between them?

4. I think sometimes people tease, name call, or 'dis other people because …

5. I think sometimes people boss others around because …

6. Two people are sort-of friends, but they put each other down a lot and then get mad at each other. What advice would you give them?

7. Why are some people labeled "popular" and others not?

8. I'd like to be friends with this one person, but I don't think my popular friends like this person. I'm scared my popular friends won't like me either if I hang around with the not-so-popular person. I could …

9. Two friends of mine are mad at each other and both are talking trash to me about the other one. I'm caught in the middle. I could make the situation worse by … Some things I could do to help are …

10. I'm hearing that a person who I thought was my friend is talking trash about me. To clear this situation up, I could …

11. When I don't like the way a friend of mine treats me, some positive things I could do are …

12. When I think a friend of mine is doing something mean to someone else, some positive things I could do are …

13. If I think a friend of mine is doing something that might get them into trouble, some things I could do to try to help are …

14. A friend of mine is getting so mad, she/he might get into a fight. Some things I could do to help are …

15. "People don't own other people." Agree or disagree? Why do people say, "That's my boyfriend/girlfriend"?

16. I've been going out with this person for a month and I like her/him as a friend, but I don't want to go out with her/him any more. I might even like someone else. To handle this situation in an honest and caring way, I could …

17. A friendship is an equal one when both people …

Thanks to Sam Diener for many of the Friendship questions.

 ## Activity: Making Things Right

Format: **Skill lesson, journaling**
Grouping: **Whole advisory, individual student tasks**
Scheduling: **One time, as needed**

Directions:
Reconciliation is an important concept and interpersonal skill. It includes apologizing, taking responsibility, making amends, and forgiving rather than holding a grudge. When someone treats another person or their belongings badly, they have changed the relationship. They have to figure out if they want to restore the relationship, and what they could say or do to do so. The person who was hurt, likewise, has the option of reengaging in the relationship or not. That is, they are not required to be passive and simply say, "That's okay." They can accept or reject the apology or gesture, they can make a request, or they can end the relationship.

Put forth a scenario to your advisees: "Let's say you said something to a friend that hurt his or her feelings." Ask advisees what they could do.

When they suggest they could apologize, question further.

- Would any apology work? Act out some apologies that would make the situation worse, and others that would work well. What's the difference?

- If you offer an apology, does the other person have to accept it? What if you had said something really unfair and embarrassing?

- What if someone insulted you in public? Is saying, "I'm sorry," enough?

- What if they broke or lost something of yours? Would an apology work then?

Introduce the idea of making amends, making things right. When a person hurts someone or their feelings, treats them unfairly, or damages their property, an apology is often not sufficient. Things can still feel out of balance. What would restore balance?

Put forth a few more scenarios using the ones listed below and/or scenarios that your advisees offer. Brainstorm at least three options for making amends in each case. Encourage advisees to be creative—they can identify things to say, give, or do.

- A friend borrowed your class notes and lost them.

- Two of your friends went to see a movie that you'd wanted to see, and they didn't invite you.

- A classmate spread a nasty rumor about you.

- A classmate has been putting you down all week.

- You've been doing most of the work on a group project that is due next week.

- A friend damaged your bicycle and doesn't have enough money to have it fixed. You don't have enough either.

- The kid who sits next to you in science kept talking during class. Your teacher thought you were the one talking and gave you a detention.

Continue with the friendship or not?

If and when someone offers a statement or gesture that attempts to make amends, the hurt person still has the right to accept or reject it, to let it go or hold a grudge. You can continue the exploration of reconciliation by asking about being on the receiving end.

- What are good reasons for accepting someone's apology or their attempt at making amends? What would you gain?

- Why might you not accept their apology or gesture? What would you gain?

- What would the consequences be of accepting or rejecting their gesture?

In this discussion, you may hear adolescents referring to the power issues involved — attempting to hold power by not forgiving, fear of losing power by forgiving, and so on. Help advisees understand that forgiving is not the same thing as forgetting, giving in, or giving up. It doesn't mean that the "bad guys" won, that you were wrong, or that you are condoning what they did. It can be a choice to disentangle oneself from the emotional impact of a situation, restore your sense of self, and move on.

The discussion of forgiveness is based on work done by William J. Kreidler.

 Activity: Peer Pressure

Format: **Organizing and representing ideas, small- and large-group dialogues, journaling, and interactive exercise**
Grouping: **Individual student task, small groups, whole advisory**
Scheduling: **One time and as needed**

Directions:
Opening the topic of differences between friends
No matter what lessons we teach, peer pressure is not going to vanish. Adolescents of all ages are sorting out issues of identity and power. They are negotiating when it's OK to be separate, how to fit in, what their preferences are, how to make their own choices, and how to test their power to influence. These are not easy tasks. We can help teenagers by steering them toward sorting out these issues with less risk rather than more, and by noting that there are positive uses of power and influence.

Use these questions for small-group listening labs, then have advisees report to the whole group.

- Do friends have to like all the same things?

- What happens when friends don't like to do the same things? Think of some good things and some risky things that might happen.

My friends like / We like / I like

Have advisees draw a Venn diagram using **Handout 12** or a chart like the one below for recording some of the ways they are similar to and different from their friends, or similar to and different from "most kids."

My friends like and do some things that I don't.	My friends and I like	What I like and do that my friends don't
_____	_____	_____
_____	_____	_____

Follow the charting exercise with a whole-group dialogue and/or journaling.

- What's good about having different preferences and interests from your friends?

- What's hard about having different preferences and interests from your friends?

- How do you communicate that you don't like to do some of the things your friend(s) like(s) to do?

- How do you feel when a friend doesn't want to do something with you? How do you react?

Preferences and pressure

Peer pressure assumes that someone is feeling pressured, and that someone is doing the pressuring. Ask students to reflect on being in both of those roles via small- or large-group dialogues and/or journaling.

- When have you felt pressured to do something that you didn't want to do? What did you do? How did the situation end up?

- When does it help to have friends pressure you? When does it hurt?

- When have you pressured a friend to do something that they didn't want to do? Did it help or hurt them? What happened to your friendship?

- What's the difference between the times when peer pressure helps and when it hurts?

Pressure from one, pressure from all

Peer pressure has a different dynamic when it involves one friend versus a whole group, so help advisees have strategies for both settings.

- What is fitting in all about?

- Is it harder to go against a friend or a group? Why?

- Why is it hard for a person to go against a group? When is it important to go against a group? What would help someone go against a group when they needed to?

- Describe a time when you acted differently from the way you really wanted to either because you wanted to fit in or because you were scared of not fitting in.

Role plays

Pass out large index cards and ask advisees to write about situations that involve peer pressure—a friend asking you to cheat or smoke, trying to convince a friend to go somewhere with you, wishing a friend would stop teasing someone, when "everyone" is wearing/doing the latest thing, or some other scene. How many people are involved? Who are they? Where and when is the scene taking place? Use their scenarios for role plays.

During the role plays, ask advisees to note when the stakes are getting higher, how the characters might feel, what the actors do that help or hurt the situation, and what else they might try. Try multiple versions of the same scenario to play out the consequences of different choices. Encourage direct as well as subtle face-saving measures, such as having code language with a friend or parent when they want help exiting a situation. This is also a time when their parents will be glad to be quoted, as in, "My parents will ground me for life if I do that."

 ## Activity: Drawing a House (or Your Room): Collaborating around Common Goals

Format: **Interactive exercise**
Grouping: **Pairs**
Scheduling: **One time**

Directions:
This activity surfaces issues about how to work cooperatively and how to negotiate and navigate relationships in school, at home, and with friends.

1. Cut easel-paper sheets in half so that each pair of students has a large piece of paper. Each pair will also need two markers of contrasting colors.

2. Divide students into pairs (random or self-selection) and say to the group, "We are going to do a drawing exercise to explore more about how people negotiate and work together. You and your partner will be drawing on the same piece of paper and each of you will use

a different colored marker to draw. From this point on, everyone needs to participate in silence—no talking, whispering, or mumbling."

3. "Now I'd like you to close your eyes and relax for a minute. In your mind's eye, imagine the house of your dreams." (You can also use the perfect room of your dreams and change what you say accordingly.) What does the outside of your house look like? What kind of materials are used to build your house? What does the roof line look like? What kinds of windows does it have? How many stories? What does the entrance look like? Now, walk out the front door. What do you see around you? What do you hear? Walk around to the back. What's there? You are really happy because you have always wanted to live in a place like this … Now open your eyes slowly and listen to the next set of instructions."

4. "Let me explain what your task is. You and your partner will be drawing one house on your paper. You will need to remain silent until you finish drawing. Here is how you will draw your house. One of you will decide to be first and you will draw one stroke on the paper with your marker. Your partner will then take her/his marker and draw one stroke on the paper. You will continue taking turns drawing for five minutes."

5. Draw examples of what one stroke can be:

Draw examples of what is one stroke cannot be:

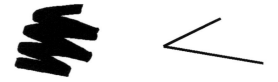

6. Ask if there are any questions. (This is the one time students can speak.) Remind students that they may not talk or write any words on their papers. Set the timer for five minutes and let the drawing begin.

7. After five minutes, call time, and ask everyone to put their markers down.

8. Debriefing involves partners first, and then the whole group.

- Give partners three minutes to talk to each other about what they drew, how they worked together, what they thought the other person was drawing, and what was confusing or frustrating about the task.

- Now, in the whole group, invite students to discuss their observations and feelings during the activity. What made this activity feel fun, frustrating, satisfying, confusing, or interesting? What did they like or not like about the activity? For the pairs who felt satisfied with their houses, how would they describe their process? For the pairs who felt frustrated, how would they describe their process?

- Chart their comments so you can refer to them for the next two questions. Expect these kinds of comments: I did one part and she did the other. I was more interested in the house, and he worked more on the landscape. I had to let go of some things I wanted, but I made sure that _____ was there on the paper. I stepped back and let her take the lead in the beginning. We had totally different ideas, but it somehow worked out. At first, I couldn't figure out where he was going, and then it started making sense to me. We totally misunderstood what each other was drawing. We were never in sync with each other. I thought we were looking down with an aerial view, and he thought we were looking at the house from straight in front of us. Sometimes we worked together and sometimes separately.

- Say, "Now think about everything that you heard about what you and your partners experienced. What does this experience have to say about student-teacher relationships, parent-child relationships, and peer-to-peer relationships?" Encourage insights about the art of negotiating. To realize a common goal everyone needs to have a voice in creating the vision and in choices for how to get there—there's never only one form a goal can take, nor only one way to reach it. Explore the issue of reciprocity—when you agree to make room for give-and-take, you don't necessarily get everything you want, but you do need to get some things that are really important to you.

9. Students may be interested in trying this exercise again (soon or even months later) to see if they can improve their negotiating skills.

Activity: Teach Win-Win Basics

Format: **Skill lesson, interactive exercise**
Grouping: **Whole advisory**
Scheduling: **One time, as needed**

Directions:

Most of us carry around the myth that conflict is always a contest where one person wins and the other person loses. In fact, nearly all conflicts can be approached from a Win-Win perspective, and many problems can be resolved using a Win-Win process (where both parties are satisfied with the outcome). If believing in the possibility of Win-Win becomes a routine way of thinking, we are more likely to participate in problem-solving processes that result in Win-Win solutions.

Chocolate Kisses

1. Begin the activity by explaining to participants:

    "We're going to play a game now. The object of the game is to acquire as many chocolate kisses as you can. We need two volunteers to come sit at this table. Each volunteer will represent one half of the larger group."

    Identify two volunteers who are approximately the same size, and share the same handedness. Then identify the half of the group that each volunteer is representing. Position volunteers so that they are facing each other across the table, their right or left elbows are on the table, and they are clasping each others' hands. This is an arm wrestling position but do not use the term. If someone says that this looks like arm wrestling, explain that it's similar, but the rules are different.

2. Continue the instructions:

    The object of the game is for each person to get as many chocolates as possible for her or his team in the time allowed. Note that you can also call the game "Points" if you don't have or don't want to use chocolates. The rules are as follows:

    *   From now on the two players may not speak to each other.

    *   Every time the back of one person's hand touches the table, the other team will receive a chocolate.

- Someone from each team needs to keep track of the number of chocolates the team receives.

- You will have 30 seconds to get as many chocolates as you can.

3. Say "Begin," and after 30 seconds, say "Stop." Participants will probably compete against each other and will probably only get a few chocolates or none. Discuss what happened.

   - "What did you see? How many chocolates did each team receive?" If the players received very few chocolates, ask, "What was the goal of the game?"

   - Ask participants if they can think of another way to play the game so teams can get more chocolates. (Usually groups will suggest ways that the two students can alternate, placing the back of the person's hand on the table.)

4. After the group offers suggestions, play one more round and ask participants to describe what was different when they played the game the second time. You might also ask:

   "What words describe the approach you used this time?"

   "How do these two approaches to the game reflect ways that you handle conflict?"

   Watch for additional aspects to debrief. Sometimes it takes a few rounds before students are cooperating easily—we can't always incorporate new ways of behaving after simply hearing them. Some student volunteers will say having an audience made it harder. Other student volunteers will bring up issues of vulnerability and trust, that is, even when they had an image of going back and forth, they didn't want to be first to "give in." Each of these comments can foster important conversations and insights.

Teach the Concept of Win-Win
Explain that the game illustrates that conflict doesn't always have to be a Win-Lose contest: "In a highly competitive society, it's easy to assume that 'For me to get what I want and need, I have to win and you have to lose.' This approach is called Win-Lose."

You might invite students to explore these questions: Think about the society in which we live. Why does Win-Lose thinking have such a powerful hold on people? In what aspects of your life do you experience the strongest Win-Lose messages? Does school reinforce a Win-Lose approach to problems or life in general?

Sometimes neither person will get what he or she wants, in which case the result is called Lose-Lose. And, like in the game, it's also possible that both people can get what they want or need in the situation. This result is called Win-Win.

Suggest that the Win-Win approach to working out problems is the one that your advisory will practice, so the first take on problems will include seeking a solution that works for everyone involved. A Win-Win solution is a solution that is nonviolent, meets some important needs of all parties involved, and helps to maintain positive relationships. Use this concept when the group negotiates how and when to do things. Ask advisees who have a problem with each other to use this process, and use it when an advisee is involved with you in a problem-solving conference around a behavioral or academic situation that needs to be resolved.

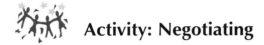 **Activity: Negotiating**

Format:	**Skill lesson**
Grouping:	**Whole advisory, small-group tasks, and individual student tasks**
Scheduling:	**One time**

Directions:

Negotiating can be accomplished by two people talking things out to solve a problem, or by a more formal process involving people, groups, or even nations. There are a few steps and concepts that make negotiating more successful. This activity includes exercises to introduce the concepts, practice the skill, apply it to an interpersonal situation, and to a group situation.

The exercises are adapted from *Dialogue: Turning Controversy into Community*, Chapter 7, by Rachel A. Poliner and Jeffrey Benson; and *Conflict Resolution in the High School*, Lesson 23, by Carol Miller Lieber.

Introducing positions and interests

Read aloud the following story:

> Two sisters ran into their kitchen, where they found an orange. It was the only orange in the house. One sister said, "I want the orange!" The other sister responded, "No, I want the orange!" This continued until their mother entered the kitchen to end the dispute. She sliced the orange in half and gave each sister half of the orange. One sister peeled her orange half, threw away the peel, and began to eat the fruit. The other sister peeled her orange half, threw away the fruit, and began to grate the peel to use for baking muffins.

Ask advisees:

- What happened in this story?

- What kept each sister from getting all that she wanted?

They will likely note that each sister got half of what she wanted, and could have gotten it all if they'd talked about it more deeply. Introduce the following concepts.

A **position** is a person's initial demand, their proposal to get what they want. It often sounds like a solution. A person can easily be focused on and quite stubborn about his or her position.

Interests are the underlying reasons for the positions, the deeper goals and concerns that the person needs to address. A person usually has several interests.

Ask advisees:

- What was each sister's position as she entered the kitchen?

- What might have been their interests?

- How could they have met their interests?

For the last two questions, encourage creative thinking. The sister who ate the fruit might have been hungry, thirsty, or in need of vitamin C, for example. And the sister who wanted the peel might have needed orange flavoring, any flavoring suitable for muffins or any baked good at all, or maybe she was just bored and wanted something to do. If the sisters had talked about it, one could have had all the fruit, while the other had all the peel. That would have been one solution. However, any of those interests could have been met in multiple ways. Stress that it is far easier to resolve differences when the people involved are not stuck on specific positions.

Practice with interests

Read each of the following scenes aloud, asking students to identify each party's starting position (their demand) and then brainstorm the interests of each party. Students will have to use their imaginations; there is no way to be sure what these interests are. The starting place for negotiating, however, is simply assuming that the other person has interests. Effective negotiators learn to listen for the interests of others and learn to recognize and speak to their own interests as well.

- Steven walked into Mr. Hollander's class wearing his new favorite t-shirt with a big slogan on it. Mr. Hollander ordered Steven to change his shirt immediately. Steven refused.

- A parent group insisted that the school eliminate two particular novels from the English curriculum. The English teachers assigned the books the next week.

- The school administration proposed that all students would have to submit to random drug testing to participate in after-school activities. Several students protested at the school board meeting.

- Angie invited Jen to go to the expensive mall to look for graduation dresses. Jen wanted to go, but said no and called Angie a snob.

- Greg and Theresa have to pick a water-related topic for their environmental science project. Greg insists on studying the state's most important river and how it's been used and abused over time. Theresa wants to focus on what the school could do to use less water.

- Tanya's family insists on a midnight curfew on Friday and Saturday nights. Tanya is in the school play; the cast party doesn't even start until 11 pm.

Journaling and pair/shares on recent conflicts

Have students write in their journals about a recent argument they had. Ask them to address the following questions:

- If a stranger overheard your argument, what would he or she have said the argument was about?

- What was your position? What were your interests?

- What was the other person's position? What do you think his or her interests were?

- As you think about the conflict now, can you name a few possible solutions that might have met some of your interests and some of their interests?

In pairs, students can share stories and help each other explore the points of view and possible outcomes.

Group negotiation

Split advisees into groups of four or five. Allow them to pick either of the two scenarios provided, and go through the steps that follow.

Scenario A: The Vacation Negotiation

Your group has received a two-week all-expenses-paid vacation to any place in the world. Your whole group must stay at the location you choose for the entire two weeks, although you may take day trips by yourself or in pairs. Where will it be and why?

Scenario B: Community Donation Negotiation

Your school has raised $5,000 to be used to better your local community. You need to decide what community project or organization will receive the donation. The donation must benefit teens who are experiencing some difficulty growing up. Who will get your donation and why?

Step 1: Silently and individually, on an index card, write your choice and three reasons for that choice.

Step 2: Read aloud just your choices (the destination or donation use), with one person recording all the choices. Do not read aloud your reasons yet.

Step 3: Was there agreement? How far apart were the choices?

Step 4: Read aloud your reasons.

Step 5: Discuss possible solutions that might serve the most important reasons from each person in the group. The solutions might have been someone's original choice, or might be a completely new idea.

When debriefing the group negotiations, discuss the following points and questions:

- How did you feel at the end of Step 2, when you heard the varied choices? Were you confident your group would find a mutual solution?

- At the end of Step 5, were you successful? How did you feel?

- What helped you succeed?

- What are the advantages of negotiating based on interests rather than on positions?

- What makes it hard for people to discuss interests?

Activity: Group Problem Solving

Format: **Skill Lesson**
Grouping: **Whole group**
Scheduling: **As needed**

Directions:
The A-B-C-D-E problem-solving process can be used for interpersonal and group problem solving. Effective problem solving takes a lot of practice, so take advantage of issues when they arise. The process is described for students on **Handout 13**.

Assess the situation and ask, what's the problem?
Invite two or three people (advisor and advisees) to describe how they see the problem and why they think it's a problem.

Ask the group if they have other thoughts about the problem—how they feel about the situation, what's not working, why it's important to solve the problem, etc. Remind students that this is not a time to point fingers, scapegoat, or criticize individuals. The task is to stay focused on the problem and problem behaviors—not attack individuals. Form a clear statement of the problem and the goal for solving the problem. Write this on the board:

> The problem is … A good solution will enable us to …

Brainstorm solutions
Invite your advisees to brainstorm potential solutions to the problem. Picture what the situation would look like if it were solved. Do this without criticizing or evaluating anything suggested.

Consider each choice carefully
Review the solutions with the class. How does each choice meet the needs and interests of everyone involved? What are the benefits of each choice? What are the negative constraints and limitations? Is the choice respectful, responsible, and reasonable? Cross out the choices that the group feels are the least effective.

Decide on your best choice and do it
Discuss the remaining choices and come to agreement on the best solution. Be mindful that the best choice might include a combination of several possible solutions. Invite students to share their preferred solutions and the reasons for their choices. Encourage as many students as possible to speak, even if their comments are in agreement with others who have already spoken. This is the way you begin to get a good sense of the groups' direction.

Summarize the comments and state what the group seems to think are the most important things to incorporate in the best choice. Use any of the following decision-making protocols to reach final agreement. Let the students be in charge as much as possible during this process. The more they feel like the owners of the solution, the more likely it is to work.

- **Reaching Consensus:** Propose the solution that sounds like most people's choice. "This sounds like the solution that has the most agreement. If there's anyone who has serious objections, this is the time to speak up and tell us what changes would make this work for you." Solicit any other changes or edits until it looks like you have the agreement of the group. Do a final consensus check by asking students to raise their hands if they fully support it as the best solution; put one thumb up if it's good enough for now; or thumb in the middle if they're not crazy about it, but can live with it.

- **Straw Poll:** If the group has narrowed the field to two or three final ideas, ask people to vote for their first preference. If there is a clear winner, modify it until the solution works for everyone.

- **Prioritize Ideas:** If the solution involves a few components, give each student three sticker dots to place on the three ideas they like best. The ideas with the greatest number of sticker dots become the highest priority to implement.

- **Small-Group Proposal:** If the information feels unwieldy, or if there are oppositional solutions with strong support, ask for a few volunteers to consider all of the data and perspectives and make a proposal to the group.

Have the advisory or a small group plan precisely how the solution will be implemented. The group should also be able to suggest ways to evaluate how effectively the solution achieves the goal for solving the problem.

Evaluate your choice after you have implemented it

At a later class meeting, or as a gathering or closing, evaluate the decision the group made. What happened? Did it work? What evidence do you have that it worked effectively? Is there anything that would help the group implement the solution more effectively?

Activity: Making Good Decisions — You Always Have Choices

Format: **Written reflection, group dialogue, project**
Grouping: **Individual student tasks, whole advisory**
Scheduling: **One time**

Directions:

1. Using these instructions, ask students to do a quick-write for five minutes:

   Make a list of all of the decisions you've made today where you made a choice among several options. Use this format:

Decision I Made	Two Other Choices I Could Have Made
1. I made a decision to_____ because _____.	1. I could have made a choice to _____ or _____.
2. I made a decision to_____ because _____.	2.. I could have made a choice to _____ or _____.
3. I made a decision to_____ because _____.	3.. I could have made a choice to _____ or _____.
4. I made a decision to_____ because _____.	4. . I could have made a choice to _____ or _____.
5. I made a decision to_____ because _____.	5.. I could have made a choice to _____ or _____..

2. Invite students to share one decision they made today, other choices they could have made, and why they thought the decision they made was the best choice.

3. Pose any of these questions, probing for examples and concrete situations that illustrate your advisees' thinking.

   • For you, what kinds of decisions are hardest to make? Why?

   • For you, what kinds of decisions are easy to make? Why?

   • In what situations are you most likely to talk about your decision with someone else before you make a final decision? How does this help?

   • In what situations are you most likely to procrastinate and avoid making a decision?

- What goes through your mind when you make a decision that you think might annoy or upset someone important to you?

4. Ask advisees to list four or five of the decisions that are toughest for them and their peers to make. Pass out **Handout 14A**: Criteria for Making Good Decisions and invite students to identify questions that would help them make good choices in those tough situations.

5. As a culminating project, ask each advisee to create a poster illustrating an important decision in their life. Review **Handout 14B**: Decision-Making Poster Project and clarify any questions about the six-step decision-making process. Make a group decision about when posters should be completed and presented.

 ## Activity: All about Conflict

Format: **Skill lesson and interactive exercise**
Grouping: **Whole advisory, small-group dialogues**
Scheduling: **One time**

Directions:
I Represent Conflict: As the facilitator, step to the center of the room and say to the group, "I represent conflict. Think about what you usually do when you disagree with someone, when you're angry with someone, when someone is bothering you. If I represent the conflict, where would you be? Place yourself somewhere in the room (or out the door!) and position your body in a way that indicates how you're most likely to respond to conflicts in your life."

Give everyone one minute to get positioned and invite students to share why they chose their place and position. Advisees will likely have chosen very different positions—in your face, behind you, crouching next to the file cabinet, to name a few we've seen—so the conversation can be very enlightening.

Conflict Styles:
1. Post lots of chart paper on the walls. Divide advisees into groups of three and ask each group to position themselves by a piece of chart paper. Give them three minutes to write down the most common conflicts they experience with friends, siblings, parents, at school, and at work. At the end of the writing time, post all chart paper on one wall so everyone can see it.

2. Then explain, "There isn't one right way to handle conflict. You always have choices. Handling conflict effectively is about choosing the best response in a given situation. Every conflict style has strengths and limitations." Pass out **Handout 15**: When it comes to conflict, you always have choices. Review these six conflict styles:

- Take charge, force, demand, protect yourself or others

- Accommodate, give in, let it go, smooth it over

- Avoid it, ignore it, drop it, or exit

- Postpone, pause and reflect; return to the problem later

- Seek out a trusted adult, a level-headed friend, or a mediator

- Problem solve:

    - CHECK IT OUT and notice, observe, and ask questions before you decide what to do

    - LISTEN AND DEFUSE when someone's upset

    - ASSERT your feelings, needs, and "No's"

    - NEGOTIATE (Let's talk it out and reach a solution that works for both of us.)

3. Mention that every conflict involves a relationship (Will my choice improve or hurt my relationship?) and involves goals (Will my choice help me get what I want or need?)

4. Use any of the conflicts on the chart paper to explore possible outcomes. Looking at the strengths and limitations of each conflict style, predict how the choice affects the relationship and predict whether the choice is likely to get you what you want or need.

Activity: Questions About Conflict

Format: Gatherings, closings, small-and large-group dialogues, or journaling
Grouping: Whole advisory or individual student task
Scheduling: Occasionally

Directions:
Use any of these questions or sentence stems for a gathering go-round, small-group listening labs, large-group structured dialogues, or individual journaling. You might try posting several of the following questions from which students can choose:

1. Share what's positive about conflict and what's negative about conflict.

2. One thing I like about the way I handle conflict is …

3. One thing I'd like to change about the way I handle conflict is …

4. In my family, one positive way I've learned to deal with conflict is …

5. In what conflict situations is it most difficult for you to listen to the other person and hear their side of the story?

6. Comment on this quotation by Martin Luther King, Jr.: "The refusal to listen is the first step toward violence."

7. When you do something wrong and get in trouble, what do you usually do first? What do you do later? Share an example that illustrates your usual modus operandi.

8. When my friends and I disagree, we usually … I wish we would … more often than we do.

9. One thing I wish people would never say to me again is …

10. One thing I wish people would say to me more often is …

Activity: Managing Your Feelings, Moods, and Attitudes

Format: Skill lesson, journaling, small-and large-group dialogues, gatherings, or personal conferencing

Grouping: Whole advisory, pairs and small groups, individuals alone or with the advisor

Scheduling: One time and as needed

Directions:

Use any or all of the following gatherings, reflection prompts, dialogue questions, and background information to help advisees manage their feelings, moods, and attitudes.

Gathering I: Feelings Check-in

Select one or more of the following categories (or other category) to have advisees describe their mood in a light-hearted way:

Today I'm feeling like ...

- What kind of weather?

- What kind of animal?

- What kind of musical instrument?

- What kind of food?

- What flavor jelly bean?

- Something connected to the current season of the year

Gathering II: Feelings Ball Toss

The first advisee holds a bean bag or other soft object and completes the sentence stem, "I feel angry when ...," then tosses the bean bag to a second student. The second student repeats what the first student said, completes it for themselves, then tosses it to a third, and so on. Each advisee repeats the prior statement and offers his or her own ending.

Self-awareness journaling or pair/share: Ask advisees to reflect on various emotions in writing or with a partner. Use **Handout 16**: Feelings, Moods, and Attitudes, to explore additional emotions.

I feel perplexed when …, so I …

I feel excited when …, so I …

I feel embarrassed when …, and what helps me is …

I feel anxious when …, and what helps is …

I feel irritated when …, so I …

If I want to feel …, I can …

Questions about anger and other emotions

Use any of these questions or sentence stems for gatherings, small-group listening labs, large-group structured dialogues, or individual journaling. Share some of the background information with students to expand the dialogues into skill lessons.

- When people start to feel angry, they usually feel it in parts of their body. These are (d)anger signals. When I feel angry, my (d)anger signals are …

- When I'm angry, I usually …

- One thing I like about how I handle anger is … Two things I'd like to do differently when I'm angry are … Three things that I can say to myself or do to calm myself are …

- When I feel annoyed, I might … When I feel furious, I might … Try other combinations that represent different intensities: embarrassed–humiliated, worried–anxious, blue–heartbroken, timid–terrified, discouraged–hopeless, etc. Having students identify more combinations will enlarge their vocabularies and deepen their understandings.

- When have you felt conflicting feelings, such as excited and afraid, at the same time? Maybe when you were on stage, tackling a new task, or feeling pressured by a friend. Think of experiences in which you had multiple and conflicting emotions. Which feeling had more influence on your choices? What was the result? What might you do next time?

- When have your feelings changed about a task, a person or an experience? Why do you think you felt differently at different times? What do you have especially strong feelings about at the moment? Can you imagine them changing?

- When I feel distracted, I can focus myself by …

- When I feel discouraged, I can motivate myself by …

- When I feel stubborn, I can coax myself by …

- I can coach myself to feel more courageous by …

- I feel most proud when …

- In my life I feel most excited and optimistic about …

Brief background and steps for managing emotions

There are more feelings than mad, bored, or fine. Having vocabulary for describing feelings is a crucial step in dealing with them. Without vocabulary or the ability to express emotions, many people act them out instead. Feelings influence behaviors and can motivate us positively or negatively. Further, we can influence our emotions more than we might think. Feelings don't make us do specific actions.

Some feelings have different intensities and change over time. We don't have to act as if each circumstance is extreme and permanent. One important goal is to make appropriate matches between what we feel and what we do. (When I feel somewhat irritated, I might … When I feel really furious, I might …) All feelings are okay, although how a person acts will have positive or negative consequences for them and other people.

Some feelings can conflict with other feelings and complicate their impact. It can be hard to navigate between competing emotions, such as feeling both attracted to and afraid of an experience, a person, or a task. With some self-awareness and self-management, people can make choices even when feeling strong or conflicting emotions.

Handout 16: Feelings, Moods, and Attitudes is not a strict list of emotions. Instead, it includes a wider range of age and cultural expressions that adolescents might use or find useful. Encourage advisees to add to the list. For students whose emotional vocabulary is comprised mainly of curse words, particularly for anger, this can be a challenging and helpful exercise.

Instead of identifying one's own emotions, many people name others' emotions, express judgements, or name behaviors. "He is embarrassed" might mean "I feel guilty." "She's a witch" might mean "I feel hurt." "I can't sit still" might mean "I am anxious." In each case, naming one's own feelings usually leads to healthier ways of dealing with those feelings and the relationships involved.

Seven steps for managing your emotions, especially anger

1. **Find words** for your feelings and others' feelings. Go beyond using the words "mad" and "bored." Don't settle for one word if you feel angry; there's probably another. Are you embarrassed and angry, sad and angry, hurt and angry? Learn the difference between thoughts and feelings. Learn words that describe the intensity of the feeling. Practice reading other people's emotions. Use **Handout 16** as a reference.

2. **Know your anger cues.** How do you know that you're getting angry? What happens to your body, your voice, your face, your stance, etc.?

3. **Identify your anger triggers.** What behaviors are "triggers" for you? Whenever someone _____, you're likely to get angry. Or whenever you experience _____, you're likely to get angry.

4. **Learn and practice reducers** that help you cool down, stay in charge and release your feelings in a healthy way. When you're feeling intense emotions, what is likely to trigger you even further? What can you do or say to yourself to feel calmer, more in control of your emotions? What can someone else say or do that will help you?

5. **Take responsibility** for your behavior—be aware of the things you do and say that lead other people to be upset and angry with you. Some of them are predictable!

6. **Communicate.** Express your feelings in ways that others can hear what you have to say. How can you say what you feel, what you need, or what's bothering you without attacking and accusing the other person?

7. **Reflect** on how you manage your emotions. Assess what's working and what's not. Congratulate yourself when you've handled a difficult situation well. Try out other strategies that might help you handle situations more constructively.

Activity: Assertive, Passive, or Aggressive — What's Your Choice?

Format: **Skill lesson**
Grouping: **Whole advisory**
Scheduling: **One time or as needed**

Directions:

Journaling:

Give advisees one to two minutes to jot down answers to the following:

- What are three things that family members or classmates do that bug you the most?

- What are three things you do that bug members of your family or classmates the most?

Share these reflections with the group.

Discussion:

1. There are three basic stances we take in responding to others' behavior. On the board write Aggressive, Passive, and Assertive. Then chart students' responses to these questions:

   - What does aggressive behavior look like and sound like?

   - What does passive behavior look like and sound like?

   - What do you think assertive behavior looks like and sounds like?

2. Read aloud each of the following statements. For each one, discuss whether the behavior would be described as Aggressive, Passive, or Assertive.

   a. You say mean things to the other person to get even.

   b. You don't express your opinion.

   c. You say how you feel when someone has done something that's upset or bothered you.

   d. You do what your friend is doing even though you don't really want to.

e. You tell a friend that you're having a difficult time this week, and you can't talk on the phone a lot.

f. You say no when you're not comfortable doing what the group is doing.

g. You yell at the other person to try and get them to do what you want.

h. You give someone the "silent treatment" after you've had an argument.

i. You accuse and blame the other person when things don't turn out the way you expect.

j. You say your preference when you and your friends are deciding what to do on the weekend.

Understandings to convey to advisees during the discussion:

- It is important to know the difference between **aggressive, passive,** and **assertive** behaviors.

- You have the power to say what's bothering you and what you need in a strong way without being mean or aggressive.

- Assertive responses give others important information. Nobody can read your mind and all of your feelings accurately.

- When you let people know what you're feeling, what's bothering you, and what you need assertively, you're taking care of yourself and taking care with the relationship.

- Assertive behavior is about more than a standard "I-message." Assertive behavior includes:

  Speaking from your own experience and perspective—sharing what you think

  Letting someone know how you feel and what you need without blaming or attacking the other person

  Giving concrete feedback to another person about what you observed and experienced

  Letting other people know when you're really feeling frustrated, angry, or upset so they don't have to guess your mood

  Pointing out how someone's decision or action impacts you

  Saying what you like and don't like, what you will and won't do

  Providing information that will help someone understand the situation

  Asking questions that will help you understand someone else's point of view

Asking for help when you need it

Making requests and stating your preferences

Saying "No" when you really need to

Journaling:

1. Review **Handout 17A** and ask students to journal about these questions:

   - For you, when is it easiest to be assertive? With whom? Why?

   - For you, when is it most difficult to be assertive? With whom? Why?

   - Read the notes that you wrote about the things that family members do that bug you. Choose one situation where you would like to behave more assertively and write down three possible things you could say or do in this situation.

2. Review **Handout 17B**: Assertive Responses and ask students to pick out a response that they would like to use more often in situations at home or at school. Write a dialogue between you and another person where this assertive response is your choice for how to deal with the situation.

 Activity: Guidelines for Giving Feedback

Format: **Personal conferencing**
Grouping: **Advisee-advisor and whole group**
Scheduling: **As needed**

Directions:

Modeling how to give and receive feedback is an essential tool for personal conferencing with students. The feedback process is also useful when you and your advisees are reflecting on the group's performance and behavior. Feedback gives us a process to share positives and negatives without being punitive or judgmental. By sharing observations about concrete, specific behaviors, constructive feedback separates the doer from the deed, providing information and insight that people can use to facilitate new thinking or a change in behavior. While criticism usually makes us feel too hurt or defensive to listen and assess what we're hearing, feedback keeps the lines of communication open and allows the other person to know you are paying attention.

There are many opportunities in advisory for students and the advisor to give and receive feedback—after presentations, when teaching each other new skills, after an advisee has facilitated a gathering or class meeting, or when an individual or the whole group is down in the dumps. Feedback can involve a private moment with a student or deal with the whole group. Use **Handout 18**: Feedback Form and the suggestions below to guide advisees. With practice, advisees can learn to be specific, speak from their own perspectives, and learn to suggest "You could try ..." rather than "You should try ..." Additionally, advisees can return to the group's agreements and consider whether to add one or more dealing with feedback.

Before giving feedback:

- Make a request or ask for permission ("I'd like to give you some feedback about ... Okay with you?").

- Consider issues of timing (now, later, much later).

- Find a private place to talk or create a group environment where feedback is non-threatening.

When you are giving feedback:

- Encourage the person or group to do some reflection and self-assessment first. Ask what they think about what they did or said.

- Begin with your positive reactions to the effort or behavior.

- Use concrete, specific language to describe your experience of what you saw, heard, read, felt, or experienced.

    - Name what you witnessed the person say or do: "When students gave their speeches you listened, you didn't fidget, you kept your eyes focused on the speaker—all of those things show respect and interest," or "You've been pretty quiet in advisory for a couple of weeks."

    - Give reactions from your perspective so you let someone know how the words or behavior affected you: "I liked it when you...," "I noticed that...," "I appreciated...," "What I understood from your comment was ...," or "If I were the audience, it would have been helpful to..."

- Invite the person to tell you more about the situation.

    - Encourage the person to clarify the problem/issue in more detail: "Can you say more about...?" or "Tell me a little more about your thinking behind this decision."

- Ask suggestive questions that might help someone shift their thinking: "Have you thought about...?", "What might a student or parent think after seeing/hearing this?", or "What would you need if..."

If the feedback is about negative behaviors:

- Express your feelings and spell out the specific problems. For example, you might say, "I'm concerned about ...", "I felt upset when I heard you ...," or, "I was surprised when I noticed you made several starts on this project and haven't yet turned in your final plan."

- Pause and invite the recipient to comment and provide more information.

- State your hopes and expectations and invite the person to generate suggestions for what they can do to make amends, self-correct, or change course. For example, "My hope is that you can meet with ... by Thursday. Tell me how you can make that happen."

- Sometimes you might want to review what happened and discuss what the person could do differently next time so the problem doesn't occur again.

When you receive feedback:

- FIRST, ONLY LISTEN. Take in what the other person is saying without interrupting.

- Then, ask yourself what aspects of the feedback ring true for you. You decide what you do with the feedback and how to use it. Think of feedback as a package you receive in the mail. You can choose to

1. return it to the sender because it came to the wrong address;

2. keep the package, open it, and use what's in it right away; or

3. keep it on the shelf for now and think about using it later.

Activity: Stress Management

Format: **Skill lesson, personal conferencing**
Grouping: **Individual student tasks, small-group dialogues, advisor-advisee**
Scheduling: **As needed**

Directions:
Quick Write: Ask student to write, "I feel stressed when ..." at the top of a sheet of paper. Then ask students to take two minutes to make a list of the situations in their lives that lead to feeling stressed, anxious, too pressured, or exhausted. Encourage students not to censor their thoughts, but to write down any situation that comes to mind. After two minutes, ask students to look back at their lists and circle the three situations that create the most stress for them right now.

Read and Reflect: Pass out **Handout 19A**: Stressed Out! and **Handout 19B**: Reducing Stress in My Life. Ask students to write next to 1, 2, and 3 on **Handout 19B** the three situations that create the most stress in their lives right now. Then read the Stressed Out! handout silently or as a whole group. Review the information and invite comments and questions from the group. You might want to share a situation that is particularly stressful for you and share the strategies you use to reduce stress in that situation.

Write: Using the information on **Handout 19A**, ask students to complete the responses for each of the three situations they named on **Handout 19B**.

Pair/Share: Ask students to turn to a partner and take three minutes to talk about one of the stressful situations they named and share the strategies they are going to try out to reduce the stress they experience in that situation.

Personal Conferencing: Invite students to talk about their big stressors in your personal conferencing time.

Activity: Wellness Week or Month

Format: **Small- and large-group dialogues, assemblies, skill lessons, project**
Grouping: **School-wide participation and mixing it up across groups, including boys-only and girls-only advisory groupings**
Scheduling: **One time**

Directions:

Create a Wellness Week or Wellness Month. Form a committee of students, advisors, the school nurse, and other prevention and student support staff to plan a week- or month-long series of activities that are launched with assemblies and continue in advisories, PE, and health classes. When topics related to physical and mental health, adolescent sexuality, and harassment call for equal doses of sensitivity and open, frank discussion, try pairing up advisories and separating into girls-only and boys-only groups for several sessions. Some issues that are sure to be on your list:

- Nutrition

- Exercise and sleep

- Healthy relationships

- Dating violence

- Eating disorders

- Suicide prevention

- Body image

- Depression

- Drugs, tobacco, and alcohol abuse

- Stress, anxiety, and relaxation techniques

- Assessing risk and risky behaviors

- Sexually transmitted diseases

- AIDS awareness

- Managing relationships at home

- Community based resources when you need help

- Peer counseling

- Planning for life after high school

To get the most out of discussions and presentations, have advisees find and share articles, interview health professionals and report back to advisory, survey their peers, study curricula, and lead activities. The more that they own the issues, the more effective their learning will be.

 ## Activity: Self-Care Check-up

Format: **Written reflection and personal conferencing**
Grouping: **Individual student tasks and advisee-advisor**
Scheduling: **After December holidays**

Directions:
January is a good time to check in with students about healthy life choices and what students do to take care of themselves physically, emotionally, and socially. Use **Handout 20** as a written reflection for students to assess how well they're taking care of themselves. After students complete the self-care survey, you might want to focus your next set of one-on-one conferences on self-care, inviting students to share their reactions to the survey, in what ways they feel they are taking good care of themselves, and where they would like to try something different.

Activity: Giving and Getting Support

Format:	**Written reflection and personal conferencing**
Grouping:	**Individual student tasks and advisee-advisor**
Scheduling:	**As needed**

Directions:

Resilient adolescents are able to reach out to an array of people in situations when another person's wisdom or support helps reduce feelings of anxiety, confusion, frustration, or loneliness. They also know how to access resources that will help them get what they need. Equally important, students who know ways to help themselves through rough periods are more likely to face challenging situations with a measure of confidence and optimism.

Handouts 21A and **21B** are surveys (Getting and Giving Support and 20 Ways to Support Yourself) that can be used in a number of ways. When you're conferencing with students who are having a tough time, some of the questions might provide useful entry points to explore what's going on in a student's life. In some situations, you can ask a student if she or he feels comfortable filling out the survey and meeting later to talk about her or his responses. Finally, some of the strategies suggested may be appropriate to explore with the whole class during particular times of the year (i.e. holidays, exams) when the general level of anxiety increases, or when a violent incident or national crisis makes everyone feel more vulnerable.

 ## Activity: The Violence Continuum

Format:	**Pair/share and group dialogue**
Grouping:	**Whole advisory**
Scheduling:	**One time**

Directions:

Use **Handout 22**: The Violence Continuum to discuss issues of violence and safety. Ask students to pair up and share their responses to the questions on the continuum. Then open up the discussion to the whole group.

Activity: Thinking and Talking about Harassment — Part I

Format: Skill lesson, small- and large-group dialogues, and journaling
Grouping: Whole advisory
Scheduling: During the first quarter

Directions:

A big part of making schools, classrooms, and advisories safe is letting students know the words and behaviors that cross the line from respect to harassment. Discussing harassment serves five purposes. First, it lets students know that you will be vigilant about listening and looking for words and behaviors that target, embarrass, or threaten others. Second, it gives you a chance to spell out the ways that you will intervene in situations that look or sound like harassment. Third, it gives students an opportunity to discuss their perceptions of harassment and to get clear about the school's harassment policy. Most students do not know this information and have a very narrow view of what harassment is. Fourth, it gives you a chance to introduce the language of aggressor, target, bystander, and ally. Having a common vocabulary makes it easier to link behaviors to the roles we choose to play in any situation. Finally, this discussion communicates that you expect students to share responsibility for making advisory a safe and respectful place for everyone.

1. Tell or read harassment stories: Use the story from *Chicken Soup for the Teenage Soul*, "The Most Mature Thing I've Ever Seen," to discuss the roles of aggressor, target, bystander, and ally. Or share another story that illustrates the various roles students play in a harassment situation.

2. Review roles people play in harassment situations, using **Handout 23**.

    -   **Aggressor:** (sometimes referred to as the bully) The aggressor engages in behaviors that harm, hurt, or intimidate someone physically, emotionally, or socially.

    -   **Target:** The target is the person being harassed by the aggressor. A target is bullied, attacked, insulted, excluded, or picked on physically, emotionally, and/or socially.

    -   **Bystander:** Someone who witnesses or hears about a situation in which an individual or group is being harassed and does not say anything or do anything to change the situation.

    -   **Ally:** Someone who works with and acts in support of the person or group who is being harassed and targeted.

3. Do a ten-minute "Speak-out" inviting students to do any of the following:

- Share a story about a time when you helped someone who was being harassed

- Share a story about a time when someone helped you when you were being harassed

- Share a story about a time when you wished someone had helped you or another person being harassed

OR

4. Invite students to choose to write about one or several of these questions:

    - What kinds of behaviors do you see around school that you think fall into the category of harassment or bullying?

    - Are there any particular groups or types of kids whom you see playing the aggressor/harasser role here at school? Why do you think individual students or groups do this?

    - What groups or types of kids are most likely to be targeted? Why do you think that is?

    - Thinking about yourself, choose to write about one of these questions in your journal.

    - Think about a time when you were targeted or harassed by an individual or group. What was the other person or the group doing or saying? How did that feel? Did anyone intervene as your ally? If not, what would you have wanted an ally to do?

    - Think about a time when you felt left out or laughed at. What was the other person or group doing or saying? How did it feel for you in that situation? How did you deal with the situation? Is there anything you wish you had done?

    - Think about a time when you witnessed someone else being targeted or harassed. What was going on? What did you do? If you witnessed a similar situation again, what would you say or do differently?

    - If you were targeted or harassed, what would you want a teacher to do? What would you want a friend to do? What would you want other peers to do who weren't friends with you?

5. Ask students to form groups of three or four to share their responses to these questions or take some time for students to share their responses with the whole group.

Activity: Thinking and Talking about Harassment – Part II

Format: **Skill lesson**
Grouping: **Whole advisory**
Scheduling: **Sometime during the first quarter**

Directions:

1. Web the word harassment. When you hear the word harassment, what words, phrases, or images come to mind?

2. Define harassment. Post the various definitions of harassment:

   Harassment is any inappropriate, unwanted, or cruel behavior that targets a particular individual or group.

   Bullying is a form of harassment when someone repeatedly and over time targets another person.

3. Brainstorm examples of various types of harassment.

4. Discuss the effects of harassment. Begin by asking, "How do students feel when they experience or witness harassment? How does harassment affect the school environment?"

   Note to advisors: In your conversations with advisees, you can refer to **Handout 24** for more detailed information about definitions and effects of harassment.

5. Now is the time to clarify schoolwide policies and procedures on harassment and explain what you will do if you witness any harassing behaviors.

Activity: Harassment Survey

Format: **Project, organizing and representing information**
Grouping: **Whole advisory**
Scheduling: **During the first quarter**

Directions:

1. Develop survey questions for interviews. With the whole group, brainstorm questions you could ask friends and family members about the topic of harassment. Here are a few examples:

   • "What kind of teasing really is upsetting to you?"

   • "Has someone bullied, teased, or harassed you in the last month? Where did it happen? What did someone say or do that you didn't like?"

   • "When you see someone being harassed, what do you usually do?"

2. Ask advisees to vote on the three questions they want to ask at least three friends or family members. Have students record their answers to each question so they can share the responses and you can collect all of the data.

3. Share interview results: Invite students to share the results from their interviews with friends and family.

 Activity: Countering Harassment and Bullying

Format: **Interactive exercise**
Grouping: **Whole advisory**
Scheduling: **Two advisory periods sometime during the first quarter**

Directions:

1. Work with a small group of students to prepare and act out a harassment role play in two scenes. Ask the audience to make observations about what they see and hear in each scene:

Scene One – The Act of Harassment: What type of harassment did you see? How do you know? What did bystanders say and do that allowed the harassment to continue or made the situation worse?

Scene Two – Countering Harassment: What did allies do to help stop the harassment and support the person being harassed?

2. Using **Handouts 25A**, **25B**, and **25C**, point out what allies can do to counter harassment.

    - Say the aggressor's name and show respect.

    - Name what you see, say why you don't like it, and tell the aggressor to stop.

    - Take action by:

    Helping the targeted person leave the scene;

    Going with the targeted person to report the incident; or

    Reporting the incident yourself.

3. Generate a quick list of four or five acts of harassment that students are most likely to witness at school.

4. Divide students into groups of five or six. Ask each group to choose one of the situations and develop a role play in two scenes as just demonstrated. Everyone in the group doesn't have to be in the role play, but the whole group has to agree on how they will act out both scenes.

5. Present each antiharassment role play.

6. Debrief each role play by using the questions in 1.

7. Pass out **Handout 25D**: Ally Pledge. Before advisees leave, ask each student to write down one thing they can do to be a good ally to students who are new at school, are shy, get picked on occasionally, or might not have many friends.

Many thanks to Sam Diener and Sherrie Gammage for their contributions to the harassment skill lessons.

Moving on to High School, College, or Career

 Activity: Imagining the Future

Format: **Written reflection, pair-shares, and gatherings**
Grouping: **Individual student task, small- and large-groups**
Scheduling: **One time**

Directions:

As a quick-write, pair-share, or gathering, invite students to imagine their future circumstances these ways:

- Imagine what your life would be like if you traveled in a time machine ten years into the future. If you're happy where you landed, what did you do to get there? If you're unhappy where you landed, what can you do now to change course?

- Make two predictions about things you will do in the next three months that set you on a course to a positive future. Collect the notes and pass them out to your advisees three months from now.

- One/five/ten/fifteen years from now...

  I won't see myself as ... Instead, I'll probably see myself as ...

  I'll probably be living ...

  I'll probably be dissatisfied with ...

  I'll be very happy because ...

Activity: Quotations about Moving On

Format: **Written reflection, pair-shares, and gatherings**
Grouping: **Individual student task, small- and large-groups**
Scheduling: **One time**

Directions:

Read any of the quotations on **Handout 26** as a gathering to start advisory sessions dealing with planning for the future, or have advisees select a quotation for journal reflections or pair-share conversations.

Activity: Personal Statements

Format: **Student presentation**
Grouping: **Individual student task**
Scheduling: **One time**

Directions:

One part of moving on to high school, career, or college is declaring your intentions, your hopes, your dreams, and your plans. Using **Handout 27**, discuss what students might say in a two-minute personal statement about themselves. Give students a week to prepare their personal statements and take time in class for students to pair up with a partner to rehearse and get feedback and suggestions. Have students pull a date slip that suggests a particular date to present their personal statement to the group. Make time for one student to share her or his personal statement every week.

Activity: Career Exploration I

Format: **Journaling, gatherings, representing ideas and information**
Grouping: **Individual student task**
Scheduling: **One time**

Directions:
Ask students to write a journal entry that describes at least three jobs or careers that seem interesting to them. This can become a starting point for:

- Investigating a career path and learning more about the skills, credentials, and personal qualities necessary to succeed in this career path

- A gathering go-round where students describe a job that interests them and one quality they have that would help them be good at this job

- A closing go-round where students link a job that interests them with something they have learned or learned how to do in a course they are currently taking

- Examining their current courses and academic plan to explore the pathway of courses and school activities that will prepare them for the kinds of career opportunities that interest them

- Brainstorming a list of all activities and responsibilities in and out of school, during the school year, and the summer that can help them develop a resume of skills and experiences that can prepare them to achieve their career goals

- Engaging in a career mapping/webbing activity where students can choose to organize their thinking by beginning with

  - a career that they name, and linking that career to skill sets, abilities, personal qualities, credentials, and work tasks linked to that career;

  - their personal assets, skills, and interests, and linking those to careers where their assets and interests are highly valued.

Activity: Career Exploration II

Format:	**Projects**
Grouping:	**Individual student tasks**
Scheduling:	**One-time activities, regularly scheduled check-ins with students about their individual career plans, and extended sessions to accommodate community-based career experiences**

Directions:

Use any of these ideas for career exploration projects:

1. Brainstorm a set of questions and topics that advisees can use in interviews with people and career site visits.

2. Choose to investigate three careers associated with the content area in one of your current courses.

3. Consult with your counselor about administering a career/interest survey to all of your advisees. Use the survey results to drive each student's career search.

4. Create a Careers in the Community scavenger hunt that requires students to investigate people, jobs, and educational opportunities nearby.

5. Create a top 50 list of the best web sites for various careers that students are investigating.

6. Use *The Teenager's Guide to the Real World,* by Marshall Brain, as a guide for reading, discussion, and career exploration.

7. Create a Career Week in which each advisory is responsible for designing and facilitating an event or activity during the week.

8. Join other advisories in developing a half-day event where students rotate among sessions with admissions and career counselors from community colleges, four-year colleges, technical schools, apprentice programs, and graduate schools to explore the links between various careers and educational opportunities.

9. Organize a job shadow program in your community where pairs of students shadow at least one person "on the job" each semester.

10. Help students link career searches to literacy skills by creating portfolios of job opportunities, applications, and other materials within a chosen career path. Students must show

evidence that they have used various means of collecting information and communicating with people (letter writing, personal interviews, internet search, phone call logs, e-mail.)

11. Make an alphabet chart from A to Z illustrating objects, concepts, skills, abilities, attributes, and work tasks associated with a particular career.

 ## Activity: Academic Planning for College and Career

Format: **Group dialogue, organizing and representing ideas**
Grouping: **Individual student task and small groups**
Scheduling: **As needed**

Directions:

Advisory is an excellent opportunity to clarify questions, concerns, "to do" tasks, and deadlines related to academic planning during high school as well as college and career plans. Work closely with your guidance department to coordinate when you take time to discuss and reflect on the following topics with your advisees:

- Registration of courses for the next semester or next school year

- Linking course selection to interest and career pathways

- Advance placement courses — what does it take and how do I enroll?

- Graduation requirements

- Tutorial opportunities and study groups that provide regular academic support during the school year

- Summer work, study, youth leadership, internship, and volunteer service opportunities

- College search and exploration

- Post-high school planning for students entering the work world, apprenticeships, or technical training

- College application procedures and deadlines

- Dealing with parental expectations concerning college and career choices

- Dealing with the anxiety of college acceptance week

 ## Activity: Practice Interviews

Format: **Large group-dialogue and guest presentations**
Grouping: **Whole advisory**
Scheduling: **As needed**

Directions:
Arrange for human resources specialists and high school or college admissions personnel to come to your advisory to role-play job and school interviews with your advisees. Make time to debrief role plays and even replay scenarios so students can walk away with some key tips that will help them present themselves in their best light.

Real World Connections and Service Learning

 ## Activity: Checking Out the World Students Live In

Format: **Gathering or closing**
Grouping: **Whole advisory**
Scheduling: **Occasionally**

Directions:

Check out what is on your students' minds—what they are reading, viewing, and listening to. One way to check into their world is to ask them occasionally what's happening out there. Sometimes when you have a minute or two of advisory remaining, ask your students one of these questions or bring in something to share that piqued your curiosity.

- "So it's the weekend. Got any suggestions for a video I should rent?"

- "I'm actually going home this afternoon right after school's out. If I wanted to take a look, is there anything good to watch on TV?"

- "In the last week, I've heard people say … a bunch of times. What does that mean to you and your friends?"

- Hold up the school newspaper or local paper and share an article that has a youth connection. Ask students what they think about the topic or issue.

- Sometimes when there's a new fad, fashion, or music group that grabs kids' attention and leaves you scratching your head, just ask kids, "I noticed/heard/saw … What's that all about?" A lot of kids are more than happy to tell you something they know that you don't.

- "If I have two hours this week just to hang out, what three websites should I check out? What TV shows should I watch? What radio station should I listen to?"

Activity: Introducing My Neighborhood

Format: **Organizing and representing data, interactive exercises, project**
Grouping: **Whole advisory, small groups, individual student tasks**
Scheduling: **One time**

Directions:
Depending on your school population, your advisees might or might not live near each other; they might or might not be familiar with each other's neighborhoods. Even within a single neighborhood, people identify different sites and markers as important. This exercise can help advisees know more about each other and their local community.

Ask each advisee to visualize their neighborhood, however they define it, then list several places that they think are the important spots in that neighborhood. They can name sites that are important for fun and social reasons, as well as historical, religious, civic, or other reasons. Advisees can then

- share descriptions of what sites they identify as being their neighborhood;

- show what they consider to be their neighborhood on a local map;

- create their own neighborhood maps;

- take a partner or small group on a tour of their neighborhood;

- note the most popular locations among the group;

- identify a nearby location that is unknown to all, and explore a site that is just beyond the familiar.

Activity: Teens and Freedom, Part I: What's Your Opinion?

Format: **Written reflection and large-group dialogue**
Grouping: **Whole advisory**
Scheduling: **One time**

Directions:
Handout 28 is a survey from USA WEEKEND. Over 200,000 teens took the survey that was distributed in the magazine, online, and in partnership with Channel One. You can give the survey to your advisees, then discuss your advisory results and compare with the national results.

 # Activity: Teens and Freedom, Part II: Making Your Case, Defending Your Point of View

Format: **Skill lesson and student presentations**
Grouping: **Individual student task**
Scheduling: **One time**

Directions:
Making your case in public and using the verbal tools of persuasion are important skills for work, for leadership, and for citizenship. Using any of the issues raised in the Teens and Freedom survey in the previous activity, require every student to make a persuasion speech of two minutes sometime during the year. At least a month in advance ask students to pick a date slip from a basket that identifies the time when each student will present her or his speech to the whole advisory.

Skill lesson: Before any students present their speeches, develop criteria for an effective and engaging presentation, and guidelines for being a respectful, supportive audience. Provide all advisees with **Handout 29** as a guide. Prepare and present your own two-minute speech on your favorite "hot button" topic and ask advisees to identify core elements of the speech.

Student presentations: Students love getting concrete feedback when they take the risk to claim their voice and be heard. You might want to pass out notecards on which advisees can write three feedback comments:

1. One thing I learned from the speech, or the most compelling idea in your speech …

2. One way you were effective in presenting your speech …

3. One thing you might add, leave out, or change to make the speech even more effective …

You can use this process when students want to to prepare and present their case statement and recommendations to faculty associations, student-faculty forums, school leadership teams, parent groups, or student government.

 ## Activity: Growing Up Then and Now

Format: **Interactive exercise, written reflections**
Grouping: **Individual student tasks**
Scheduling: **One time**

Directions:

This is an opportunity for students to interview family members and other adults they know to get a picture of their experiences growing up. Make copies of **Handouts 30A** and **30B**. Ask students to fill out their handouts describing their current experience and ask students to interview at least three people who were born in different decades, using any of these ideas:

• Invite students to choose questions they think would be most interesting to compare.

• What were the most surprising or unusual responses in their interviews?

• In what ways does growing up feel most similar and in what ways does it feel most different from one generation to the next?

• Find out more about the most admired people from other generations.

• Find out more about the music of other generations.

Then, share the data in advisory.

Activity: What's Doing around Town?

Format: **Reading and announcements**
Grouping: **Individual student task and team challenge**
Scheduling: **A few times a year**

Directions:

Very few students read newspapers these days. If your community has a Newspapers in Education program, check to see if you can get multiple copies several times a year. Choose to reserve papers for a day of the week when the newspaper runs youth columns or runs weekend highlights. If you spend an advisory session reading newspapers, here's a suggestion for closing the activity.

Post sections of the paper on the board before students begin reading, divide students into teams of four or five, and ask students to circle articles they read in at least three different sections. At the end of the period take ten minutes to call out sections of the paper and invite any team member to give a 20-second summary of an article in that section. Tally points for each team.

 ## Activity: Rant and Rave about the Real World

Format: **Written reflection**
Grouping: **Individual student tasks**
Scheduling: **Occasionally**

Directions:

Rants: Sometimes there's nothing like writing a good rant to get something off your chest. According to Dr. James Seitz (University of Pittsburgh) a rant is "a bombastic form of speech in which one talks extensively and excitedly without interruption." (How perfect for adolescents!) Rants often take the form of a lengthy, vehement complaint about something that the speaker finds especially annoying, or it could be a scathing expression of outrage about something the speaker feels is unfair, unjust, or just plain wrong-headed. Invite students to write a rant about a real situation at school, in their community, in the US, or in the world that triggers intense feelings of annoyance or outrage.

Raves: Writing a rave (or a panegyric to be more precise) may be a bit more challenging for some students. A panegyric is a speech in which someone or something is elaborately praised. Invite students to write a panegyric in praise of:

- a sports figure, musician, or artist who embodies perfection in pursuit of her/his craft or discipline;

- a favorite place, street, natural setting, city, building, or other site;

- the perfect meal;

- a perfect day at;

- the perfect dress or outfit;

- the perfect boyfriend/girlfriend;

- the best car on the market;

- or anything else that deserves your accolades.

 ## Activity: Quotations about Living in the Real World

Format: Journaling and written reflection, group dialogues, gatherings, closings
Grouping: Whole advisory, small groups, and/or individual student tasks
Scheduling: Occasionally

Directions:
The quotations on **Handout 31** introduce the words and ideas of prominent people who have spoken and written passionately about the roles we play in the world around us. Give students these quotations or others that you select. Use them as a springboard for any of the following activities:

1. Ask students to read the quotations, selecting two or three that capture their attention. Divide students into groups of five. Have students participate in "round robins," taking a minute each to discuss a quotation of their choice and explain why that quotation has particular meaning for them.

2. Choose any of the quotations to use as a premise for an extended journal entry, developing the ideas contained in the quotation.

3. Find news clippings, cartoons, photographs, or articles that illustrate the main idea contained in a quotation of your choosing.

4. Write about or discuss a quotation with which you strongly agree or one with which you strongly disagree.

5. Ask advisees to discuss a quotation that speaks to them, one that reflects their inner thoughts and feelings.

6. Cut the quotations into strips, put them in a basket, and ask every student to pull one. Invite students to read their quotations and make connections between themselves and the idea expressed in their quotation.

7. Use quotations to practice critical reading and reasoning skills:

   a. **Paraphrasing** — Using your own words, choose particular sentences to rewrite, while keeping the idea intact.

   b. **Summarizing** — Summarize in one clear sentence the idea contained in one of the longer quotations.

   c. **Looking for evidence** — Ask students to identify the kinds of evidence and data that would validate the truth as it is expressed in one quotation.

Activity: Exploring and Mapping Your Community

Format: **Project, organizing and representing data**
Grouping: **Whole advisory**
Scheduling: **Preparation sessions before the field trip, a field trip day, and several advisory sessions after the field trip**

Directions:
Democracies depend on an educated, engaged citizenry willing to invest their time and talents in making their communities work. Many young people have too few opportunities to genuinely explore public life in their own communities. In this mapping project, students will:

- Name, investigate, and describe institutions, organizations, programs, and places that are part of public life in their community

- Use various documentation tools to explore public life in their community

- Use their discoveries and data to construct maps of what they learned about their community

- Create several giant maps that reflect their discoveries about their community

The objectives of this project are to explore, become more familiar with, and feel more a part of one's community. If this design is more involved than your advisory can handle, you can use simpler formats, like a treasure hunt of civic and historical places. Using maps and collecting facts, photos, and rubbings will still be worthwhile.

Before the field trip you will need to:
- Arrange permission for a field trip day (during a mild weather season) for your students. Ideally, you will need two busses for four to five hours, so that students can be dropped off and picked up at various places in the community to gather information and document their experiences. You will also need to reserve a space in a local park for lunch.

- Arrange to have enough volunteers (parents or other adults) go with you on the field trip so that each student group has an adult with them, and each bus has a bus route guide who tracks drop-offs and pickups for different groups during the field trip.

- Gather documentation tools that students will use on their field trip, such as cameras (regular, panorama, and telephoto disposable cameras are terrific for this kind of activity), tape recorders, note cards, clipboards, pencils, sketch paper, crayons for rubbings, sticky notes to attach to artifacts, etc.

- Gather street maps of your community (each student group needs at least one).

- Before the field trip, collect five dollars from each student for lunch and artifact purchases. You will be pooling all the money, so if some students are not able to bring in money, it's okay.

- Map out the bus route ahead of time. Arrange for drop-offs and pickups of different groups during the field trip.

- Gather project materials for construction of maps (large poster board, construction paper, scissors, staplers, tape, glue sticks, string, rulers, markers, etc.) and equipment for printing and publishing.

Pre-Field Trip Instructions

1. Explain that students will be taking a field trip to explore public life in their community. They will document their discoveries and use all of their data to create giants maps that depict what they've learned. Students will be working in four different groups to gather data during the field trip.

2. Divide students into four task groups. These groups will continue to work together during the field trip and afterwards when they create their maps. Post the four tasks on newsprint, summarized as follows:

   1. Document the commercial and business life of your community and the public spaces, "street furniture," and signage found there.

   2. Document the cultural, educational, recreational, and spiritual life of your community.

   3. Document the human and health-care services in your community.

   4. Document the civic life in your community (local, state, and federal government institutions).

   Elicit examples of each sector of civic life and pass out and review **Handout 32A**: Places and Institutions in Public Life. Remind students that they can use this handout as a reference for their exploration.

3. Have students arrange themselves in their task groups and pass out general instructions, **Handout 32B**, and specific instructions for their group, **Handout 32C**, **D**, **E**, or **F**. As you monitor groups, remind them that every student needs to take primary responsibility for one of the four tasks on her or his instruction sheet. Make sure that interview questions for tasks 3 and 4 have been formatted into interview survey forms, so that each group member

has at least ten forms to use for obtaining interviews. Ask one or two people in each task group to be prepared to summarize what they will be doing on the field trip.

4. Pass out final instructions for the field trip. Add any other necessary instructions, suggestions, or notes to the instructions below

Things You Will Need To Do

- Ask for several bags along the way for collecting your stuff.

- Take photographs at each stop, including pictures of people, objects, and places. Record the number of each photo with its location.

- Every person in your group should complete at least five interviews.

- Create several sketches, drawings, or crayon rubbings of objects and places at each location.

- Attach sticky notes to each object, artifact, and document you collect to note where it's from.

5. Divide the money you have collected into five portions. (You need to use the fifth portion to purchase drinks, cups, utensils, and plates for the picnic.)

6. Give one portion to each group with the following charges:

Group 1--->You have $_____ to purchase artifacts from places you visit. You must spend all of your money.

Group 2--->You have $_____ to purchase enough snacks, fruit, desserts, and finger food to provide lunch for the whole class.

Group 3--->You have $_____ to purchase enough main entree food to provide lunch for half the class.

Group 4--->You have $_____ to purchase enough main entree food to provide lunch for half the class.

Field Trip Day

1. Make sure all arrangements have been made.

2. Leave about 45 minutes at the end of the field trip for lunch. Collect the film from each group, and have it developed before the next advisory.

After the Field Trip

1. Have all the materials available for groups to use for their projects.

    *   Groups need a large piece of poster board for each street or location that they explored, a map showing the locations of the places they visited, and all of the things they collected.

    *   Groups need to decide how they will design a map of each location, showing directions and locations of each place they visited.

    *   Groups need to decide how they will display and attach objects, documents, and photos to the map.

    *   On each map, groups need to place a title, a legend, and any written annotations to explain photos, drawings, etc.

    *   Survey question groups need to collate and summarize their data, highlight the most frequent and surprising responses, and put their findings in a graphic display.

Final Period

1. Give each group about ten minutes to explain their maps to the rest of the class. Ask each person to highlight something they discovered that was interesting, surprising, curious, or compelling.

2. Share final thoughts about the project, using any of the following questions:

    *   Before this project, I thought … Now I think …

    *   Before this project, I didn't know … Now I understand …

    *   I wonder what would happen if …

    *   I wish we had more time to …

    *   I still don't understand why/how …

    *   I thought it was fun when we …

    *   Before this project, I never thought I would …

Assessment

Ask each student to write about what she or he learned in this project using any of these questions:

1. What three things did you like best about your group's project?

2. What's one thing you liked about each of the other groups' projects?

3. What five things did you learn about public life in your community that you didn't know before?

4. Who was the most interesting person you encountered? What made this person someone people should know?

5. What did you do in this project that you've never done before?

6. If you were the mayor, what recommendations would you make to improve the physical environment and improve the civic life of the community?

7. What parts of this project did you like the best? Like the least? What was most challenging for you about this project?

Plan to display the mapping projects in your school, the local library, or an elementary school where they can be used by younger students in their studies of the local community.

 ## Activity: Service-Learning Projects

Format: **Projects**
Grouping: **Individual student tasks, small groups, or whole advisory**
Scheduling: **Multiple sessions, possibly including an extended single block**

Directions:

Short-term and long-term service-learning projects are rich opportunities for advisees to learn about their communities and the larger world and about their own passions and sense of efficacy, as well as how to collaborate. Some schools require students to find and carry out their own projects; others engage the whole group, perhaps on a community service day.

The following principles will make the experience more successful:

- Attend to the service component and to the learning component. To have the opportunity to research why the service is needed and to reflect on how to have an impact are what turn a service project into a service-learning project.

- Students should finish service-learning projects with the feeling that they are capable of having an impact, not overwhelmed about the enormity of problems that they cannot understand or change. Choose projects that are developmentally appropriate, manageable, and will offer some sense of success.

- Look to make connections or follow a theme across projects, and from projects to classes. Students will learn that service takes commitment and understanding.

- Service-learning projects employ many interpersonal and intrapersonal skills. Interpersonal skills needed will minimally include group decision-making, collaborating, listening, and feedback. Intrapersonal skills needed are likely to include motivating oneself, persevering, fulfilling commitments, and self-reflection. Both sets of skills should be supported proactively.

- Short-term as well as long-term projects are likely to employ many academic skills, such as research, writing, organizing data, or planning a budget, so supporting the application of those skills will also be important.

- Each stage of a service-learning project has its own learning value, though advisees may be eager to jump into the service stage. Try to find a pace that engages them in planning and research, neither of which are required to be done purely from the classroom. Early stages might include collecting data, interviews, or other active processes.

- Be careful not to foist an adult concern onto young people. Kids should not finish a service-learning experience and think adults have abdicated their responsibilities.

As you and your group think about possible service-learning projects, reflect on the goals of your advisory program as a whole. Goals of career preparation, the development of social responsibility, or adolescent health and wellness, for example, might point toward certain choices over others.

There is an infinite array of service-learning opportunities that can be excellent experiences for your advisory group, whether advisees pick their own individual projects, work in small groups, or work with the whole advisory group. Part of the learning is in the choosing of a project. Some ways to start the selection process are:

- Doing a community study, noting needs that could be addressed

- Interviewing community leaders and members and/or reading local newspapers to identify needs

- Holding a large-group dialogue focused on the question: What's great about our community? What would make it a better place to live? Depending on your goal and frame of reference, you could look beyond your immediate community to state, national, and global issues as well.

- Asking advisees in a large-group dialogue: What are the issues that you and your peers have to deal with these days? What service might be of use to teenagers?

- Brainstorming possible topics, followed by pairs of students investigating what might be involved and reporting back to the whole group

- Asking advisees: What issues really interest or concern you?

- Read a story about making a difference or changing neighborhoods, and see what ideas it inspires. (See *Seedfolks* example below.)

Below is a sampling of service-learning projects.

- As a group, read the (very short) book, *Seedfolks* (Paul Fleischman, 1997). Through 13 points of view statements, *Seedfolks* describes neighbors who get to know each other and build a community by turning a vacant lot into a garden. Advisees might be inspired to tackle a vacant lot, to record and share important stories, to collect evidence of a culturally changing community, or to organize a cultural celebration.

- Any of the projects described above could be done without connecting to a novel and still go in many potential directions. Advisees who interview neighbors of a vacant lot or building, for example, might find out what residents need most and make a proposal to their local government.

- Sign up as a group or individually for work in a service-providing agency, such as homeless shelters, soup kitchens, day care centers, animal shelters, or many other organizations. Serving over a period of time will encourage deeper learning, as well as well-structured preparation and follow-up reflections. Why are people homeless? How did you feel during your first visit to the shelter? How did that change over time? Or, why is it good to read to little kids? How do you pick good books to read to them? What would it take for them to have more books of their own?

- Consider environmental projects, such as monitoring acidity in a local lake and reporting results to a state agency, or monitoring and reducing electricity or water use at school. While some schools define service as directly helping other people, others define it more broadly — helping people, animals, or our planet.

- Select an issue that affects students in your school, such as needing information about health issues, or what is available to do in the afternoons. Advisees might identify health resources for peers, conduct a survey, make a proposal, or organize an ongoing study café, weekly frisbee afternoons, or a club of some sort.

- Focus on a topic that could influence how students relate to the school neighborhood, such as local shopkeepers or neighboring residents. Do store owners think shoplifting is a problem? How does it affect them? Advisees could run a campaign to influence their peers.

- The advisory group can sign up individually or together for a walkathon or other worthy fund-raiser. The service and learning can be more than raising money for a good cause. Advisees can do research the issue, advocate to parents and neighbors why it is important, and learn coordinating and planning skills.

- Service-learning can focus on advocacy, learning to have a voice in a democratic society. Students can research local, state, or national issues, then speak or write to appropriate leaders.

- Offer a service, such as snow shoveling for elderly neighbors, or baby-sitting for single moms.

Be sure to provide opportunities to reflect on the project in writing and/or in discussions at various stages. What do you expect to learn? What skills will be needed? What skills might you improve during this project? What did you learn about the issue, about our community, and about yourself? How would you assess your skills at the end of the project?

 Activity: Discussing World Events and Global Crises

Format: **Gatherings, journaling, small- and large-group dialogues**
Grouping: **Pairs, small groups, and whole advisory**
Scheduling: **Occasionally**

Directions:
Starting the Conversation
When discussing national or world events that generate controversy and deeply divided opinion, use an inquiry-based model of dialogue. Begin by describing the event or issue in a few phrases; then assess what students know, and follow their questions. You can begin with four basic questions:

- What are you fairly certain you know?

- What do you think you know, but are not sure of?

- What are your questions?

- What are the sources of your information?

These questions will raise the issues that are most salient for your students. Helping students to be more conscious of the ideas, values, and evidence upon which they base their opinions and make informed judgments is vital preparation for citizenship in a democracy.

Ethics and International Crises

Crisis events provide an opportunity to think through the many kinds of ethical dilemmas associated with global conflicts. Invite students to consider the ethical standards by which we should judge the actions of the US and those of other nations. The following questions can be starting points for exploring ethical standards of behavior in any national or international crisis:

1. Does the action inflict more or less harm on all or some groups affected by the action?

2. Does the action force anyone to engage in immoral or illegal acts?

3. Does the action contribute to greater safety and security in the short run and/or the long run?

4. Do the goals and desired outcomes of an action justify the means?

5. Does what is right, fair, and moral for one group or government conflict with what is right, fair, and moral for another group?

6. Is the desired action safe, smart, legal, and equitable for all/some groups?

7. Does the desired action meet important interests of all groups involved in the situation?

How can I deal with the wide range of opinions students may have?

When discussing issues of war and peace, violence, and terrorism, it's helpful to distinguish between issues of patriotism and opinions of specific government policies. In addition, we can encourage students to clarify whether their opinions are about the character and actions of nations/governments or those of the people who are citizens within a particular nation/government. We can also communicate to students that different viewpoints add to our understanding of an issue rather than subtract from it. As Gandhi said, "Everyone has a piece of the truth." The right for all voices to be heard is at the heart of what it means to live in a democracy.

When discussing controversial issues, teach students how to engage in nonadversarial dialogue, rather than debate. In dialogue, the goal is to listen, to learn from others' perspectives, to understand ourselves and others more deeply, and to be open to shifting our beliefs and opinions. Debate emphasizes proving that you are right and that the other person/group is wrong. Structure the conversation as a dialogue, where there is time to explore various positions and the specific needs and interests underlying these positions. This is an opportunity to hear a diversity of feelings and opinions and a chance to learn from each other.

You may want to have students formalize a respectful way of disagreeing by asking them to state their disagreements by saying, "I see things differently. I think that …", rather than telling other students that they are wrong. It is important that you and your students find ways to affirm different perspectives even if they are unpopular. Take time for students to process their thoughts and feelings.

Although controversial issues can produce tensions and strong feelings, these are the very qualities of conversation that engage adolescents' intense interest and curiosity. Whether you make time every week to talk about what's happening in the world or set aside a few minutes once in a while, these dialogues can help students complicate their thinking and gain confidence in their ability to talk about what's going on around them. If we allow students' questions and concerns to shape the conversation, we will have taught and listened well.

Personal Passions, Hobbies, and Interests

 Activity: How Do You Like to Learn?
What Do You Like to Do?

Format: **Reading, organizing, and representing ideas and information**
Grouping: **Individual student task**
Scheduling: **One time**

Directions:
Handout 33 is a quick guide to Howard Gardner's theory of eight intelligences. This can be used in the following ways:

- Students can identify strengths, preferences, and growing edges — ways of learning that are outside their comfort zone.

- Students can discuss the matches between what they like to do and courses they are taking. What courses offer the best matches? What's the evidence that these courses are a good match?

- In what courses are there very few or no matches? How can you use your preferred intelligences more strategically to get more out of these classes?

- Students can map or chart their intelligence preferences on a large piece of paper and use this as a gateway to career exploration within your advisory or in conjunction with other career exploration activities sponsored by the guidance department.

- Students can set goals for building new competencies in one intelligence every quarter.

- If independent learning projects are part of your advisory program, you might require students to use at least three intelligences in developing a presentation or creating a product.

 ## Activity: Personal Interest Inventory

Format: **Written reflection**
Grouping: **Individual student task**
Scheduling: **One time**

Directions:

Invite students to complete these sentence stems or invite students to choose two or three to write about more expansively, sharing specific experiences that illustrate a particular interest.

1. Something I do outside of school that is very important in my life is …

2. One thing I can teach others is …

3. Three things I love to do with my friends are …

4. My favorite music group/TV show/movie/website/athlete/radio station is …

5. Something I like/enjoy doing that would surprise people is …

6. Three jobs I expect to have sometime in my life are …

7. The job I want most in my life is …

8. Three things I will need to do to get this job are …

9. Things in which I participate at school are: sports/community service/clubs/special groups/other …

10. Before I finish high school, I would like to learn how to …

Activity: Passionate Presenters

Format: **Student or guest presentations**
Grouping: **Whole advisory**
Scheduling: **Regularly scheduled throughout the year**

Directions:
Ask each student to make a presentation at least one time during the school year. Students can choose to

- share something about a topic on which they are an expert;

- teach something to everyone in the group;

- read a passage that has personal meaning for them;

- facilitate a discussion of a topic of their choice.

For guest presentations, you might hold the expectation that each student invite a guest to advisory to share her or his stories, experiences, career, or unusual hobby. Each student should make the arrangements for the guest to come and introduce the guest to the advisory group.

 ## Activity: Wall of Fame

Format: **Announcements**
Grouping: **Individual student task**
Scheduling: **Weekly or monthly**

Directions:
Create a Wall of Fame in your room where you and students can post pictures and articles about students in your advisory or about groups and events in which your advisees are involved outside or inside school.

Activity: Teen Trading Bin

Format: **Project**
Grouping: **Whole advisory**
Scheduling: **Ongoing**

Directions:
Create a Teen Trading Bin. Place a box somewhere in your classroom where kids can drop in magazines, paperback books, computer games, tapes, etc., that they don't want anymore and want to trade for something else. As long as they've put something in the box, they can take something out.

 ## Activity: Exploratorium

Format: **Games and projects**
Grouping: **Small groups and individual student tasks**
Scheduling: **Regularly scheduled**

Directions:
If you have advisory every day or several times a week, you can schedule a weekly or bi-monthly Exploratorium where you and your advisees can explore different interests, issues, projects, and topics. Here are a few ways to set up a regularly scheduled Exploratorium.

- Brainstorm a list of activities and projects people would like to do during the year. Then each student can vote for three to five choices on the list. Once you have the top ten preferences, you and the students can create a schedule for when to do what during the course of the school year.

- Another option is to reach consensus on two or three activities that your advisory will do on a weekly or biweekly basis for six to eight weeks. Each student signs up for one activity and continues to meet and work with that activity group for each Exploratorium session.

Activity: Passion Project

Format: **Project**
Grouping: **Individual student task**
Scheduling: **Regularly scheduled**

Directions:

Many schools want to encourage students to explore their personal passions and interests more deeply, but don't know how to carve out the time within regular course work to make this happen. Advisory can be the container for a yearly independent project where students choose to become experts about something that captures their attention, long-term interest, and motivation. Passion projects enable students to meet standards across disciplines, use research and investigation tools to explore their chosen topics, sustain an effort over extended time, and use a variety of media to communicate and demonstrate what they have learned. These projects can strengthen home-school communication if advisors and parents are expected to check in with students at various stages of project planning, research, and completion.

 Activity: Did You Know?

Format: **Announcements**
Grouping: **Whole advisory**
Scheduling: **Occasionally**

Directions:

We've never met a kid who didn't perk up when asked to talk about her or his unusual experiences or special knowledge. When you have opportunities, invite students to share their unique perspectives by saying, "We have a resident expert on ... What can you tell us about ...?"

Rituals, Celebrations, Transitions, and Closure

 ## Activity: Thought or Story of the Week

Format: **Announcements**
Grouping: **Whole advisory**
Scheduling: **Weekly**

Directions:
During the year, ask each advisee to contribute a thought or story for the week. If you make this a weekly routine, every student will have at least a turn or two before the year is over. Keep books around that students can draw from: *Chicken Soup for the Teen-age Soul, Seven Habits for Highly Effective Teens, Golden Nuggets*, books of quotations and meditations for young people. This kind of activity does triple duty: every student chooses something to share with the whole group; every student plays the roles of both speaker and audience; and every week you've created an opportunity for quiet listening and reflection.

 ## Activity: Team Congratulations

Format: **Announcements**
Grouping: **Whole advisory**
Scheduling: **As earned**

Directions:
When every student has completed a project, performed satisfactorily on an assessment, or accomplished something as a team or house—do something special to acknowledge how much you appreciate their efforts. You might consider

1. composing a written thank-you note that you read to the group and post on the class's bulletin board space;

2. a public announcement by the principal;

3. posting a giant "Congratulations" sign when every student in the advisory has endured and successfully completed a particularly challenging project or lesson;

4. naming or eliciting from students the qualities and skills the group used successfully to accomplish a task;

5. Passing out colored ballpoint pens that you've bought in bulk.

 ## Activity: Give Them Something to Cheer About!

Format: **Assembly**
Grouping: **Mixing it up across groups or school-wide participation**
Scheduling: **Occasionally or seasonal benchmarks**

Directions:
Here are some ideas that give large groups something to cheer about:

- Celebrate important milestones and accomplishments of individual faculty and students, student groups and faculty departments, grade levels, or the whole school. Do this in a way that crosses groups and interests, highlights people's significant contributions and achievements within school and in their lives outside of school, recognizes personal milestones (a new baby, 30 years on the job, perfect student attendance) and collective accomplishments (increased grade point average for the 10th grade, the biology department's results of its community-based investigation of toxic waste dumps, the school's collective volunteer hours in the community, the number of students who participated in …, etc.).

- Create opportunities for advisories to share their service learning projects or internships.

- Kick off "theme weeks" by thanking those who organized it, announcing the week's events and activities, and providing a five-minute inspirational story, quotation, or challenge to think about as the week unfolds.

- Celebrate progress and solutions to problems that impact most people in the building. Give student-faculty committees or task forces an opportunity to discuss the problem, the data they collected, the criteria and constraints they needed to consider in developing possible solutions, and their recommendations.

Activity: Recognize Individual Accomplishments In and Out of the Classroom

Format: **Gathering, journaling, or pair-shares**
Grouping: **Whole advisory**
Scheduling: **A week or so before longer vacations**

Directions:

Recognizing individual accomplishments is as important as recognizing whole-group successes. Our competitive "I win, you lose" culture too often doesn't support taking pleasure in the accomplishments of others. Create opportunities that encourage students to appreciate the efforts of their peers.

In addition, we don't often recognize students' talents and competencies if they aren't used in the classroom. When you acknowledge that students do important things in their lives outside of school, you have the power to help students broaden their definitions of success and excellence, as well as break down stereotypical views of their classmates. Every time a student says to herself, "Wow, I didn't know that about …. That's awesome!," something good has happened in your advisory group.

Activity: Transitions to Holidays

Format: **Gathering, journaling, or pair-shares**
Grouping: **Whole advisory**
Scheduling: **A week or so before longer vacations**

Directions:

Holidays and vacations are not always entirely positive times for young people, from the interruption of reassuring school routines to the loss of daily social connections, to stressful family dynamics when who's "family" looks different and involves more people. For many students, school is the place where ongoing peer friendships and important relationships with adults can make conflicts and stresses at home more manageable. It's helpful for students to think about how things change when school's not in the mix for a couple of weeks or months. Invite students to talk with each other (in pairs or small groups), share their responses to any of these questions with the class, or write in their journals.

Winter Vacations

- What do you look forward to the most/the least during the holidays?

- What's particularly fun and/or stressful about the holidays for you?

- What kinds of plans are you making so you can connect to people in ways that are important to you?

- When you feel stressed, what are two or three things you can do that help you take care of yourself?

- What's one special thing you want to do for a family member that lets her/him know you care about them?

- What's one way you help keep peace in the family over the holidays? If you could have it or do it, what's something that would make this vacation a good experience for you?

 ## Activity: Preparing for the End of the School Year

Format: **Gatherings, journaling, personal connections, and closings**
Grouping: **Whole advisory**
Scheduling: **End of the year**

Directions:

Late spring comes with many challenges for students about attending fully, staying focused, meeting deadlines, studying for exams, and preparing for time out of school. Advisory groups can help coach and coax students through the last several weeks of school more responsibly and gracefully. Questions and topics below are discussion starters.

1. Helping students stay focused

- Why am I here? What is my goal today/this week?

- What makes it hard to focus during this time of the year? Do problem-solving about each of the reasons that are stated.

- Calculate the number of hours from now till the end of the year, set specific goals so those many hours will be well spent.

- Plan advisor sessions for outside the building with conversation before (about goals and commitments) and after (did it work to be outside?).

2. Anxiety about leaving for the summer

- What are your plans for the summer? Brainstorm ideas.

- What's one goal you have for yourself this summer?

- What's great about leaving for the summer? What's hard about it?

- What questions are you asking yourself about the summer?

- What are your resources or support during the summer?

- See if advisees want to set times with each other for getting together.

- (If you want to make this offer) Advisor offers one or two get-togethers.

- Discuss the sentences: Time is scary. Time is powerful.

- Do research to find out what you could do/see around town. This could be done as an advisory field trip. If done in jigsaw fashion, each advisory would take a different part of town or set of sites, go there, gather information, then all meet together for lunch and the afternoon to share information and make plans. This could include anything from museums and historic walks to service projects and gardening.

3. Exam-related issues

- Acknowledge anxieties; talk about them out loud.

- Talk through good preparation.

- Map out time lines and specific plans for getting ready.

- Count down days with tips and reminders.

- Invite students to write a card that includes self-talk and encouraging statements that will help them get through exam week.

Activity: 10 End-of-the-Year Rituals

Format: **Gatherings, journaling, personal connections, and closings**
Grouping: **Whole advisory**
Scheduling: **End of the year**

Directions:

Activities that focus on closure and celebration are important aspects of big events like graduation and awards assemblies, but they are not perceived as central to life in the classroom. We get so caught up in the testing and grading cycle that it takes incredible discipline to invite students to stop and reflect on the school year. Develop rituals that give students the opportunity to reflect on what they've learned, appreciated, and experienced in your advisory program and throughout their daily lives at school. Here are some starting points.

1.   **Appreciation Notes:** Give every student the name of someone in the advisory. Their task is to write a note to that person that might include something they appreciated about this person as an advisory member; something they got to know about this person that they found interesting; something this person did in advisory that they thought was cool, funny, smart, impressive, or unexpected; something they'll remember about this person. Collect the cards and pass them out on the last day.

2.   **Create a Memories Bulletin Board:** Students can write their responses to any of these sentence starters:

     •   One thing I won't forget about advisory is ...

     •   I'm no longer uncomfortable about ... Advisory has helped me ... about ...

     •   For me, the best thing about this year has been ...

     •   In September, I thought ... Now, I think ...

     •   Advisory got me to think more about ...

     •   The biggest challenge for me this year was...

     •   I surprised myself this year by ...

     •   The one thing I never want to do again is ...

     •   One thing I really learned how to do well this year is ...

- Goodbye … Hello …

3. **Closing Thoughts:** In your last advisory session, ask each student to share a response to one of the sentence starters above.

4. **Closing Journal Entries:** If students kept a journal, ask them to write about any of the sentence starters above or any of the questions suggested in the letter-writing activity below.

5. **Stories:** Share some memorable moments and stories from this year.

6. **Assessing Your Advisory Goals:** Review the big goals and expectations you set for advisory this year. Discuss whether and how successfully your advisory met them.

7. **Banners:** Create a congratulations banner or poster that acknowledges what students have accomplished during the year.

8. **Thank You Notes to Staff:** Invite students to spend a few minutes writing thank you notes to teachers, administrators, and unsung friends and helpers at school.

9. **Appreciation Notes or Appreciation Tokens to Advisees:** Make the time to write a personal note to each advisee, noting something you appreciated about them this year, a positive change you noticed as the year progressed, a challenge they met, one way they earned your respect and admiration, and/or something you will remember about them. Another option is to find a little toy or trinket that reflects something important that you learned about each of your advisees this year. Give each student an appreciation token when you share your story about him or her.

10. **Letter to New Advisees:** 6th or 9th graders can write letters to students who will be entering their school. Here are some ideas for what students might include in their letters.

    - What can you look forward to doing/learning/contributing in advisory?

    - What are two things you liked best this year and two things they could try to change?

    - What was your biggest challenge this year? How did you meet this challenge? What did you learn about yourself?

    - What did you find fun or interesting?

    - What was the biggest surprise for you this year?

    - If students want to learn the ropes to be successful in school, what should they know?

Rainy-Day Fun Stuff

These are activities to do

- when you and your group have hit the wall and everyone needs a break from the routine;

- when you want to surprise everyone just for the fun of it;

- when you're not prepared and just don't have it together;

- during exam weeks, high school and college acceptance week, and other times when kids are winding down from a particularly grueling week;

- and of course, when you've had a relentless run of bad weather that's made everyone a little cranky!

 **Activity: Time Out for Games**

Format: **Games**
Grouping: **Small groups**
Scheduling: **Monthly**

Directions:
Everyone loves games and puzzles of some sort. Invite students to contribute board games, word games, puzzles, mazes, or brain twisters to your "rainy day" box and set aside one day a month for game day when students can facilitate games they know and learn to play games they don't.

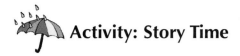 **Activity: Story Time**

Format:	**Reading**
Grouping:	**Whole advisory**
Scheduling:	**As needed**

Directions:
A lot of children's literature rings true for people of any age. Read some of your favorite picture books, especially ones that are filled with humor, wisdom, and/or silliness. [*The Stupids....* books (James Marshall), *Click, Clack, Moo: Cows That Type* (Doreen Cronin), *Oh, The Places You'll Go!* (Dr. Seuss), *How Are You Peeling?: Foods with Moods* (Saxton Freymann and Joost Elffers) are some of our favorites!]

 **Activity: Let's Eat**

Format:	**Gathering**
Grouping:	**Whole advisory**
Scheduling:	**As needed**

Directions:
Bring fruit and cookies, do a pot-luck breakfast, do a theme party with snacks, or have a DESSERTS-is-STRESSED-spelled-backwards party.

 **Activity: Afternoon or Evening at the Movies**

Format:	**Project**
Grouping:	**Whole advisory**
Scheduling:	**One extended advisory time or after school**

Directions:
Schedule a time to go see a movie that generates high interest from the students and will provide interesting conversation afterwards. Reserve a place to go after the movie for snacks and good conversation.

 **Activity: Cafeteria Birthday Party**

Format:	**Gathering**
Grouping:	**Whole advisory**
Scheduling:	**Quarterly**

Directions:
Every quarter, meet your advisees in the cafeteria for a quarterly birthday celebration. Reserve a table, bring a tablecloth, get plates and utensils from the cafeteria, provide a cake (encourage students to pitch in a dollar or volunteer to bake a cake), have everyone sign a card for each birthday recipient, and get other ideas from students that will make this a fun celebration.

 Activity: Stand Out in the Crowd

Format:	**Project**
Grouping:	**Whole advisory**
Scheduling:	**One time**

Directions:
This activity definitely has a goofy quotient of ten, and sometimes that's just what you need to lighten up the load that everyone's feeling. Bring any one of the following items to advisory, so that your advisees can stand out in the crowd for the rest of the day:

- glitter fingernail polish so that everyone can paint their pinky finger nails

- face paint and costume makeup to liven up one side of everyone's face

- temporary, wash-off tattoos to put on arms, ankles, or wrists

- all kinds of stickers to create a graphic touch on the leg of your pants or the back of a shirt or jacket

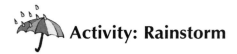 **Activity: Rainstorm**

Format: **Gathering**
Grouping: **Whole advisory**
Scheduling: **One time**

Directions:

When you've had too much dreary rainy weather or everyone is wishing for some rain, here's an energizer that gets everyone up and moving and takes about ten minutes. Participants "make a rainstorm" by making a series of sounds in sequence. (Think of the wave in baseball stadiums.)

1. Gather everyone standing in a circle. As the facilitator, stand in the middle of the circle and say:

   "We are going to make a rainstorm from the first sounds of a shower, to the sounds of a downpour, to the end of the storm. We will make four different sounds. Follow me as I do them."

   1. Rub your hands together to make a swishing sound.

   2. Snap your fingers — right hand, left hand, right hand, left hand, etc.

   3. Slap your thighs — right, left, right, left — very fast.

   4. Stamp your feet — right, left, right, left — very fast.

2. "Now, I need a volunteer to be first. Okay, I will start by rubbing my hands together and you do exactly what I do every time I turn back to you in the circle. For everyone else, when the person on your right starts making a sound, you make exactly the same sound, and you keep making that same sound until the person on your right begins making another sound. Then you make the new sound. At the end, as I turn around in the circle the last time, I will keep criss-crossing my open hands — that is the signal to stop making all sound — so you stop after the person on your right has stopped. Any questions? Okay, let's try it."

3. Keep rotating around the circle, making the first sound until you again face the person who began making the first sound. Then change to the second sound and continue around the circle, changing sounds each time you arrive at the person who began the rainstorm. Here's the sequence:

1. Rub your hands together

2. Snap your fingers alternately

3. Slap your thighs alternately

4. Stamp your feet alternately

5. Slap your thighs alternately

6. Snap your fingers alternately

7. Rub your hands together

8. Criss-cross your open hands (palms outward) as a signal to stop all sound

4. You can conclude by saying, "That sounded great. We created something together that we could not create by ourselves. Give yourselves a hand."

Handouts

Community-Building, Group Cohesion, Group Maintenance

Orientation, School Citizenship, and School Business

Personal Goal-Setting, Reflection, and Self-Assessment

Tools for School and Learning

Life skills, Healthy Development, and Self-care

Moving On to High School, College, and Career

Real World Issues and Service Learning

Personal Passions, Hobbies, and Interests

HANDOUT 1

Silent Squares Puzzle Problem

Enlarge each square to 6 inches by 6 inches.

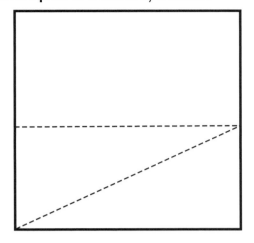

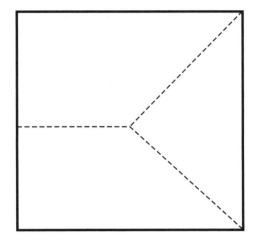

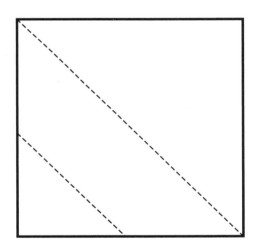

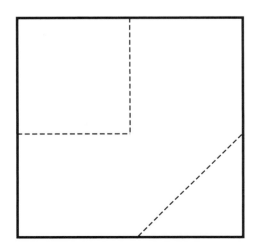

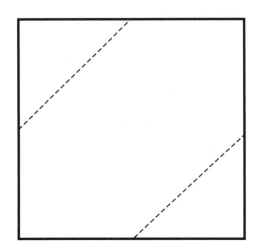

HANDOUT 2

Who's Going to the Concert?

Answer: Juan, Peter, Sam, David, Abdul, Carlos, Pang, Jill, and Kim

Who will be going to the concert?

The concert takes place on this coming Saturday night.

After being given a free ticket to the concert, Juan has decided to go.

Kamal, Keisha, and Jeff are good friends; they've agreed never to go to a concert unless all three of them can go together.

Susan will be going to the concert as long as she doesn't have to baby-sit that night. She baby-sits Juan's little brother on Friday or Saturday every week.

Jennifer is new in town. She knows only one person, her next-door neighbor, Rachel. Jennifer will go if Rachel goes.

Peter doesn't really like pop music, but he's good friends with Sam; so if Sam goes, Peter will go.

Sam got a poor grade on his last Biology lab and he can't go to the concert unless someone can help him understand genetics and prepare for the next exam.

David wants Sam to go to the concert, since it's Sam's favorite group. David is a science whiz. He will tutor Sam in genetics.

Michael has a 10 p.m. curfew on weeknights and a midnight curfew on weekends.

The concert is scheduled from 9:30 p.m. until 12:30 p.m.

Abdul will go to the concert if an adult drives them and picks them up.

Carlos's father will drive Carlos to the concert and will volunteer to give other kids a ride.

Kamal, Keisha, and Jeff have pooled all of their money, but they still don't have enough for three tickets.

Rachel just bought a bunch of new CD's and doesn't have enough money for a concert ticket.

Pang had an argument with Jill, and Jill stomped off without resolving it. Pang won't go to the concert if Jill goes, unless Jill apologizes and agrees to resolve the conflict.

Jill feels bad about leaving after she got mad at Pang. Jill's decided to call Pang, apologize, and talk it out so they can resolve the conflict.

Kim will go if the group is less than ten people. Kim doesn't like big groups, because they're too much of a hassle, and it's too easy to get in trouble.

Juan's family needs Susan to baby-sit this Saturday night.

HANDOUT 3

Adding or Subtracting — What's My Impact?

The Positives

There are many different skills and behaviors that add to a group's effectiveness. When everyone knows about these skills and behaviors and can talk about them, the group can more easily improve the way it works together. On the chart below, rate yourself on a scale from one to five, where
1 is low (you don't like or are not great at this role) and
5 is high (you like this role and play it well).
Then think of a person—in or out of school—who uses this skill really well.

Positive group skills, Behaviors that encourage collaboration	Rate yourself low----high	Name a role model
Initiating/problem-solving: proposing ideas, suggesting next steps, experimenting, carefully confronting disruptive behaviors	1 2 3 4 5	
Organizing/coordinating: keeping the group on track, focusing on goals, suggesting timelines, proposing fair division of labor	1 2 3 4 5	
Seeking: identifying what information and resources are needed, doing research, connecting different ideas, asking related questions	1 2 3 4 5	
Encouraging: encouraging everyone's participation and thinking, praising efforts, staying positive	1 2 3 4 5	
Harmonizing: checking on feelings, sensing when the group needs a break or a heart-to-heart talk, suggesting ways to work better together	1 2 3 4 5	
Clarifying/summarizing: clearing up confusion, checking to see if everyone understands and if the topic has been discussed enough, offering conclusions	1 2 3 4 5	

The Negatives

Everyone has moments when they make it harder for their group to work, when they subtract ideas and energy. When we use any of the behaviors below, we push the group off track, undermine confidence, or damage the way people talk and work together. What can you do to get out of this role next time?

Negative group roles, Behaviors that discourage collaboration	Your experience • When have you fallen into each role? • What helped you get out of the role?
Dominating: telling others what to do, insisting my ideas are better than others', hogging the spotlight and the credit	
Distracting: talking about everything except the task at hand, fidgeting, telling jokes, calling attention to myself	
Blocking: being stubborn, rarely offering an idea but always finding flaws in others' ideas, disagreeing without listening carefully, playing the devil's advocate long after it's useful	
Withdrawing: being consistently silent or out of the loop, not sharing ideas, not doing a fair share of the work, drifting along	
Doom and Glooming: expecting the group to fail, claiming projects won't work and ideas are bad, spreading a sour mood	

HANDOUT 4

First Week Student Profile

Last name: _____

First name: _____

Middle name: _____

Birth date: _____

Three words that best describe me are _____, _____, and _____.
Two things I do well are _____ and _____.
I was born in ❑ United States or ❑ _____.
My first language is ❑ English or ❑ _____.

Home Address:

Street _____ Apartment _____

City/Town _____ Zip Code _____

How long have you lived at your current address? _____ years or _____ months
How long have you lived in this community/town/city? _____ years or _____ months
Home Phone Number (_____)_____ E-mail Address_____

Family Information:

Full name of parent/guardian   Full name of parent/guardian

_____   _____

Place of work _____   Place of work _____

Occupation _____   Occupation _____

Born in ❑ US or ❑ _____   Born in ❑ US or ❑ _____

First Language: **First Language:**
❑ English ❑ Other_____   ❑ English ❑ Other_____

Names and ages of brothers and sisters:

Name _____ Age_____   Name _____ Age_____

Name _____ Age_____   Name _____ Age_____

Name _____ Age_____   Name _____ Age_____

Educational Information:

This is my ❏ first ❏ second ❏ third ❏ fourth year at this school.

The last school I attended was _____.

Are there any health issues that might affect your attendance, on-time arrival to class, or class participation?
❏ No or ❏ Yes _____

During the school year, I work at _____ about _____ hours per week.

After high school graduation, I am currently planning to:
❏ Get a full-time job
❏ Work part-time and go to college part-time
❏ Attend a 4-year college full-time
❏ Attend community college full-time
❏ Attend technical school
❏ Get an apprenticeship
❏ Serve in the military

Course Schedule: (to be filled out later in the week)

Class Period	Name of Course	Class Period	Name of Course
1st		5th	
2nd		6th	
3rd		7th	
4th		8th	

HANDOUT 5

Personal Pathway

Personal Pathway for _____

Think about your life experiences, people who are important to you, and goals. Fill in the areas along your path with drawings or writing representing where you have been, people and events along the way, and where you might be headed.

Where I started - family, neighborhood, state, country

Someone or something that influenced me along the way

Three things I've liked learning or doing

A turning point in my life; I used to…, but now I …

Where and when I sometimes stray off-course

A goal for this term or year in school and out of school

Where I might be headed

H A N D O U T 6

Life Skills Check List

Cluster #1: Self-awareness, self-expression, and self-management skills

1. Recognize and name your own feelings

2. Express feelings appropriately and assess the intensity of your feelings accurately (on a MAD scale of 1 to 10, I feel...)

3. Understand the cause of your feelings and the connection between your feelings and your behavior

4. Manage your anger and upset feelings (know your cues, triggers, and reducers)

5. Know what you do that bothers others and accept responsibility when you mess up

6. Self-reflect on your behavior; be able to learn from it, self-correct, redirect, and change when you need to

7. Make responsible choices for yourself by analyzing situations accurately and predicting consequences of different behaviors

8. Deal with stress and frustration effectively

9. Exercise self-discipline and impulse control

10. Say, "NO" and follow through on your decisions not to engage in unwanted, unsafe, unethical, or unlawful behavior

11. Seek help when you need it

12. Focus and pay attention

13. Set big and little goals and make plans

14. Prioritize and "chunk" tasks, predict task completion time, and manage time effectively

15. Activate hope, optimism, and positive motivation

16. Work for high personal performance and cultivate your strengths and positive qualities

17. Assess your skills, competencies, effort, and quality of work accurately

Cluster #2: Interpersonal communication and problem-solving skills

18. Exercise assertiveness; communicate your thoughts, feelings, and needs effectively to others

19. Listen actively to demonstrate to others that they have been understood

20. Give and receive feedback and encouragement

21. "Read" and name others' emotions and nonverbal cues

22. Empathize; understand and accept another person's feelings, perspectives, point of view

23. Analyze the sources and dimensions of conflict and utilize different styles to manage conflict

24. Use WIN-WIN problem solving to negotiate satisfactory resolutions to conflicts that meet important goals and interests of people involved

25. Develop, manage, and maintain healthy peer relationships

26. Develop, manage, and maintain healthy relationships with adults

Cluster #3: Cooperation, group participation, and leadership skills

27. Cooperate, share, and work toward high performance within a group to achieve group goals

28. Respect everyone's right to learn, to speak, and to be heard

29. Encourage and appreciate the contributions of others

30. Engage in conscious acts of respect, caring, helpfulness, kindness, courtesy, and consideration

31. Recognize and appreciate similarities and differences in others

32. Counter prejudice, harassment, privilege, and exclusion by becoming a good ally and acting on your ethical convictions

33. Exercise effective leadership skills within a group

34. "Read" dynamics in a group; assess group skills accurately; identify problems; generate, evaluate, and implement informed solutions that meet the needs of the group

35. Use a variety of strategies to make decisions democratically

HANDOUT 7A

Quarterly Goal-Setting — Academics

Name_____

Quarter (or Trimester) from _____(date) to _____(date)

Academic Goals: Choose an academic goal for each of your courses—a quarterly grade you want to earn; specific skills you want to use and improve; something you want to learn how to do well, or content knowledge you want to master.

Name of Course	
By the end of this quarter I will…	
Why does this goal matter to me?	
Three steps I will take to achieve this goal	
Two obstacles and what I can do to overcome them	
Three indicators that I'm on my way to reaching my goal	
Who will I talk with about my goal? What support do I need?	

Comments during the quarter: _____

_____

Results at the end of the quarter: _____

What worked? What didn't? What will I do differently next quarter? _____

_____

What did I learn about myself? _____

_____

HANDOUT 7B

Quarterly Goal-Setting — Work Habit

Name_____

Quarter (or Trimester) from _____(date) to _____(date)

Academic Goals: Chose a work habit that you want to improve and use regularly.

Work Habit Goal	
By the end of this quarter I will…	
Why does this goal matter to me?	
Three steps I will take to achieve this goal	
Two obstacles and what I can do to overcome them	
Three indicators that I'm on my way to reaching my goal	
Who will I talk with about my goal? What support do I need?	

Comments during the quarter: _____

_____

Results at the end of the quarter: _____

What worked? What didn't? What will I do differently next quarter? _____

_____

What did I learn about myself? _____

_____

HANDOUT 7C

Quarterly Goal-Setting — Personal Goals

Name_____

Quarter (or Trimester) from _____(date) to _____(date)

Choose a goal related to in-school or out-of-school activities, leadership, service or a personal passion.

Personal Goal	
By the end of this quarter I will…	
Why does this goal matter to me?	
Three steps I will take to achieve this goal	
Two obstacles and what I can do to overcome them	
Three indicators that I'm on my way to reaching my goal	
Who will I talk with about my goal? What support do I need?	

Comments during the quarter: _____

_____

Results at the end of the quarter: _____

What worked? What didn't? What will I do differently next quarter? _____

_____

What did I learn about myself? _____

_____

HANDOUT 8

Personal Assets and Qualities of Character

Analytical	Forgiving	Precise
Appreciative	Friendly	Prepared
Assertive	Generous	Problem-solver
Attentive	Gentle	Principled
Careful	Goal-oriented	Prudent
Caring	Hardworking	Purposeful
Collaborative	Helpful	Reasonable
Committed	Honest	Responsible
Communicative	Humorous	Reflective
Compassionate	Idealistic	Reliable
Competent	Imaginative	Resourceful
Concerned	Inclusive	Respectful
Confident	Independent	Responsive
Consistent	Industrious	Self-aware
Cooperative	Initiating	Self-disciplined
Courageous	Insightful	Self-motivated
Creative	Intuitive	Self-regulating
Curious	Joyful	Sensitive
Decisive	Kind	Skeptical
Detail-oriented	Leader	Skillful
Determined	Logical	Spirited
Effective	Loving	Steady
Efficient	Loyal	Studious
Empathetic	Observant	Supportive
Energetic	Open-minded	Tactful
Encouraging	Optimistic	Thorough
Enthusiastic	Organized	Thoughtful
Ethical	Patient	Tolerant
Fair	Perceptive	Trustworthy
Flexible	Persevering	Understanding
Focused	Powerful	Warm

Weekly Time Log

Name_____ From _____ (date) To _____ (date) Write total hours for the week in the first column.

Activity Type	Sunday	Monday	Tuesday	Wednesday	Thursday	Friday	Saturday
Family time with parents, siblings, relatives____	___/___ Total: ___hr.___min.	___/___ Total: ___hr.___min.	___/___ Total: ___hr.___min.	___/___ Total: ___hr.___min.	___/___ Total: ___hr.___min.	___/___ Total: ___hr.___min.	___/___ Total: ___hr.___min.
Time with friends—in person, by phone, on-line____	___/___ Total: ___hr.___min.	___/___ Total: ___hr.___min.	___/___ Total: ___hr.___min.	___/___ Total: ___hr.___min.	___/___ Total: ___hr.___min.	___/___ Total: ___hr.___min.	___/___ Total: ___hr.___min.
Time in class	___/___ Total: ___hr.___min.	___/___ Total: ___hr.___min.	___/___ Total: ___hr.___min.	___/___ Total: ___hr.___min.	___/___ Total: ___hr.___min.	___/___ Total: ___hr.___min.	___/___ Total: ___hr.___min.
School activities, sports, clubs, etc.____	___/___ Total: ___hr.___min.	___/___ Total: ___hr.___min.	___/___ Total: ___hr.___min.	___/___ Total: ___hr.___min.	___/___ Total: ___hr.___min.	___/___ Total: ___hr.___min.	___/___ Total: ___hr.___min.
Out-of-school activities, events	___/___ Total: ___hr.___min.	___/___ Total: ___hr.___min.	___/___ Total: ___hr.___min.	___/___ Total: ___hr.___min.	___/___ Total: ___hr.___min.	___/___ Total: ___hr.___min.	___/___ Total: ___hr.___min.
Homework, study time, research, tutoring____	___/___ Total: ___hr.___min.	___/___ Total: ___hr.___min.	___/___ Total: ___hr.___min.	___/___ Total: ___hr.___min.	___/___ Total: ___hr.___min.	___/___ Total: ___hr.___min.	___/___ Total: ___hr.___min.
Personal alone time: TV, music, interests, grooming, Internet, video games, etc.	___/___ Total: ___hr.___min.	___/___ Total: ___hr.___min.	___/___ Total: ___hr.___min.	___/___ Total: ___hr.___min.	___/___ Total: ___hr.___min.	___/___ Total: ___hr.___min.	___/___ Total: ___hr.___min.
Sleep	___/___ Total: ___hr.___min.	___/___ Total: ___hr.___min.	___/___ Total: ___hr.___min.	___/___ Total: ___hr.___min.	___/___ Total: ___hr.___min.	___/___ Total: ___hr.___min.	___/___ Total: ___hr.___min.
Volunteer service	___/___ Total: ___hr.___min.	___/___ Total: ___hr.___min.	___/___ Total: ___hr.___min.	___/___ Total: ___hr.___min.	___/___ Total: ___hr.___min.	___/___ Total: ___hr.___min.	___/___ Total: ___hr.___min.
Work	___/___ Total: ___hr.___min.	___/___ Total: ___hr.___min.	___/___ Total: ___hr.___min.	___/___ Total: ___hr.___min.	___/___ Total: ___hr.___min.	___/___ Total: ___hr.___min.	___/___ Total: ___hr.___min.

Total hrs. per day ___hr.___min. ___hr.___min. ___hr.___min. ___hr.___min. ___hr.___min. ___hr.___min. ___hr.___min.

HANDOUT 10

Task Log for the Week

Name_____ From _____(date) To _____(date)

First, write your To Do list in the middle column. Second, review and edit your list by using the PREP tips in the left column. At the end of the week, check (✔) the tasks that you completed, and circle three uncompleted tasks that are on the top of your list for next week.

Review Your List Using PREP Tips

Prioritize — Sort the tasks into three groups – 1s are absolutely essential for having a productive, successful week at school, 2s are important for your physical and mental health and your relationships with family and friends, 3s are everything else.

Reorganize — Predict how much time the most important tasks will take. Write in a day of the week next to each 1 task and each 2 task. These are the two things each day that you will make sure you do. If you have multiple tasks that will take significant amounts of time, spread them out.

Eliminate — Cross out two things from your list that are either unrealistic expectations for this week or things that won't have a negative impact in your life if they don't get done.

Plan ahead — Forecast three important To Do's that you know you will need to schedule time for during the next week.

To Do List for the Week Write down everything you want to get done over the next week.	1s 2s 3s	Day	✔

HANDOUT 11

Habits and Strategies Check List

Habits and Strategies That Help You Do School – What works for you?	I do this a lot and it works	It would help if I did this more often	I'd like to try this out	This would never work for me
1. Sometimes I let my parents know what I need to do so they can help me keep my commitments by checking in with me or helping me stick to a schedule that keeps me on track.				
2. I know how to use my parents as a shield to protect my time and avoid doing things that might get me in trouble. (For example, I can say, "Look, my parents won't let me go out after eight on school nights." or "You know, if my parents find out, I'll be grounded for a month. I think I'll pass this time.")				
3. I know how to check myself before I say something out loud—I've got a handle on what's okay to say publicly, what's better to say privately, and what's best left unsaid.				
4. I know when it's not a good idea to "free-style"—I know the times when I need to do things exactly "by the book."				
5. When I've got a problem at school I've got friends or family I can talk with who can help me sort things through to come up with a solution.				
6. When I'm upset or angry I know how to "chill out" and not make a major production out of it in class. I can postpone dealing with it until later.				
7. I can walk away from ignorant comments directed at me, especially when I think there's not much I can do that will change this person's behavior. I have learned, "It's just not worth my time and energy."				
8. Around school I know the teachers and administrators who will cut me some slack and those who won't.				

Habits and Strategies That Help You Do School – What works for you?	I do this a lot and it works	It would help if I did this more often	I'd like to try this out	This would never work for me
9. I can tell the difference between quality work and work that is shoddy. I know what I do differently when I make an effort and when I don't.				
10. I manage my time to meet school obligations week in and week out.				
11. I prioritize tasks and responsibilities.				
12. I map out plans for completing a complex task. I identify the steps and materials needed to complete it. I "chunk" a big task into smaller parts so it is easier to check what I have accomplished and what I have left to do.				
13. I make good choices about when and where to do what homework. (For example, I know what is easier to do when I'm tired and what kind of work requires me to be totally focused and alert with no distractions.)				
14. I accurately predict how long it will take to do various kinds of school tasks and assignments.				
15. I know that there will be some peak times during the year when I need to gear up and crank out school work at the exclusion of most other activities.				
16. I know when it's important to use standard English and when it's okay to use different dialects and slang.				
17. I ask myself questions that will help me get ready and organized to do work.				
18. When I'm distracted I use strategies that will help me refocus and pay attention.				

Habits and Strategies That Help You Organize Information – What works for you?	I do this and it's pretty easy	I do this but it's hard	I'd like to learn how to do this	This won't work for me
19. I use graphic organizers.				
20. I use Post-it notes for summarizing information, for reminders, for markers of things I need to read over or review.				
21. I number chunks of information that I need to remember in a specific order.				
22 I highlight or circle words and concepts that might be hard to remember.				
23. I create a picture in my mind that includes all the things that are related to the same concept or category.				
24. I draw pictures and symbols to make connections between concepts and ideas.				
25. I rewrite information on note cards that will help me review and study.				
26. When I take notes I leave space to correct things, add new information, and write summary points.				

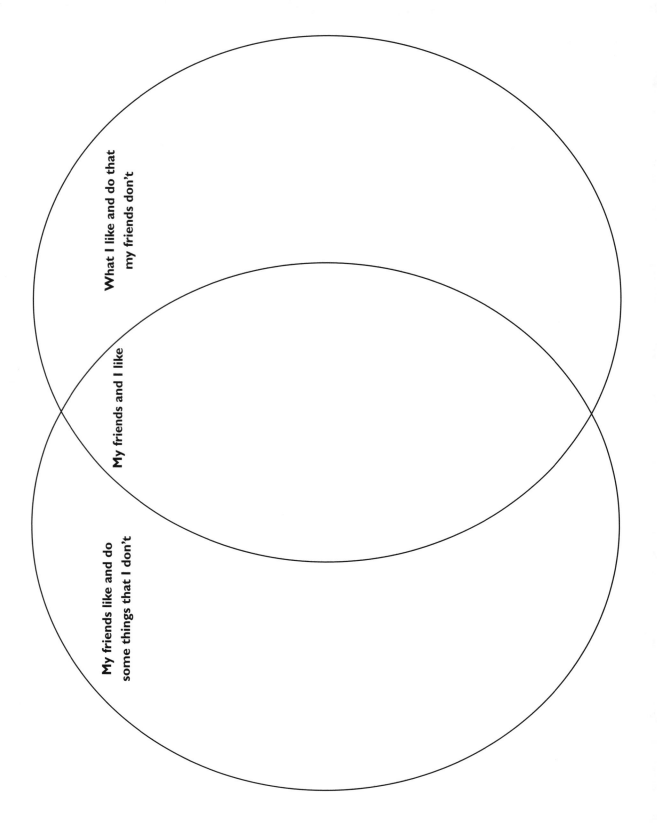

My Friends Like / We Like / I Like

What I like and do that my friends don't

My friends and I like

My friends like and do some things that I don't

HANDOUT 13

A-B-C-D-E Problem Solving

ASSESS the situation and ASK, what's the problem?

Describe the problem and say why it's a problem. How do you feel about the situation? What's not working? Why is it important to solve the problem? This is not a time to point fingers, scapegoat, or criticize individuals. The task is to stay focused on the problem and problem behaviors — not attack individuals. Form a clear statement of the problem and the goal for solving the problem.

The problem is _____.

A good solution will enable us to _____.

BRAINSTORM solutions

Brainstorm potential solutions to the problem. Picture how the situation would look if it were solved. Do this without criticizing or evaluating anything suggested.

CONSIDER each CHOICE Carefully

Review the solutions. How does each choice meet the needs and interests of everyone involved? What are the benefits of each choice? What are the drawbacks and limitations? Is the choice respectful, responsible, and reasonable? Cross out the choices that are the least effective.

DECIDE on the best choice and DO it

Discuss the remaining choices and come to agreement on the best solution. Be mindful that the best choice might include a combination of several possible solutions. Share your preferred solutions and the reasons for your choices. Summarize the comments and state what the group seems to think are the most important things to incorporate in the best choice. Use one of these decision-making protocols to reach final agreement.

- Reaching Consensus: Propose the solution. Solicit any final changes or edits. Ask students to raise their hands if they can fully support this solution; do "thumbs up" if it's good enough for now; do "thumbs in the middle" if they're not crazy about it but can live with it; or do "thumbs down" if it's unacceptable. Keep working on the solution until everyone raises a hand or does "thumbs up."
- Straw Poll: If the group has narrowed the field to two or three final ideas, ask people to vote for their first preference. If there is a clear winner, modify it until the solution works for everyone.
- Prioritize Ideas: If the solution involves a few components, give each student three sticker dots to place on the three ideas they like best. The ideas with the greatest number of sticker dots become the highest priority to implement.
- Small-Group Proposal: If the information feels unwieldy, or if there are opposing solutions with strong support, ask for a few volunteers to consider all of the data and perspectives and make a proposal to the group.

Plan precisely how the solution will be implemented. The group should also be able to suggest ways to evaluate how effectively the solution achieves the goal for solving the problem.

EVALUATE your choice after you have implemented it

Evaluate the decision. What happened? Did it work? What evidence do you have that it worked effectively? Is there anything that would help the group implement the solution more effectively?

HANDOUT 14A

Criteria for Making Good Decisions

☐ Does it meet an important need in my life?

☐ Does it feel reasonable to me and others? Given who I am, does it make sense to me and others?

☐ Is it do-able? (Am I asking myself to do something that might be somewhat challenging, but is not impossible to do? Do I have the time, skills, and resources to do it? Does it take into consideration any constraints or limitations?)

☐ Is it moral? (Does it hurt anyone? Is it fair and just? Is it destructive in any way to property or the environment?)

☐ Is it safe?

☐ Is it a healthy choice?

☐ Is it responsible?

☐ Is it legal?

☐ Does it respect the rights and needs of other people involved in the decision or affected by the decision?

☐ Is it smart? (Does this decision help me stay on the right track or get me on the right track? Does it help me create a positive future for myself?)

☐ Does this decision make me a better person, a better student, friend, or family member, a better worker, a better citizen?

HANDOUT 14B

Decision-Making Poster

Posters need to include:
1. Details that show your thinking about the decision-making process
2. Creative design and layout
3. Easy-to-read type or printing

Decision-Making Process

Step One: Describe an issue that requires you to make an important choice within the next week, month, or year (choices about your education, work, family or peer relationships, or personal habits and routines).

- By _____, I need to decide
  - Whether I will_____
  - When I will _____
  - If I Should _____
  - How I will _____
  - What I will _____
  - What to_____

- I am making this decision because I want_____.

- This decision will help me_____.

Step Two: Gathering Information – Identify the information you have gathered from people and other resources that will help you make a good decision.

Step Three: Identifying Choices – Describe at least three possible choices in detail.

Step Four: Evaluating Choices – List the advantages and disadvantages, constraints or limitations, and hopes and fears associated with each choice.

Step Five: Deciding on the Best Choice
- Explain your decision in detail (What you will do; when and where you will do it; how you will do it; the resources you need to do it; any steps involved in implementing your decision).
- Explain why this choice is better than the other choices.
- Indicate at least three ways that this choice meets criteria for good decision making. How do you know that your decision meets the three criteria you selected? (See **Handout 14A**.)

Step Six: Evaluating My Decision – If you are able to implement your decision, share the results of your decision in this way. What did you want? How did the decision help you to get what you wanted? What was the outcome? In what ways did the decision positively or negatively affect your life? If this decision involves your future, write how you imagine this decision will play out in your life.

HANDOUT 15

When it comes to conflict, you always have choices. You can ...

→ Take charge, force, demand, protect yourself or others

→ Accommodate, give in, let it go, smooth it over

→ Avoid it, ignore it, drop it, or exit

→ Postpone, pause and reflect; return to the problem later

→ Seek out a trusted adult, a level-headed friend, or a mediator

→ Problem solve:

- CHECK IT OUT, notice, observe, and ask questions before you decide what to do

- LISTEN AND DEFUSE when someone's upset

- ASSERT your feelings, needs, and "No's"

- NEGOTIATE ("Let's talk it out and reach a solution that works for both of us.")

HANDOUT 16

Feelings, Moods, and Attitudes

accepted	depressed	grossed out	nervous	shocked
afraid	desperate	guilty	obstinate	shut down
affectionate	determined	happy	open	shy
agitated	disconcerted	hateful	optimistic	silly
aggressive	discouraged	heartbroken	overwhelmed	sorrowful
aggravated	disappointed	helpless	pained	spiteful
amazed	disgusted	hopeful	panicked	stubborn
ambivalent	disillusioned	horrified	paranoid	stuck
amused	disrespected	hostile	peaceful	sulky
angry	distracted	humiliated	peeved	supported
annoyed	down	hurt	perplexed	surprised
anxious	eager	hysterical	playful	suspicious
appreciative	ecstatic	impatient	persecuted	sympathetic
argumentative	elated	independent	pessimistic	tenacious
arrogant	embarrassed	indifferent	positive	tense
ashamed	empty	indignant	powerful	terrific
awestruck	energized	inferior	powerless	terrified
awkward	enraged	inspired	prepared	ticked off
bad	enthusiastic	intimidated	proud	threatened
belligerent	envious	irate	psyched	thrilled
bored	exasperated	irritated	puzzled	timid
brave	excited	jazzed	reflective	trusted
calm	excluded	jealous	refreshed	uncertain
cautious	fearful	jolly	regretful	uncomfortable
cheerful	fearless	joyful	rejected	uneasy
closed	focused	juiced	relieved	unsafe
comfortable	foolish	jumpy	remorseful	up
confident	frenzied	livid	repulsed	upset
confused	friendly	lonely	respected	vengeful
contemptuous	frightened	loved	righteous	victimized
content	frustrated	loving	sad	victorious
courageous	furious	mad	safe	vindictive
crabby	good	malicious	satisfied	warm
cranky	goofy	mellow	scared	wary
curious	grateful	mischievous	secure	weary
defeated	greedy	miserable	self-assured	weird
defensive	grief-stricken	mortified	self-conscious	wistful
delighted	grouchy	negative	self-pitying	worried

Aggressive, Assertive, and Passive Behavior —What's the Difference?

Aggressive ~ I get what I want and need at the expense of others – by dominating or hurting others physically or emotionally	Assertive ~ I take care of myself by expressing my needs, thoughts, and feelings, while showing respect and concern for others	Passive ~ I allow others to take advantage of me. I choose not to act. I don't express my feelings, needs, or thoughts honestly.
Sounds like You put down the other person, attack, and accuse: "You're such a ...;" "You always ...;"; "You never ..." You blame, assume, stereotype; you're argumentative and interrupt a lot. Your voice is loud, dramatic, hostile. Your language is often mean, negative, rude, abusive, sarcastic.	**Sounds like** You share your needs, requests, and opinions honestly and openly: "I need to ...; "I feel ... when ... because ..." You listen attentively even if you disagree, and appreciate others' efforts to listen. You speak up. You take responsibility when you mess up. Your voice is even, calm, friendly. Your language is respectful, neutral or positive.	**Sounds like** You never really say what you feel, want, and need: "Whatever, it doesn't really matter to me", "I guess so..." You're silent or withhold information; you speak so softly others can't really hear you; you apologize a lot and blame others. You go along even if you really don't want to. You whine and wear people down.
Looks like Getting in someone's face; eye-rolling; threatening, confrontational posture; invading someone's personal space; dramatic arm movements; pointing fingers	**Looks like** Relaxed; open expression and posture that invites conversation; matching how the other person is sitting or standing; side by side rather than eyeball to eyeball	**Looks like** Shoulder shrugs; you look weighted down; you don't make eye contact; you look withdrawn, like you're trying to hide; you pout, frown; you look flustered
Payoffs You get what you demand most of the time; you stay in control; others see you as powerful ; you protect yourself	**Payoffs** You keep your dignity and self-respect; you get your needs met more often; you maintain respect for others; you value others; you use your power positively	**Payoffs** You avoid confrontation or taking responsibility. You don't get blamed. Using the silent treatment, you can ruin someone's good time without being aggressive.
Costs Your behavior can be dangerous and destructive; you may alienate and use other people. People may not like you. You fear not being in control and then lose control when you don't get what you want. You put on a front for others and can isolate yourself.	**Costs** It takes time. You may experience more conflict, although you have more tools to handle it effectively. Even when you're sensitive to others' needs and feelings, they can still feel uncomfortable with your directness and reject what you're saying.	**Costs** You don't feel in control of your emotions very often; you get anxious, resentful, angry a lot. Instead of expressing it, you seethe inside; you lose your self-respect; you give up being yourself. Other people walk over you. You don't have many real friends.

HANDOUT 17B

Assertive Responses

Here's what I need for right now_____.
Can you live with that?

I'd really like some help with _____.

I'm feeling _____ about_____ _____.
Can we talk about this?

I need to say no for right now. That's how it's going to have to be. Can you live with that?

I see your point and here's how I see the situation _____.

Help me understand why _____. Can you say more about_____?

It really bothers me when you _____. I'd prefer_____.

I know you didn't mean any disrespect, but that's how it felt. Please don't _____.

I would really like to_____.

It would work out better for me if _____.

293

H A N D O U T 18

Feedback Form

Opening on a positive note:
What did you like that [name of person] said or did? _____

_____

What worked well? _____

What was effective? _____

Constructive Suggestions:
What might have made it even more effective? _____

_____

What's one thing you might have changed, added, left out, or done differently? _____

_____

Closing on a positive note:
I appreciated _____

• •

Feedback Form

Opening on a positive note:
What did you like that [name of person] said or did? _____

_____

What worked well? _____

What was effective? _____

Constructive Suggestions:
What might have made it even more effective? _____

_____

What's one thing you might have changed, added, left out, or done differently? _____

_____

Closing on a positive note:
I appreciated _____

HANDOUT 19A

Stressed Out!

What is stress? Stress is the body's automatic response to any physical or mental demands or pressures from external circumstances that create internal tension within you. When you experience these demands or pressures, your safety and well-being feel threatened and your body rushes to defend itself.

What is the body's stress reaction? First, the body experiences ALARM when it recognizes a stressor and prepares for it by secreting hormones that

- raise your blood pressure
- heighten your awareness
- increase your perspiration
- increase your breathing rate
- make your mouth feel dry
- produce butterflies in your stomach
- make your hands feel cold and clammy
- increase your heart rate
- make your muscles tense up

The body seeks release and relief from the stressor (stressful situation). If you don't do something to reduce or relieve the stressor, you are unable to cope with the immediate situation effectively, will feel exhaustion, increased discomfort or fear, and may feel frozen in the moment (I'm stuck and I can't get out!).

Is stress bad? Not all stress is bad. The stress reaction is necessary and can be beneficial. It allows us to respond quickly in threatening situations and can give us a boost of energy to deal with the situation.

What is bad stress? Stress can be harmful when there isn't any relief from it, when it doesn't go away or lessen. It makes it very difficult to function normally and feel okay about yourself. When too much stress happens too often, the result can be a constant state of exhaustion.

What is good stress? Stress can be good and can bring a sense of pride and accomplishment when it results from successfully rising to a challenge, overcoming an obstacle, and stretching one's abilities.

What causes stress?
fear of failure
feeling alone in the world
too much to do and not enough time
upcoming tests and deadlines
too many choices to think about
a family crisis

feeling overloaded or overwhelmed by a particular event or situation

not feeling ready or prepared for what's coming up

a friendship or dating relationship with too much conflict or tension

one-sided relationships where you give, but you don't feel you get enough back

severe peer pressure to do things you're not comfortable doing

what you want for yourself is different from what you think others want of you or for you

not enough quiet time or down time for yourself

not feeling you can meet expectations from teachers, parents, friends

events and crises that shake your sense of security

What are the results of feeling stressed?

low energy	irritability	lack of enthusiasm
distance from peers	exhaustion	crying
procrastination	arguing constantly	sleeping too much or too little
muscle aches	headaches	changes in sleeping habits
distance from family	loss of sense of humor	changes in eating habits

What is stress management?

Stress management is the ability to manage excessive demands from people, events, or situations in ways that feel constructive and productive.

What are some strategies for managing stress?

1. Remove yourself from the situation and give yourself a break, even if it's only a few minutes.
2. Notice your physical reactions and do something immediately to relax and release the tension (walk, exercise, listen to music you love, daydream for little while, meditate, etc.).
3. Take a nap or catch up on sleep one day of the week.
4. Talk to a friend or family member.
5. Make a "To Do" list of three to five things you want to accomplish this week.
6. Learn to say NO to excessive demands.
7. Be assertive and let others know what you need.
8. Rethink an old routine or habit and do it in a different way.
9. Break up a task into chunks so you feel a sense of accomplishment when you complete each part of the task.
10. Tackle a difficult task when you have the most energy and feel fresh.
11. Eat healthy foods. They give longer-lasting and more stable energy.
12. Let the small stuff go. Decide which situations are not worth fighting about. What would take less energy to do than to fight about not doing?
13. Every day, try to balance a really demanding task with doing something that's fun, easy, and satisfying.

HANDOUT 19B

Reducing Stress in My Life

1. I feel stressed when _____
   _____

   The stress reaction I experience is _____
   _____

   The cause of this stress is probably _____
   _____

   The results of feeling this stress include _____
   _____

   I want to try out these two things to manage this stressful situation more effectively:
   I can_____
   I can_____

2. I feel stressed when _____
   _____

   The stress reaction I experience is _____
   _____

   The cause of this stress is probably _____
   _____

   The results of feeling this stress include _____
   _____

   I want to try out these two things to manage this stressful situation more effectively:
   I can_____
   I can_____

3. I feel stressed when _____
   _____

   The stress reaction I experience is _____
   _____

   The cause of this stress is probably _____
   _____

   The results of feeling this stress include _____
   _____

   I want to try out these two things to manage this stressful situation more effectively:
   I can_____
   I can_____

HANDOUT 20

Self-Care Check-Up

Read through the following habits, routines, and activities. Put a ☆ next to things that you do regularly in your life. Put a ✔ next to things you do occasionally. Put an (X) next to things you've never done. Then reread the list and circle five things you'd like to try that might make a positive difference in how you feel physically, emotionally, interpersonally, and spiritually.

Taking Care of Your Physical Self

_____ Eat a healthy balanced diet

_____ Eat three meals a day and keep snacks to once a day

_____ Exercise, work out, or walk regularly

_____ Get regular medical care and check-ups

_____ Get enough sleep so I feel rested (at least seven hours a night)

_____ Make space for quiet time away from all things electronic

_____ Participate in a physical activity regularly (dance, individual or team sports, martial arts, yoga,

drill team, etc.)

_____ Create a daily personal hygiene and skin care routine

_____ Dress and fix your hair the way you like

_____ Take time off every week to catch up on rest

Taking Care of Yourself Emotionally

_____ Take time for self-reflection (How am I doing? How am I feeling? What do I need to do to feel okay?)

_____ Write in a journal

_____ Check yourself (Listen to your inner thoughts, feelings, conscience, and beliefs before acting)

_____ Say no when you feel like you're on overload

_____ Reread favorite books, rewatch favorite movies, listen to favorite music

_____ Use self-talk for personal encouragement and motivation

_____ Identify comforting activities, surroundings, and treasured objects and seek them out

_____ Visualize yourself (imagine yourself in your own movie) accomplishing tasks that lead you to feel proud,

competent, or successful

_____ Rehearse hard conversations that you want to have with a friend, family member, or teacher

_____ Find things that make you laugh

_____ Allow yourself to cry

Interpersonal Self-Care

_____ Allow people to get to know who you really are

_____ Connect with important people in your life on a regular basis

_____ Take time to play

_____ Do something nice, unexpected, helpful, or special for a friend or someone in your family

_____ Make space for new people in your life

_____ Connect by phone or e-mail with friends and family whom you don't see often

_____ Confide your hopes and fears to a friend, family member, or mentor who listens to you with full attention

_____ Participate in a youth group outside of school

Nurturing Your Spirit

_____ Spend time in nature

_____ Take care of a pet, plants, or a garden

_____ Sing or play music

_____ Do something that gives you pleasure and doesn't cost any money

_____ Create, perform, compose, construct, or write something of your own making

_____ Do something that you haven't tried before

_____ Participate in a religious/spiritual community or congregation

_____ Contribute your time and resources to something you believe in

_____ Attend a support group with peers who are working through a similar personal issue or family situation

HANDOUT 21A

Giving and Getting Support

Everybody needs support. Think about the people in your life right now who can support you to do and be your best, listen to you, have a good time with you, and be there for you when you need them. Then think about how you play a support role with others.

1. I have friends my own age who really care about me, who can talk with me about my problems, and who can help me out when I'm having a hard time.

   Name_____ Name_____

   If there isn't someone like this in your life right now, who would you like to be there for you in this role? _____

   _____

   What are two things you could do to make this relationship happen? _____

   _____

   Are there any friends your own age, or brothers or sisters, for whom you play this role in their lives?

   Name_____ Name_____

   What is one thing I can do to be more supportive to them? _____

2. I have friends my own age who I can study or do homework with, who I can talk to when I'm having a problem in a class, and who are happy for me when I do well in school.

   Name_____ Name_____

   If there isn't someone like this in your life right now, who would you like to be there for you in this role? _____

   _____

   What are two things you could do to make this relationship happen? _____

   _____

   Are there any friends your own age, or brothers or sisters, for whom you play this role in their lives?

   Name_____ Name_____

   What is one thing I can do to be more supportive to them? _____

3. I have a parent or other adult close to me who expects me to follow rules, and who helps keep me on track when things get a little confusing, a little crazy, or just plain difficult.

   Name_____ Name_____

   If there isn't someone like this in your life right now, who would you like to be there for you in this role? _____

   _____

   What are two things you could do to make this relationship happen? _____

   _____

Adapted with permission from Healthy Kids Survey, developed by WestEd for the California Department of Education (www.wested.org/hks)

4. I have a parent or other adult close to me who is interested in my school work, who believes I will be successful, who always wants me to do my best.

Name_____ Name_____

If there isn't someone like this in your life right now, who would you like to be there for you in this role? _____

_____

What are two things you could do to make this relationship happen? _____

_____

5. I have a parent or other adult close to me who listens to me when I have something to say and who talks with me about my problems.

Name_____ Name_____

If there isn't someone like this in your life right now, who would you like to be there for you in this role? _____

_____

What are two things you could do to make this relationship happen? _____

_____

6. I have a parent or other adult close to me who counts on me to listen and be supportive to them when they are having a hard time.

Name_____ Name_____

What's one thing you can do to show them that you care about them? _____

7. At my school, there is a teacher or some other adult who really cares about me, who listens to me when I have something to say, who works with me when I need help.

Name_____ Name_____

If there isn't someone like this in your life right now, who would you like to be there for you in this role? _____

_____

What are two things you could do to make this relationship happen? _____

_____

8. At my school, I have several teachers who notice when I do a good job, who believe I will be successful, who always want me to do my best.

Name_____ Name_____

If there isn't someone like this in your life right now, who would you like to be there for you in this role? _____

_____

What are two things you could do to make this relationship happen? _____

_____

HANDOUT 21B

20 Ways to Support Yourself

There are good reasons to get good at doing the things for ourselves that can help us keep on track and moving in a positive direction. Often there is no one around to give us the support we would like. At other times, we get satisfaction from working things out by ourselves or doing things that build our inner resources and self-confidence. Take a look at these statements and see what you already do in the way of self-support and what you might like to try out.

20 Ways to Support Yourself	I already do this a lot	I'd like to do this more	I'd like to try this	This doesn't work for me
1. I can work out my own problems if I need to.				
2. I'm willing to try new things that can help me achieve my goals.				
3. I stand up for myself without putting others down.				
4. When I'm feeling down, I can imagine myself in a special place that feels safe and calming.				
5. When something is particularly hard for me, I try to picture myself doing that thing.				
6. When I feel overloaded, I can make a realistic plan that will help me get out of the hole.				
7. When friends are pressuring me to do something that's not a good choice for me, I go someplace private and quiet where I can think things through.				
8. I try to understand what other people go through when they are having a bad time. It helps me know that I'm not the only one who has bad days and bad times.				
9. I have some favorite music I listen to that helps me feel calm when I'm upset.				
10. When I've made a good choice for myself that was really hard to make, I go over what I did in my mind so I can use this experience in the future.				
11. Sometimes I write down my thoughts to help me get a clearer sense of what I'm thinking or feeling.				

Adapted in part with permission from Healthy Kids Survey, developed by WestEd for the California Department of Education (www.wested.org/hks)

20 Ways to Support Yourself	I already do this a lot	I'd like to do this more	I'd like to try this	This doesn't work for me
12. When I'm feeling pressured, I don't try to please everyone or try to do everything at once. I can feel good about just accomplishing one thing.				
13. Sometimes helping other people or doing something special for someone will lift up my own spirits.				
14. When I can't solve a problem by myself, I know where to go to for help.				
15. When I've made a bad choice, it doesn't mean that all my choices are bad ones. I have confidence that I can make a better choice next time.				
16. When things are bothering me or I don't feel quite myself, I feel okay about letting someone else know.				
17. After I've done something well, I like going over it again in my mind.				
18. I try to understand my own moods and feelings before I jump to conclusions or do something impulsive.				
19. I'm willing to share my opinions about things even when they may be different from others.				
20. I'm willing to change what I'm doing when things are not working out.				
Is there anything else that you do to give yourself support when you need it?				

HANDOUT 22

The Violence Continuum

Violence is using force to injure, hurt, threaten others, or do harm to property or to the physical environment.

What kinds of violence occur most frequently in your school?

What kinds of violence worry you the most in your school?

Are there any types of violence you would add to the continuum?

Murder

Rape

Criminal gang activity

Hate crimes

Use of weapons to threaten or harm

Physical abuse and assault

Sexual harassment and abuse

Alcohol and drug abuse

Physical fighting

Bullying

Threats and intimidation

Stealing

Property damage and vandalism

Trash talk

Put-downs, prejudicial remarks, and rumors

Disrespect

Discourtesy and rudeness

Ignoring or excluding people

Invisibility

▲BEGIN HERE

HANDOUT 23

Roles People Play in Harassment Situations

Aggressor: (sometimes referred to as the bully) The aggressor engages in behaviors meant to harm, hurt, or intimidate someone physically, emotionally, or socially. These behaviors include unwanted physical contact of any kind (hitting, kicking, shoving, spitting), nonverbal gestures meant to threaten, embarrass or call attention to someone in a negative way, verbal attacks meant to hurt someone's feelings or damage someone's relationships with others (taunting, teasing, racial slurs, name calling), and social exclusion. Aggressors may pick on one person repeatedly or lash out randomly. Aggressors instigate the harassment, egg on others to do the harassing, or sometimes join in the harassment later.

Target: The target is the person being harassed by the aggressor. A target is bullied, attacked, insulted, excluded, or picked on physically, emotionally, and socially. Targets often feel helpless to respond to the aggressor in an effective way that makes them stop.

Bystander: Someone who witnesses or hears about a situation in which an individual or group is being harassed and does not say anything or do anything to change the situation. Bystanders often play the role of enabler. The enabler allows a harmful situation, like harassment, to continue and grow worse. Examples include:

- Stopping to watch

- Laughing when you hear about a harassment incident

- Telling your friend to just ignore the harassment — it will go away

- Laughing, telling or showing your friend(s) graffiti on the bathroom wall

- Making excuses for the harasser's behavior

- Not reporting harassment to school staff

- Saying "boys will be boys"

- Saying "If they weren't so ... then they would not get picked on."

- Not taking harassment seriously

Ally: Someone who speaks and acts in ways to support the person or group who is being harassed and targeted; someone who speaks up against harassment in front of other peers; someone who is friendly with kids who are shy, isolated, or less popular at school.

HANDOUT 24

What Is Harassment?

- Harassment is any inappropriate, unwanted, or cruel behavior that targets a particular individual or group.

- To harass is to physically or verbally hurt, aggravate, frighten, tease, taunt, threaten, or insult a targeted group or individual.

- Harassment can include behaviors like spreading rumors, gossip, using social exclusion, and sometimes stalking. Harassment makes both targets and bystanders feel uncomfortable, embarrassed, isolated, and angry.

- Harassment is sometimes an act of discrimination based on prejudice.

- Harassment is mean, harmful, illegal, and doesn't belong in schools or anywhere else.

- In addition, harassment often leads to bullying. A person is bullied when she or he is exposed, repeatedly and over time, to the negative actions of one or more people. Bullies use their power or strength to dominate, intimidate, or attack the targeted person physically or verbally. Bullying behavior can include pressuring someone repeatedly to do something that she or he doesn't really want to do. The student who is being bullied may feel she or he has no power to stop the bully.

- If someone is doing or saying something to you that leads you to feel unsafe, uncomfortable, or embarrassed, it's probably harassment.

- Even if someone is "just joking," no one has the right to say things that make you feel targeted (singled out). No one has the right to touch you unless you say it's OK.

- You have the right and a responsibility to tell students to stop the harassing behavior or to report the behavior to a teacher, counselor, your parents, or, in some cases, to legal authorities.

Types of Harassment

- Racial or ethnic harassment includes attacks or negative comments associated with someone's skin color, ethnicity, native language, or national origin.

- Size-ist harassment means taunting someone because of their height or weight.

- Look-ist harassment includes attacks based on someone's looks. For example, calling someone ugly, a dog, or grease ball.

- Class-ist or social group harassment includes targeting someone based on how much money or possessions they or their family have or don't have; targeting someone because of their association with a particular social group; or a social group as "losers."

- Sexual harassment includes unwanted, unwelcome sexual comments or actions that target an individual or group and/or make spectators uncomfortable; unwanted touching, gestures, sexually-based insults; sexual rumor spreading; staring; unwanted "compliments" that have a sexual reference. Sexually harassing comments can be spoken or written, using graffiti, slams, pagers, cell phones, or the Internet.

- Sexual orientation harassment includes antigay, antibisexual, antilesbian attacks. Examples include calling someone a "fag" or "lesbo," or calling something you don't like "gay" or "queer."

- Religious harassment includes attacks on someone's religious beliefs, practices, or group.

- Able-ist harassment includes insulting a person based on a real or assumed physical or mental disability. Examples include habitually calling someone "retard," "dummy," or "stupid," or insulting them because they use crutches, a hearing aid, glasses, or a seeing-eye dog.

Effects of Harassment

The target of harassment may

- feel uncomfortable, embarrassed or threatened;

- fear going to school and feel that school is unsafe;

- avoid going to school;

- have lowered self-esteem;

- be depressed;

- do poorly in school;

- feel isolated;

- start to withdraw from friends, family, or normal activities;

- feel angry and powerless;

- seek revenge, retaliate with violence.

HANDOUT 25A

When someone is being harassed, you can be an ally when you...

1. Say the aggressor's name and show respect

2. Name what you see, say why you don't like it, and tell the aggressor to STOP

3. Take action...

- Help the targeted person to leave the scene.

- Go with the targeted person to report the incident.

- Report the incident yourself.

When someone is harassing you, you can...

1. Stop what you're doing or saying and pause for a few seconds.

2. Think - What can I say that will help me take care of myself, send a strong message, and deescalate the situation?

3. Say your message –

- Say the person's name and show respect.

- Say, "I don't like it when you _____. I want you to stop."

4. Exit - Don't wait for an apology or change of attitude. You said what you needed to say, and now you need to leave the scene, walk the other way, or focus your attention elsewhere.

HANDOUT 25B

Tips for Countering Harassment

- If you're upset or uncomfortable, you have the right to speak up. Ignoring it sometimes works, but often harassment continues unless people act positively to stop it.

- Many targets of harassment laugh in the beginning, because they are nervous or embarrassed and hope that they can "laugh it off." Often the bystanders and the person doing the harassing misinterpret the laughter, thinking the targeted person doesn't mind. Sometimes people joke back and forth, but when one person gets too aggressive or goes too far it escalates into cruel teasing and harassment, and can result in bullying.

- If you speak to the aggressor, use a voice that sounds strong, confident, and assertive, because you have the right not to be harassed. If possible, talk with the person privately or in a safe space after the incident.

- If it feels unsafe, if you're very upset, or if the harassment continues, speak with a teacher, counselor, parent, or other trusted adult. If you're nervous about confronting a person who is a known bully, that's a good indication that it's time to inform adults about the problem. If informal conversation doesn't work and/or it's a serious incident, you can also file a formal harassment complaint. You have a right to a safe environment, and teachers, counselors, and administrators are required by law to respond.

- Often, the harasser is angry about something (though being angry does not justify harassment) that has nothing to do with the targeted person. It can help to ask, "What's up? What are you angry about?" or "What are you frontin' for?" or "Where did that come from?" Using insults or threats escalates the conflict, and you can get in as much trouble as the person who started it.

- When two or more allies speak up, the message to stop the harassment is even stronger. The power of several voices can prevent the harasser from turning on allies who take a stand. If you see an ally getting targeted, act as an ally for them.

HANDOUT 25C

Find the Right Words to Respond to Harassment

Don't go there. This isn't funny anymore.

That's harassment. I don't like it and I want it to stop.

That looked like harassment to me. Don't do that anymore.

We don't say that around here. So knock it off, okay?

If you had said that to me, I'd feel 'dissed. Please don't say that stuff when I'm around.

This is getting old. Can you just drop it already?

I wouldn't want anyone to say that to me. Cut it out.

It really bothers me when you _____. I'd want you to _____.

I'm not going to start with you, so don't start with me.

I know you think this is just playing around, but it crosses the line of respect.

Ally Pledge

Here's what I can do to be a good ally to students who are harassed, who are new at school, who are shy, or who might not have many friends.

I can _____

_____

_____.

_____
Signed

_____
Date

HANDOUT 26

Quotations about Moving On in My Life

For every one of us that succeeds, it's because there's somebody there to show you the way out. The light doesn't necessarily have to be in your family; for me it was teachers and school.

Oprah Winfrey

If you don't know where you're going to, you will end up somewhere else.

Lewis Carroll, Alice in Wonderland

That's the risk you take if you change: that people you've been involved with won't like the new you. But other people who do will come along.

Lisa Alther

Every exit is an entry somewhere.

Tom Stoppard

To accomplish great things, we must not only act, but also dream; not only plan, but also believe.

Anatole France

"No" can be one of the most positive words in the world. No, I will not be defeated. No, I will not give up.   *Martha Williamson*

Hold fast to dreams, for if dreams die, life is a broken winged bird that cannot fly.

Langston Hughes

If Plan A isn't working, I have Plan B, Plan C, and even Plan D.   *Serena Williams*

Life consists not in holding good cards but in playing those you hold well.   *Josh Billings*

Live out of your imagination, not your history.

Stephen Covey

You may encounter many defeats, but you must not be defeated. In fact, it may be necessary to encounter the defeats, so you can know who you are, what you can rise from, how you can still come out of it.   *Maya Angelou*

How defeated and restless the child that is not doing something in which it sees a purpose, a meaning! It is by its self-directed activity that the child, as years pass, finds its work, the thing it wants to do and for which it finally is willing to deny itself pleasure, ease, even sleep and comfort.

Ida M. Tarbell

Failure is an event, not a person.

William D. Brown

Failure is more interesting than success.

Max Beerbohm

Never be bullied into silence. Never allow yourself to be made a victim. Accept no one's definition of your life; define yourself.

Harvey Fierstein

HANDOUT 27

Your Personal Statement

Prepare a two-minute personal statement that you will write and share with your advisory.

Jot responses to any of the questions below. Then decide what words and phrases most accurately describe who you are and who you want to become. There is no correct formula for writing a personal statement. How you want to express yourself is your choice.

What makes you happy?

What do you love to do?

What do you really want to learn about, become an expert at doing?

What personal talents do you want to develop and strengthen?

What three things in life matter most to you?

What do you want to accomplish in your life?

What people in life do you most admire?

What words would your friends, family, and teachers use to describe you?

What makes you different from every other person on earth?

What do you want people to remember about you?

What inspires you?

What motivates you?

What have you learned from your family about living a good life?

What will you need to do to live the life you want to live?

What keeps you going when you feel down and discouraged?

What messages or self-talk guide you through the day?

What are your hopes for your own future?

What are your hopes for the world you live in?

What do you imagine yourself doing ten years from now?

What will it take to make your dreams a reality?

Teens and Freedom, Part I: What's Your Opinion?

This is a survey from USA WEEKEND. Over 200,000 teens took the survey that was distributed in the magazine, online, and in partnership with Channel One.

1. Today's teens have:

Too much freedom	16%
Not enough freedom	47%
The right amount of freedom	37%

2. Do you think adults today are trying to limit teens' freedoms too much?

Yes	70%
No	30%

2a. If yes, who is most responsible for the restrictions?

Parents	44%
School officials	16%
Law enforcement officials	26%
Politicians	14%

3. Do you now have the freedom to: (percentage saying yes)

Listen to whatever music you want	87%
Pick your own friends	92%
Decide how to spend your money	81%

4. Some communities are imposing curfews on teenagers at night to reduce crime. Is that:

Fair	50%
Unfair	50%

5. If you have children, will you be:

Stricter than your own parents or guardian	4%
Not as strict	44%
About the same	52%

6. Do you think public school officials should have the right to tell students what to wear at school?

Yes	21%
No	79%

7. Which do you think should or should not be banned by school dress codes?

	Banned	Not banned
Hats	15%	85%
Baggy clothes	19%	81%
Short skirts	35%	65%
Cutoff pants	20%	80%
Exposed midriffs	42%	58%
Earrings on boys	19%	81%
Nose, lip, tongue, or eye rings	44%	56%
Clothes with gang symbols	75%	25%

8. I think uniforms in public school are:

A good idea	17%
A bad idea	83%

9. If the national anthem is played before sporting events at your school, students should:

Be required to stand	69%
Have the right not to stand	31%

10. Should public schools be allowed to lead students in prayer?

Yes	43%
No	57%

11. Which of the following should school officials be allowed to enforce to protect students? (percentage saying yes)

Restrict foul language in writing assignments	58%
Censor what students write in the school newspaper	38%
Ban books, newspapers, and magazines considered offensive	31%
Search a student's locker for drugs or weapons without permission	58%

12. Do you think your parents trust you:

Enough	65%
Not enough	35%

13. The respect you get from your parents or guardian should be:

Earned	46%
Automatic, unless I abuse it	54%

14. Parents today should have the right to ... (percentage saying yes)

Install a V-chip in the TV to block violent or offensive shows	35%
Install a special device in the car allowing them to monitor teens' driving speed	30%
Install a computer program limiting what teens can access	36%

15. Should there be restrictions on teens' use of the Internet?

Yes	30%
No	70%

15a. If yes, which do you favor? (percentage saying yes)

There should be limits on how much time teens can spend on the Internet	28%
There should be limits on where teens can go on the Internet	87%

16. How well do you know the lyrics to the music you listen to?

Very well	61%
Somewhat well	34%
Not very well	4%
Not at all	1%

17. How well do your parents or guardian know the lyrics to the music you listen to?

Very well	12%
Somewhat well	27%
Not very well	30%
Not at all	31%

Results originally appeared in *USA Weekend* Magazine's 1997 Teen Survey: Teens and Freedom. Used by permission of *USA Weekend* Magazine.

HANDOUT 29

Making Your Case and Defending Your Point of View

Tips for Presenting Your Ideas Effectively

1. Do you have an opener, a compelling story, incident, quote that sets the context and personalizes the problem so that the audience understands how this issue affects real people?

2. Do you define and describe the problem clearly in ways that illuminate the problem, identify what's not working, or describe what needs are not being met?

3. Have you given the audience the facts (specific examples, data, statistics, comparisons, illustrations, and anecdotes) that connect conditions and situations to real individuals and groups)?

4. Have you told the audience why doing something is important? What might happen if nothing is done or nothing changes? How does this problem affect students, the school, or the larger community?

5. Have you shared suggestions for solutions? Do you compare this solution to other possible solutions? Why is this a better idea? What needs to be done? What is the plan? Who will make it happen? How much will it cost? Where will the money come from?

6. Have you made an appeal to your audience? What do you want your audience to think about, reconsider, or do after they listen to your speech?

HANDOUT 30A

This *Is* Your Life as an Adolescent!

I was born in _____ (year).

1. What I like most about school is _____

    _____

2. What I like least about school is _____

    _____

3. The three most serious discipline problems at school are:

    _____

    _____

    _____

4. What are the most popular hair styles and fashion trends among your friends?

    _____

5. What are the fashion trends that make your parents crazy?

    _____

6. What's your favorite music or musical group? _____

    _____

7. How many telephones are in your house? _____

    How many TVs?_____ How many cars in your family? _____

    What is the latest electrical gadget that everyone wants? _____

8. Who is a public figure you admire or want to be like?_____

    _____

9. What are the popular slang words and phrases that your crowd uses?

    _____

10. What do you do for fun on weekends? Where do you hang out? _____

_____

11. What clubs, groups, and organizations do you belong to?

_____

_____

12. What is your favorite radio or TV show?

_____

13. What book or magazine have you been reading lately? _____

14. How old were you when you had your first date? _____

15. Do you get an allowance? How much? _____

16. How are you most often punished? What consequences do you have for messing up?

_____

17. What do you do that bothers your parents/guardians/extended family the most? _____

_____

18. What worries you the most growing up? _____

_____

19. Are there any issues or problems in society that trouble you right now? If so, what are they? _____

_____

20. What are two or three phrases or expressions that you hear from your family over and over again? _____

_____

_____

HANDOUT 30B

This *Was* Your Life as an Adolescent!

I was born between
1. 1926 - 1935
2. 1936 - 1945
3. 1946 - 1955
4. 1956 - 1965
5. 1966 - 1975
6. 1976 - 1985

Think back to when you were a teenager—when you were between 13 and 18 years old.

1. What I liked most about school was _____

   _____

2. What I liked least about school was _____

   _____

3. The three most serious discipline problems at school were:

   _____

   _____

   _____

4. What were the most popular hair styles and fashion trends among your friends?

   _____

5. What were the fashion trends that made your parents crazy?

   _____

6. What was your favorite music or musical group? _____

   _____

7. How many telephones were in your house? _____

   How many TVs?_____ How many cars in your family? _____

   What was the latest electrical gadget that everyone wanted? _____

8. Which public figure did you admire or want to be like? _____

   _____

9. What were the popular slang words and phrases that your crowd used?

_____

_____

10. What did you do for fun on weekends? Where did you hang out?_____

_____

11. What clubs, groups, and organizations did you belong to?

_____

_____

12 What was your favorite radio or TV show?

_____

13. What was a favorite book or magazine?_____

14. How old were you when you had your first date?_____

15. Did you get an allowance? How much?_____

16. How were you most often punished? What were the consequences for messing up?

_____

17. What did you do that bothered your parents/guardians/extended family the most?_____

_____

18. What worried you the most growing up? _____

_____

19. Were there any issues or problems in society that troubled you then? If so, what were they? _____

_____

20. What were two or three phrases or expressions you heard from your family over and over again?

_____

HANDOUT 31

Quotations about Living in the Real World

You have to stand for what you believe in. And sometimes you have to stand alone.

Queen Latifah

Our character is what we do when we think no one is looking.

H. Jackson Brown, Jr.

I was taught that the world had a lot of problems; that I could struggle and change them; that intellectual and material gifts brought the privilege and responsibility of sharing with others less fortunate; and that service is the rent each of us pays for living.

Marian Wright Edelman

A loving person lives in a loving world. A hostile person lives in a hostile world. Everyone you meet is your mirror.

Ken Keys

The least I can do is speak out for those who cannot speak for themselves.

Jane Goodall

Its name is Public Opinion. It is held in reverence. It settles everything. Some think it is the voice of God.

Mark Twain

There's a world of difference between truth and facts. Facts can obscure truth.

Maya Angelou

The ultimate measure of a man is not where he stands in moments of comfort, but where he stands at times of challenge and controversy.

Martin Luther King, Jr.

We are living beyond our means. As a people, we have developed a lifestyle that is draining the earth of its priceless and irreplaceable resources without regard for the future of our children and people all around the world.

Margaret Mead

We are citizens of the world. And the tragedy of our times is that we do not know it.

Woodrow Wilson

One isn't necessarily born with courage, but one is born with potential. Without courage, we cannot practice any other virtue with consistency. We can't be kind, true, merciful, generous, or honest.

Maya Angelou

Most of the important things in the world have been accomplished by people who have kept on trying when there seemed to be no hope at all.

Dale Carnegie

The problems that exist in the world today cannot be solved by the level of thinking that created them.

Albert Einstein

The refusal to listen is the first step toward violence.

Martin Luther King, Jr.

Everybody has a piece of the truth.

Gandhi

The most violent element in society is ignorance.

Emma Goldman

What you need is sustained outrage ... there's far too much unthinking respect given to authority.

Molly Ivins

And so, my fellow Americans, ask not what your country can do for you; ask what you can do for your country.

John F. Kennedy

Never doubt that a small group of thoughtful, committed citizens can change the world. Indeed, it is the only thing that ever has.

Margaret Mead

In every deliberation, we must consider the impact of our decisions on the next seven generations, on those faces who are yet beneath the ground.

The Great Law of the Six Nations, Iroquois Confederacy

There are no warlike peoples—only warlike leaders.

Ralph Bunche

There can be no daily democracy without daily citizenship.

Ralph Nader

It just seems to me that as long as we are both here, it's pretty clear that the struggle is to share the planet, rather than to divide it.

Alice Walker

Nothing can bring you peace but yourself.

Ralph Waldo Emerson

My definition of a free society is a society where it is safe to be unpopular.

Adlai E. Stevenson

You can't hold a man down without staying down with him.

Booker T. Washington

The only thing necessary for evil to triumph is for good men to do nothing.

Edmund Burke

HANDOUT 32A

Places and Institutions in Public Life

Some Examples...

Civic Life — Municipal services (police, fire department, courts, judicial services, trash collectors, street and sewer maintenance, etc.); government offices and agencies, post offices, armed services; political action organizations, initiatives, and campaigns; safety and consumer protection organizations and regulatory agencies; housing authorities; planning and development agencies

Human and Health-Care Services — public housing, social agencies, hospitals, clinics, medical research and technology labs, doctors' offices, services for children, families, people with disabilities, and the elderly, rehabilitation services

Spiritual Life — churches, synagogues, mosques, funeral homes, retreat and spiritual centers

Economic Life — places of employment; professional, trade, and labor associations; commercial, service and industrial properties, banks, restaurants, shopping areas

Media — TV (commercial, public, and cable), radio, newspapers, movies, magazines, billboards

Education — preschools, public, private, and parochial schools, college, universities, and other higher education and vocational institutions, community education centers, public awareness initiatives

Cultural, Recreational, and Voluntary Organizations — parks, green spaces, recreational centers, theaters, arenas, performing arts and visual arts centers, libraries, YMCA, camps, museums, historical, architectural, preservation, and cultural heritage organizations

HANDOUT 32B

Mapping Public Life

1. Using the handout "Places and Institutions in Public Life," make a list of all the specific places and institutions that are part of public life in your community, linking them to the roles that citizens play in these places and institutions. Make sure to include specific places and institutions that you are familiar with, places and institutions that you and your family visit and participate in. Since you will be mapping these places later, you need to know their location.

Place or institution	Location in your community	The roles that citizens play in this place or institution

2. Using any phone books and directories available, categorize the various kinds of youth services and centers found in your community. Then make a map legend that categorizes these places and identify their location on a community map.

HANDOUT 32C

Exploring Public Life (Commerce and Business)

Group 1: Document the commercial and business life of your community and the public spaces, "street furniture," and signage found there.

1. Using street maps, "yellow pages," and any other community directories from the Chamber of Commerce or other organizations, identify and locate two or three locations or streets in your community that contain the most commercial and business activity. On three separate sheets, list the commercial and business places in each location.

2. Using the lists and locations generated in 1, brainstorm three lists:

   - What can you photograph that will give people a vivid picture of "public life" (people, places, and spaces) in these locations?

   - What kinds of free documents and "artifacts" do you think you can get from various places that you can attach to your map? (For example, you can get boxes and containers of products sold, menus, business cards, etc.)

   - If your group has $20.00, what kinds of "artifacts" could you purchase that would help illustrate places, products, and services that you find in your exploration. These "artifacts" need to be small enough to attach to the map that you create. (For example, you might find a post card of something in your community or purchase a "part" or inexpensive item that illustrates various services offered or products sold in the places you visit.)

3. Create "people on the street" questions that will help you understand what people think of your community. For example, "What are the two best things and the two worst things about this community?" or "In three words, how would you describe your community?" or "What's one change you would recommend that would make this community a better place to live?"

4. Create questions you can use to interview owners and employees of commercial and business places you visit. What kinds of information will give you a good picture of the history and "health" of business and commerce in your community?

HANDOUT 32D

Exploring Public Life
(Culture, Education, Recreation, and Spiritual Life)

Group 2: Document the cultural, educational, recreational, and spiritual life of your community.

1. Using street maps, "yellow pages," and any other community directories, identify and locate three or four locations or streets in your community that contain the most cultural, educational, recreational, and religious institutions. On separate sheets, list the specific places found in each location.

2. Using the lists and locations generated in 1, brainstorm two lists:

    *   What can you photograph that will give people a vivid picture of "public life" (people, places, and spaces) in these locations?

    *   What kinds of free documents and "artifacts" do you think you can get from various places that you can attach to your map? (For example, you can get newsletters, schedules, announcements, business cards, etc.)

3. Create questions directed to members, participants, and volunteers who are part of these institutions and organizations. Frame questions that will help you understand what people think about these institutions and their roles in your community. For example, "How does this place _____ make this community a good place to live?" or "What are your reasons for membership or participation in this institution?" or "What's one change that would help this institution serve the community better?"

4. Create questions you can use to interview employees of the places you visit. What kinds of information will give you a good picture of the history and "health" of these institutions and organizations?

HANDOUT 32E

Exploring Public Life
(Human Resources and Health Care)

Group 3: Documenting the human resources and health-care services in your community

1. Using street maps, "yellow pages," and any other community directories, identify and locate three or four locations or streets in your community that contain the most human and health care services and institutions. On separate sheets, list specific places found in each location.

2. Using the lists and locations generated in 1, brainstorm two lists:

   • What can you photograph that will give people a vivid picture of "public life" (people, places, and spaces) in these locations?

   • What kinds of free documents and "artifacts" do you think you can get from various places that you can attach to your map? (For example, you can get newsletters, schedules, announcements, business cards, etc.)

3. Create questions directed to consumers of various services and volunteers who participate in these institutions and organizations. Frame questions that will help you understand what people think about these institutions and their roles in your community. For example, "How does this institution_____ make this community a good place to live?" or "What are your reasons for using this service?" or "What's one change that would help this institution serve the community better?"

4. Create questions you can use to interview employees of the places you visit. What kinds of information will give you a good picture of the history and "health" of these institutions and organizations?

HANDOUT 32F

Exploring Public Life (Civic Institutions)

Group 4: Documenting the "civic life" in your community (local, state, and federal government institutions that provide benefits and services to the public)

1. Using street maps, "blue pages," and any other community directories, identify and locate three or four locations or streets in your community that contain the most government offices, services, and institutions. On separate sheets, list specific places found in each location. Be sure you identify each place as part of the local, state, or federal government.

2. Using the lists and locations generated in 1, brainstorm two lists:

    *   What can you photograph that will give people a vivid picture of "public life" (people, places, and spaces) in these locations?

    *   What kinds of free documents and "artifacts" do you think you can get from various places that you can attach to your map? (For example, you can get newsletters, schedules, announcements, business cards, etc.)

3. Create questions directed to consumers of various services and volunteers who participate in these government services and programs. Frame questions that will help you understand what people think about these institutions and their roles in your community. For example, "How does this institution/service/program benefit you and make this community a good place to live?" or "What are your reasons for using this service or participating in this program?" or "What's one change that would help this institution serve the community better?"

4. Create questions you can use to interview employees of the places you visit. What kinds of information will give you a good picture of the history of these places in your community and the successes, controversies, and challenges that they face?

How do you like to learn? What do you like to do?

Are there one or two intelligences where you are a match for almost every statement in the list?

What statements most closely reflect learning tasks that you find particularly appealing or feel like a natural fit for you?

What statements reflect learning tasks that are difficult or boring for you?

Logical/Mathematical

- I like solving logic puzzles.
- I like working with numbers and solving problems with numbers.
- I like to do experiments.
- I like to estimate things and make predictions.
- I like to use tools and equipment.
- I like to reason things out and look for solutions to problems.
- I like to label, order, and categorize information.
- I like working with theories and models.
- I like to design programs on the computer.
- I like things to be logical and orderly.
- I like sorting out and analyzing data.
- I like statistics.
- I like having structures and formulas that will help me get the right answer.
- I like playing games that require strategy.
- I like finding evidence and proving that something is correct.
- I like making lists.
- I like to know how things work.

Kinesthetic

- I like doing things with my hands.
- I like testing my physical strengths and skills.
- I like working with tools and equipment to make and fix things.
- I feel more myself when I'm active, moving, playing, or exercising.
- I like to dance.
- I like to play sports.
- I take care of my body and I'm interested in doing things that keep me healthy.
- I like to perform in plays and skits.
- I like to try out and test things by physically doing something.
- I like to create movements or gestures as a way to remember or give something meaning.
- I like expressing myself physically.
- I prefer doing something rather than reading about it or listening to an explanation of it.

Interpersonal

- I like hanging out with my friends.
- I like to work with others to learn something.
- I'm good at working out conflicts and differences with others.
- I like parties and gatherings with friends or family.
- I like to organize and plan activities and events.
- I'm good at communicating my needs and feelings to others.
- I like helping others.
- I like being a leader.
- I like to figure out what makes people do what they do.
- I like being part of a team or group that has a purpose.
- I'm sensitive to the moods and feelings of others.
- I make friends pretty easily and get along with most people.
- I like to talk to others before making a decision.
- I'm a good participant in a group.
- I like meeting new people in different settings.
- I like learning about different people and cultures.

Naturalist

- I feel more myself when I'm outside in nature.
- I like learning about the natural world.
- I like animals and I like to take care of them.
- I like plants and gardening.
- I'm tuned in to the sensory world outside (water, sky, outdoor sounds and smells, weather, the earth).
- I like to camp, walk, hike, climb, canoe, sail, etc.
- I like to spend time outdoors by myself.
- I like to observe the natural world in different settings in all its detail.
- I connect other things to nature images and analogies.

- I like exploring new places.

- I like returning to the same place over and over to see what's changed.

- I like to see the connections between living things.

- I like doing field studies in the natural environment.

Visual/Spatial

- I like to draw, paint, or create three-dimensional forms.

- I like to look at art, architecture, and the built environment.

- I like to work with color, pattern, space, and form.

- I like to present things visually using pictures, charts, graphs.

- I like to do lettering and calligraphy.

- I like to design things.

- I remember things by creating mental pictures and images.

- I like to spend time imagining things.

- I like to transform objects and spaces into something new.

- I can find my way around different spaces and environments easily.

- I notice details about the spaces I'm in.

- I like solving spatial and pattern puzzles.

- I like making maps and diagrams.

Musical/Rhythmic

- I like listening to music.

- I play a musical instrument.

- It's easy for me to remember musical lyrics.

- I find myself looking for a beat, trying to discover the rhythm of things.

- I like to sing.

- I can recognize different kinds of music and different composers.

- I like participating in musical performances.

- I like attending musical performances.

- I remember things by making up a song.

- I like to hum or whistle or have music playing when I'm working.

- I like creating rhymes and sayings that have a beat.

- I like practicing a musical piece until I get it right.

Verbal/Linguistic

- I like the experience of reading.

- I like writing things as a way of remembering.

- I like learning new words and exploring their meaning.

- I like playing with words and making up words.

- I like explaining things to others.

- I like discussing issues with others.

- I like telling stories and making up stories.

- I like poetry.

- I like to write poetry.

- I like creative writing where I can express myself in words.

- I like to write reports and essays.

- I like learning languages.

- I prefer listening to or reading about something, rather than watching something or actually doing something physical.

- I like making a good argument.

- I like word games.

- I like listening to stories.

- I like crafting a good sentence.

- I like to analyze and discuss literature.

Intrapersonal

- I like to spend time thinking by myself.

- I am very aware of my own moods and feelings.

- I like being alone.

- I like working independently.

- It's easy for me to make goals for myself and accomplish them.

- I usually know what's the right decision for me without asking others.

- I trust my own judgment.

- I feel comfortable "in my own skin."

- I know who I am and like who I am.

- I have a good sense of what works for me and what doesn't.

- I like sitting back and watching and observing others.

- I like reflecting about what I've done and experienced.

- I like to write my thoughts in a journal.

- I like school work that has a personal meaning for me.

Additional Resources

Boorstein, Gail. "A Study of Advisory." ERIC No. ED408544, 1997.

Cole, Claire. *Nurturing a Teacher Advisory Program.* Westerville, OH: National Middle School Association, 1992.

DaGiau, Bette J. "A Program of Counseling and Guidance to Facilitate the Transition from Middle School to High School." ERIC No. ED413562.

Daniels, Harvey, Marilyn Bizar, and Steven Zemelman. *Rethinking High Schools.* Portsmouth, NH: Heinemann, 2001.

Goldberg, Mark F. *How to Design An Advisory System for a Secondary School.* Alexandria, VA: Association for Supervision and Curriculum Development, 1998.

Gulassi, John P., Suzanne A. Gulledge, and Nancy D. Cox. *Advisory: Definitions, Descriptions, Decisions, Directions.* Westerville OH: National Middle School Association, 1998.

Lieber, Carol Miller. *Partners in Learning.* Cambridge, MA: Educators for Social Responsibility, 2002.

Mathews, Jay. "An Extra Dose of Emotional Support." The Washington Post, (February 12, 2001).

Mizelle, Nancy B. "Helping Middle School Students Made the Transition into High School." ERIC No. ED432411, 1999.

National Middle School Association, "NMSA Research Summary #9." NMSA Website.

Rost, Jacquie and Marceil Royer. "Evaluating the Effectiveness of Charger Connection Class." ERIC No. ED430189, 1999.

Silva, Peggy and Robert A. Mackin. *Standards of Mind and Heart: Creating the Good High School.* New York: Teachers College Press, 2002.

Activity Resources

Hanson, Mark Victor and Kimberly Kirberger. *Chicken Soup for the Teenage Soul.* Deerfield Beach, FL: Health Communications Publishers, 1998.

Hoversten, Cheryl, Nancy Doda, and John Lounsbury. *Treasure Chest: A Teacher Advisory Source Book.* Westerville, OH: National Middle School Association, 1991.

Kreidler, William J. *Conflict Resolution in the Middle School.* Cambridge, MA: Educators for Social Responsibility, 1997.

Kreidler, William J. and Rachel A. Poliner. *Conflict Resolution in the Middle School Workbook and Journal.* Cambridge, MA: Educators for Social Responsibility, 1999.

Lieber, Carol Miller. *Conflict Resolution in the High School,* Cambridge, MA: Educators for Social Responsibility, 1998.

McFarlane, Evelyn and James Saywell. *If…Questions for Teens.* New York: Random House, 2001.

Poliner Rachel A. and Jeffrey Benson. *Dialogue: Turning Controversy into Community.* Cambridge, MA: Educators for Social Responsibility, 1997.

Rohnke, Karl and Jim Grout. *Back Pocket Adventure.* Beverly, MA: Project Adventure, 1998.

About the Authors

Rachel A. Poliner and Carol Miller Lieber have worked and learned together for years as a school consulting team and as program leaders for Educators for Social Responsibility. *The Advisory Guide* grew out of their experiences working with schools across the United States, as they helped faculty and administrators to imagine, create, and implement effective programs.

Rachel A. Poliner is an Educational Consultant, based in Boston, Massachusetts focused on schools reforms dealing with personalization or social and emotional learning; and on management, change, and conflict. A former teacher, she has worked with public and independent schools in New England and across the U.S. Her recent efforts include consulting on advisory programs and high school redesign; designing and implementing K-12 social and emotional learning reforms district-wide; shaping faculty culture; and integrating character development, conflict resolution, and service learning through all subject areas.

While with ESR, Rachel was a faculty member of ESR/Lesley University's joint masters' degree program and developed the Stories Program: Conflict and Character through Literature and Language Arts. She has co-authored various ESR curricula, including *Dialogue: Turning Controversy into Community; The Power of Numbers*, an integrated mathematics and social studies curriculum; and *Conflict Resolution in the Middle School Student Workbook and Journal.*

Carol Miller Lieber is a national leader in integrating principles of prevention, personalization, and youth development into everyday practices and structures for secondary schools. Carol has taught students at all grade levels and in 1973 co-founded a small urban secondary school in St. Louis. She has served on education faculties at University of Missouri, and National-Louis, Lesley, and Washington Universities.

Facilitating healthy development and academic success for every student has been at the heart of her work with Educators for Social Responsibility. She has supported principals, leadership teams, and faculty in their efforts to personalize learning in large and small schools, create more coherent systems of discipline and student support, and develop effective teaming and professional learning communities. She is the author of many books, including *Partners in Learning* about best practices in secondary classrooms, and *Conflict Resolution in the High School.*

About ESR

ESR is a national non-profit organization that was founded in 1982. Our mission is to make teaching social responsibility a core practice in education so that young people develop the convictions and skills to shape a safe, sustainable, democratic, and just world. We are a national leader in educational reform. Our work spans the fields of social and emotional learning, character education, conflict resolution, diversity education, civic engagement, prevention programming, youth development, and secondary school improvement. ESR offers comprehensive programs, staff development, consultation, and resources for adults who teach children and young people preschool through high school, in settings including K-12 schools, early childhood centers, and afterschool programs. For more information about ESR visit our website, www.esrnational.org.

About Partners in Learning Professional Development

Over the last 10 years, Educators for Social Responsibility has helped secondary educators design and implement practices and programs that have a proven track record of improving school climate, increasing student achievement, and reducing aggressive and disruptive behaviors. We support continuous school improvement, small school start-up, and secondary school redesign through our school change work called Partners in Learning. We combine a consultative process with "nuts and bolts" training and coaching to assist faculty, principals, and leadership teams in creating schools where everyone feels safe, welcomed, respected, and connected. We customize all of our programs to meet each school's specific needs and entry points. To find out how ESR can help you visit our web site at www.esrnational.org or call 1.800.370.2515.

Essential Resource

Partners in Learning: From Conflict to Collaboration

Good teaching not only supports the intellectual development of adolescents-it nourishes their spirits and touches their hearts. *Partners in Learning* is an essential tool for helping secondary classroom teachers make this happen. *Partners in Learning* is a practical and hands-on guide organized around ten core practices that will enable students and teachers to work together toward common learning goals. Each practice includes classroom-tested tools, strategies, and routines that make a positive difference in students' motivation to learn and succeed. This guide also includes a chapter on classroom management and discipline, a guide for setting up the classroom to support these practices, and a detailed plan for integrating community building, student orientation, and course content into the first month of school. With hundreds of activities and tips, this guide is an essential for every high school classroom teacher. For more information or to order, call us at 1-800-370-2515 or visit our online store at www.esrnational.org.